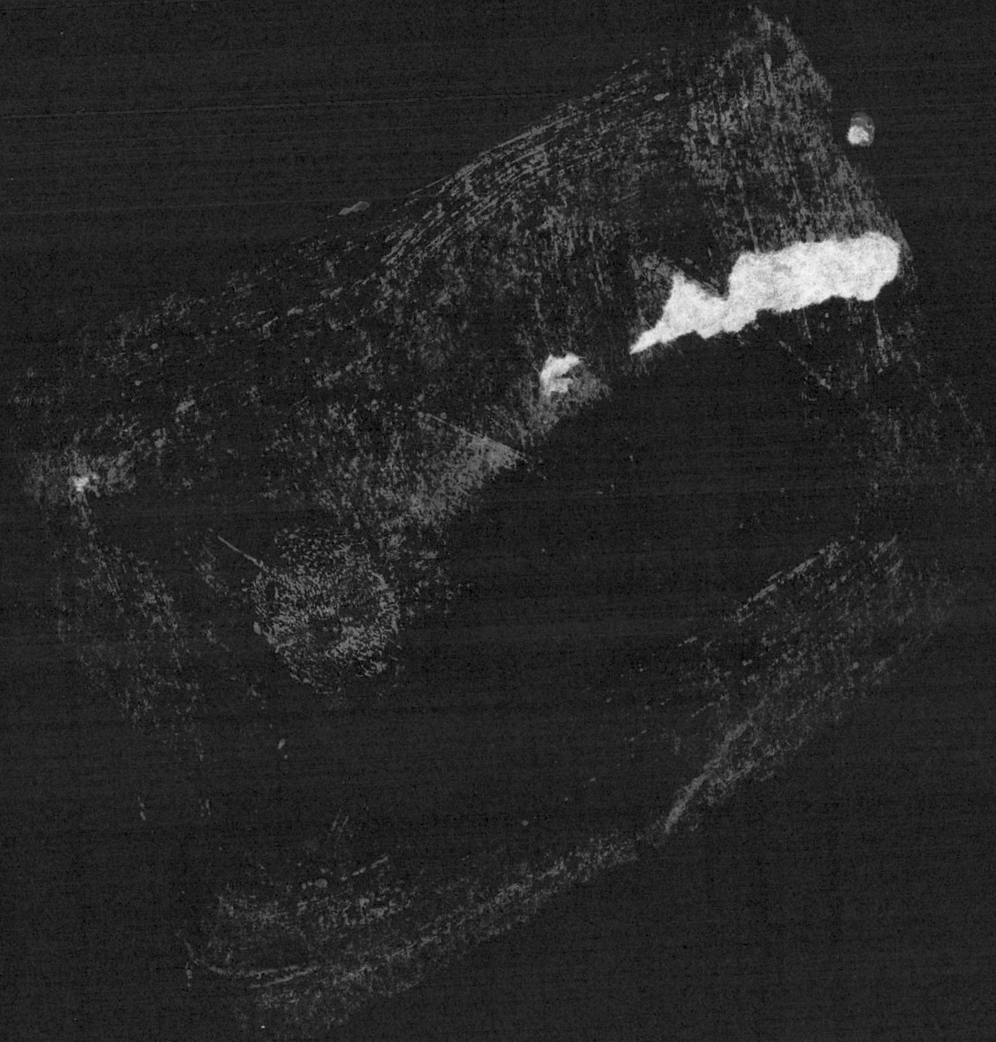

GER 3693 , C. König / F. Kloe
während der Internationalen
Deutschen Meisterschaft der
Korsare , Steinhuder Meer.

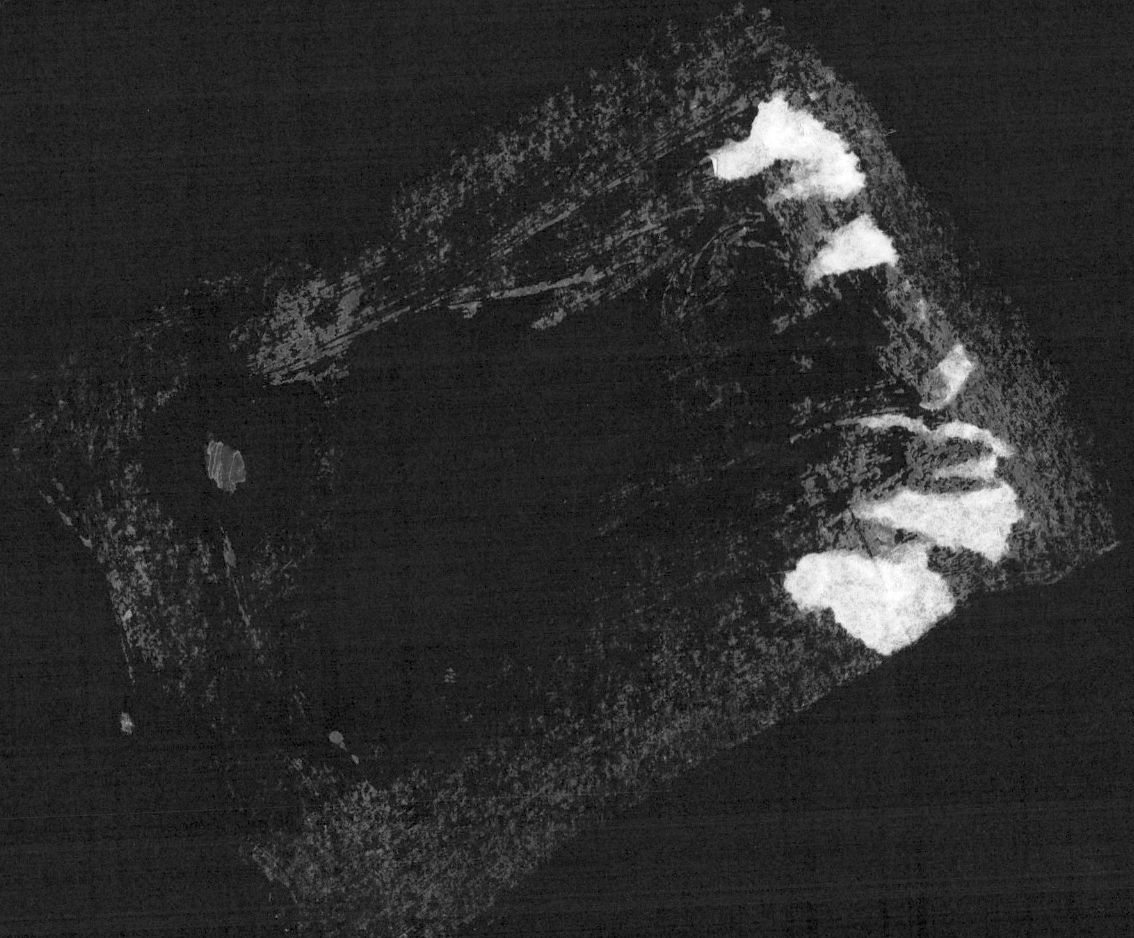

Für meine Töchter Henrike und Lotte
und deren Mütter Annett und Philine

For my daughters Henrike and Lotte
and their mums Annett and Philine

Das Steinhuder Meer – Eine Liebeserklärung

Mit Fug und Recht kann ich sagen, dass dieses Buch von meinen über zwanzig bisher veröffentlichten Büchern mein persönlichstes ist. Es knüpft an mein Steinhuder-Meer-Buch von 2015 an und ist dennoch ganz anders. Besonders freue ich mich, dass ich Freundinnen und Freunde, Bekannte sowie Kolleginnen und Kollegen überzeugen konnte, über ihre Zeit am und mit dem Steinhuder Meer zu schreiben und am Buch mitzuwirken. Sei es, dass sie am Steinhuder Meer leben, dort arbeiten oder ihre Kindheit oder Jugend dort verbrachten.

Durch meinen Beruf bin ich die letzten drei Jahrzehnte viel herumgekommen auf der Welt, habe Sonnenuntergänge an weit entfernten Ozeanen gesehen, in Melbourne vier Jahreszeiten an einem Tag erlebt, die schönsten Orte in Europa oder sonst irgendwo gesehen, und trotzdem zog es mich – sobald ich in der Heimat war – unmittelbar zu meiner kleinen Jolle an das Steinhuder Meer.

Es ist der Reiz der Vielfältigkeit des Naturparks: das Wasser, die Landschaften, die Tiere und Menschen, alles was dazu gehört. Selbst das wechselhafte Wetter hat seinen Reiz. Auch die Historien der reizvollen Orte, die zum Naturpark gehören, üben ihren Reiz aus. Als ich mich mit meiner Kamera rund ums Meer begab, fiel mir auch auf, welch wundervolle Kirchen im Naturpark stehen. Sie gehören, oftmals jahrhunderte Jahre alt, mit dazu. Sind sie doch Zeugnisse vergangener Kulturen, Baustile und einer besonderen Kunst, und begeistern oftmals uns Menschen, unabhängig ob man nun religiös ist oder nicht.

Zur Vielfalt gehört auch die Möglichkeit, unsere Zeit je nach Gemütszustand am Steinhuder Meer zu verbringen. Egal ob actiongeladen, mit Freundinnen und Freunden, auf oder am Wasser oder beschaulich mit sich selbst. Und mit der Natur.

Das macht es aus, unser Steinhuder Meer.

Mir war in den letzten zweieinhalb Jahren kein Aufwand zu groß, um das Buch so mit dem Inhalt zu füllen, wie ich ihn mir vorstellte. Egal ob Zeit für Aufnahmen, die dazugehörenden unzähligen Kilometer, die ich fuhr, Texte schreiben, lesen und korrigieren, Telefonate und E-Mails mit Co-Autorinnen und Co-Autoren oder einfach nur, um Genehmigungen für Aufnahmen einzuholen.

Trotz allem kann dieses Buch keinen Anspruch auf Vollständigkeit erfüllen. Zu groß ist der Naturpark und zu groß die Unterschiede, was jede Betrachterin bzw. jeder Betrachter möglicherweise von einem Buch über den Naturpark Steinhuder Meer erwartet.

Was ich mir wünsche, ist ein Lächeln, das sich zeigt, wenn ein Mensch irgendeine Stelle im Buch findet, die ihn besonders berührt – dann war es jeglichen Aufwand wert.

Lake Steinhuder Meer – A declaration of love

I can justifiably say that this book is my most personal of the more than twenty books I have published so far. It follows on from my Lake Steinhuder Meer book from 2015 and yet it is completely different. I am particularly pleased that I was able to persuade friends, acquaintances and colleagues to write about their time at and on Lake Steinhuder Meer and to contribute to the book. Whether they live on Lake Steinhuder Meer, work there or spent their childhood or youth there.

Due to my job, I have travelled the world a lot over the last three decades, seen sunsets on distant oceans, experienced four seasons in one day in Melbourne, seen the most beautiful places in Europe, Africa or South America, and yet as soon as I was back home, I was immediately drawn to my little dinghy on Lake Steinhuder Meer.

It is the appeal of the diversity of the nature park: the water, the landscapes, the animals and people, everything that goes with it. Even the changeable weather has its charm. And the history of the charming places that are part of the nature park. As I was travelling around the lake with my camera, I also noticed what wonderful churches there are in the nature park. They are part of it, often centuries old. They are evidence of past cultures, architectural styles and a unique art, and often inspire us humans, regardless of whether we are religious or not.

This variety also allows us to choose how to spend our time at Lake Steinhuder Meer depending on our mood. Whether action-packed, with friends, on or by the water or enjoying a contemplative moment by yourself. And always with nature.

That's what makes our Lake Steinhuder Meer so special.

Over the last two and a half years, no effort was too great for me to fill the book with the content I had in mind. It didn't matter whether it was the time I spent taking photos, the countless kilometres I drove, writing, reading and correcting texts, phone calls and emails with co-authors or simply obtaining permission to take photos.

Despite everything, this book cannot claim to be complete. The nature park is too large and the differences are too great, which is what every viewer might expect from a book about the Lake Steinhude Nature Park.

What I would like to see is a smile when someone finds a place in the book that particularly touches them – then every effort has been worthwhile.

Herzlichst, Sincerely

Heinrich K.-M. Hecht

Liebe Leserinnen und Leser,

im Oktober 1974 unterzeichnen die Vertreterinnen und Vertreter der heutigen Region Hannover, des damaligen Landkreises Nienburg und des Landkreises Schaumburg-Lippe die Übereinkunft zur Gründung des Naturparks Steinhuder Meer. Er ist bis heute bundesweit ein Modell, wie sich Naturschutz und Tourismus in Einklang bringen lassen. Jährlich rund zwei Millionen Besucherinnen und Besucher zeigen, dass dies mit behutsamer Lenkung bestens funktioniert.

Auch die landschaftliche Vielfalt ist unter den über hundert Naturparken Deutschlands einzigartig: Auf 426 km² Fläche finden sich Moore, schwimmende Wiesen, uralte Baumbestände, eiszeitliche Moränen und nicht zuletzt das Steinhuder Meer selbst – der größte Binnensee Nordwestdeutschlands. Der See und sein Umland zählen zu den schönsten und wertvollsten Schutzgebieten Deutschlands; es ist Heimat vieler selten gewordener Tier- und Pflanzenarten.

Der neue Bildband von Heinrich K.-M. Hecht zeigt in beeindruckenden Aufnahmen die ganze Vielfalt dieses besonderen Naturraums und führt die Leserinnen und Leser auch durch idyllische Dörfer abseits des Ufersaums, üppige Wälder und zu ungeahnten Kulturschätzen. Die Insel Wilhelmstein wird ebenso fotogen in Szene gesetzt wie der Wassersport in einem der traditionsreichsten Segelreviere Deutschlands.

Blättern Sie, lesen Sie und überzeugen Sie sich von der „Faszination Naturpark Steinhuder Meer" – gerne auch als Gast in einer der Ausstellungen des Naturparks, auf einer Wanderung, einer Radtour oder einer Einkehr in einem der typischen Fischrestaurants.

Wir freuen uns auf Ihren Besuch!

Dear readers,

In October 1974, representatives of what is now the Hannover region, the former district of Nienburg and the district of Schaumburg-Lippe signed the agreement to establish the Lake Steinhude Nature Park. To this day, it is a nationwide model of how nature conservation and tourism can be harmonised. Around two million visitors a year show that this works very well with careful management.

The diversity of the landscape is also unique among the more than one hundred nature parks in Germany: the 426 square kilometres of moors, floating meadows, ancient tree populations, glacial moraines and, last but not least, the Lake Steinhuder Meer itself – the largest inland lake in north-west Germany. The lake and its surroundings are among the most beautiful and valuable protected areas in Germany; it is home to many rare animal and plant species.

The new illustrated book by Heinrich K.-M. Hecht shows the full diversity of this special natural area in impressive photographs and also takes the reader through idyllic villages away from the shore, through lush forests and to unexpected cultural treasures. The island of Wilhelmstein is presented in a photogenic way, as are the water sports in one of Germany's most traditional sailing areas.

Browse, read and experience for yourself the "Fascination of Lake Steinhude Nature Park" – also as a guest in one of the nature park's exhibitions, on a hike, a cycle tour or a stop at one of the typical fish restaurants.

We look forward to your visit!

Jörg Farr
Landrat Landkreis Schaumburg

Steffen Krach
Regionspräsident der Region Hannover

Detlev Kohlmeier
Landrat Landkreis Nienburg/Weser

Inhaltsverzeichnis / Contents

Vorwort / Preface	5
Grußwort / Greeting	7
Inhaltsverzeichnis / Contents	8
Naturpark Steinhuder Meer / Lake Steinhude Nature Park	11
Moor / Peat bogs	23
Tiere / Animals	29
Aale / Eels	41
Störche / Storks	43
Wassersport / Water sports	51
Baltische Segler-Vereinigung / Baltic Sailing Association	63
Hannoverscher Yacht-Club / Hannover Yacht Club	67
Segel-Club Mardorf / Mardorf Sailing Club	71
Schaumburg-Lippischer Seglerverein / Schaumburg-Lippe Sailing Club	73
Yachtclub Steinhuder Meer / Steinhuder Meer Yacht Club	77
Holzboote / Wooden boats	81
Torfkähne / Peat barges	81
Auswanderer / Emigrants	85
Auf der Planke rund ums Steinhuder Meer / On the plank around Lake Steinhuder Meer	87
Bootswerft Bopp&Dietrich / Boatyard Bopp&Dietrich	91
Großenheidorn	95
St.-Thomas-Kirche / St Thomas' Church	106
Fliegerhorst Wunstorf / Wunstorf airbase	109
Steinhude	119
Vom Glück des Zurückkehrens / The happiness of returning	125
Petruskirche / St Peter's Church	130
Insel Wilhelmstein / Wilhemstein island	133
Im Nebel der Erinnerung / In the mist of memory	139
Fort de Lippe	145
Kalimandscharo	147
Idensen	153
Sigwardskirche / Sigward's Church	156
Auhagen	159
Sachsenhagen	165
Elisabethkirche	168

Hagenburg	171
St.-Nikolai-Kirche / St Nicholas' Church	174
Wiedenbrügge	177
Bergkirchen	
St.-Katharinen-Kirche / St Catherine's Church	180
Wölpinghausen	185
Münchehagen	187
Hardichhaus / Hardich House	191
Ehemalige Klosterkapelle / Former monastery chapel	196
Dinopark / Dinosaur Park	199
Rehburg-Loccum	211
St.-Martini-Kirche / St Martin's Church	214
Bad Rehburg	217
Friederikenkapelle / Friederike Chapel	220
Kloster Loccum / Loccum Monastery	223
Winzlar	235
Fachwerkkapelle / Half-timbered chapel	238
Mardorf	241
Christuskapelle / Christ Chapel	244
Schneeren	251
Kirche zum guten Hirten / Church of the Good Shepherd	262
Heckrinder / Heck cattle	265
Brokeloh und Husum	269
St.-Jacobi-Kirche / St Jacob's Church	274
Linsburg	277
Neustadt am Rübenberge	283
Liebfrauenkirche / Church of Our Lady	288
Kloster Mariensee / Mariensee Monastery	290
Danksagung / Acknowledgments	296
Die Autorinnen und Autoren / The authors	298
Partner / Partners	310
Quellenverzeichnis / Bibliography	312
Bildnachweise / Picture credits	312
Impressum / Imprint	312

↑ Das Feuchtgebiet Internationaler Bedeutung (FIB) am Steinhuder Meer macht seinem Namen alle Ehre: Scharen von Wasservögeln brüten, mausern, rasten und überwintern hier.

↑ The Wetland of International Importance (FIB) on Lake Steinhuder Meer lives up to its name: flocks of water birds breed, moult, rest and hibernate here.

Naturpark Steinhuder Meer

Lake Steinhude Nature Park

Doreen Juffa

**50 Jahre Naturpark Steinhuder Meer –
Ein „Großschutzgebiet" blickt in die Zukunft**

Was macht eigentlich einen Naturpark aus? Im Bundesnaturschutzgesetz ist er definiert als ein großräumiges Gebiet, das überwiegend aus Schutzgebieten besteht, eine große Arten- und Biotopvielfalt aufweist und sich besonders für Erholung und Naturerleben eignet. Neben dieser gesetzlichen Definition zeichnet den Naturpark Steinhuder Meer die einzigartige und faszinierende Landschaft sowie die engagierten Menschen für Natur und Kultur vor Ort aus.

In Deutschland gibt es 105 Naturparke, davon vierzehn in Niedersachsen. Sie stehen für Naturschutz, Umweltbildung, Erholung und Regionalentwicklung. Die Naturparke machen über ein Viertel der Fläche Deutschlands aus. Etwa 30 km vor den Toren Hannovers liegt der Naturpark Steinhuder Meer. Ein einzigartiges Naturparadies: ausgedehnte Moorflächen, schwimmende Wiesen, eiszeitliche Moränenlandschaften, Binnendünen, Berge und Niedersachsens größter Binnensee – das Steinhuder Meer. Das Gebiet des Naturparks erstreckt sich über die Landkreise Nienburg/Weser und Schaumburg sowie die Region Hannover, die die Trägerschaft übernommen hat.

Keine Zukunft ohne Vergangenheit – und auf die können wir in Niedersachsen auch ziemlich stolz sein. Wenn in einem der beiden Infozentren des Naturparks ein Trophäenschrank stünde, er wäre gut bestückt. Seit seiner Gründung im Jahr 1974 hat das Großschutzgebiet reichlich Anerkennung, Preise und Zertifikate für die dort geleistete Arbeit eingeheimst. Etwa für das vielfach kopierte „Honigtopfsystem".

**50 years of Lake Steinhude Nature Park –
A "large protected area" is looking to the future**

What actually constitutes a nature park? The Federal Nature Conservation Act defines a nature park as a large area that consists predominantly of protected areas, has a great diversity of species and biotopes and is particularly suitable for recreation and experiencing nature. In addition to this legal definition, the Lake Steinhude Nature Park is characterised by its unique and fascinating landscape as well as the local people's commitment to nature and culture.

There are 105 nature parks in Germany, fourteen of which are in Lower Saxony. They stand for nature conservation, environmental education, recreation and regional development. The nature parks cover over a quarter of Germany's surface area. The Lake Steinhude Nature Park is located around 30 kilometres from the gates of Hannover. A unique natural paradise: Extensive moorland areas, floating meadows, glacial moraine landscapes, inland dunes, mountains and Lower Saxony's largest inland lake – the Steinhuder Meer. The nature park covers the districts of Nienburg/Weser and Schaumburg as well as the Hannover region, which has taken over sponsorship.

No future without a past – and we can be pretty proud of that in Lower Saxony. If there was a trophy cabinet in one of the nature park's two information centres, it would be well stocked. Since it was founded in 1974, the nature reserve has received plenty of recognition, awards and certificates for the work it has done. For example, for the widely copied "honey pot system". An ingenious way of carefully guiding the streams of visitors – around 60,000 people on beautiful, warm weekends –

↑ Aus den Hütten lassen sich Vögel und andere Tierarten hervorragend beobachten. Sich in den Hütten ruhig verhaltene Menschen werden von den Tieren nicht als Bedrohung wahrgenommen.

↑ Birds and other animal species can be easily observed from the huts. People behaving quietly in the huts are not perceived as a threat by the animals.

Ein ausgetüfteltes Angebot, um die Besucherinnen- und Besucherströme – rund 60.000 Menschen an schönen, warmen Wochenenden – auf Erlebniswegen und Aussichtstürmen behutsam zu lenken und so den Menschen spannende Naturerlebnisse zu ermöglichen, ohne die Natur zu stören.

Dem Goldstandard „Qualitäts-Naturpark", nach den Kriterien des Verbandes Deutscher Naturparke (VDN), genügt das Steinhuder Meer schon seit 2006 im Fünf-Jahres-Turnus – ohne Unterbrechung. Was dem Naturpark trotz S-Bahn und dichtem Busnetz aber fehlte, war ein Fernbahnhof im Einzugsbereich, um den Naturpark „entspannt und klimafreundlich" erleben zu können. Aber auch hier: Aufgabe inzwischen gelöst und Haken dran. Denn im Jahr 2018 ist der Naturpark Steinhuder Meer kräftig gewachsen. Er umfasst seitdem eine Fläche von 426 km². Ein Zugewinn von 110 km² – mit dem Bahnhof Neustadt am Rübenberge als Station im deutschen Schienennetz. Mehr Gebiet mit dem Meer als Kernstück, das sich nun zwischen Leine und Fulde erstreckt; es reicht vom Kloster Mariensee bis zum Kloster Loccum. Zu den kommunalen „Neulingen" im Drei-Landkreis-Gebiet zählen neben der Kernstadt Neustadt die Orte Poggenhagen, Mariensee, Nöpke, Hagen, Dudensen, Wulfelade, Loccum, Münchehagen und Sachsenhagen.

Mit diesen neuen Partnern sind weitere kulturelle und landschaftliche Highlights dazugekommen, die die Attraktivität des Naturparks steigern. Dazu gehört, dass der Naturpark auch in der Fläche noch präsenter wird. An den Ufern und auf dem Wasser hat sich in dieser Hinsicht in den letzten Jahren

along adventure trails and viewing towers, enabling people to experience nature in an exciting way without disturbing nature.

The Lake Steinhuder Meer has met the gold standard "Quality Nature Park", according to the criteria of the Association of German Nature Parks (VDN), every five years since 2006 – without interruption. What the nature park lacked, however, despite the suburban railway and dense bus network, was a long-distance train station in the catchment area so that visitors could experience the nature park in a "relaxed and climate-friendly" way. But here too: Task now solved and ticked off. The Lake Steinhude Nature Park grew considerably in 2018. It now covers an area of 426 square kilometres. A gain of 110 square kilometres – with Neustadt am Rübenberge station as a stop on the German rail network. More territory with the lake as its centrepiece, which now stretches between the Leine and Fulde rivers; it extends from Mariensee Monastery to Loccum Monastery. The municipal "newcomers" in the three-county area include the towns of Poggenhagen, Mariensee, Nöpke, Hagen, Dudensen, Wulfelade, Loccum, Münchehagen and Sachsenhagen in addition to the centre of Neustadt.

With these new partners, further cultural and scenic highlights have been added that increase the attractiveness of the nature park. This includes making the nature park even more present in the area. A lot has happened in this respect on the banks and on the water in recent years: on the Neustadt side, the Nature Park House opened on the Mardorfer Uferweg. The two-storey building in passive house standard houses the in-

↑ Morgenstimmung im Naturschutzgebiet Meerbruchswiesen – eines der landesweit bedeutendsten Schutzgebiete.

↑ Morning atmosphere in the Meerbruchswiesen nature reserve – one of the most important protected areas in the country.

einiges getan: Auf der Neustädter Seite eröffnete am Mardorfer Uferweg das Naturpark-Haus. Das zweigeschossige Gebäude im Passivhausstandard beherbergt die interaktive Ausstellung „Vom Torfabbau zum Klimaschutz" zum Thema Moor, vermittelt Informationen für alle interessierten Besucherinnen und Besucher und beherbergt den Sitz der Naturpark-Verwaltung. Mittlerweile sind zwei Ranger als Ansprechpartner vor Ort unterwegs – mit besonderem Augenmerk darauf, dass Naturschutz und Tourismus am Binnensee Hand in Hand gehen.

Auch die Infoscheune Steinhude, der Expo-Standort im historischen Scheunenviertel, hat 2022 eine Runderneuerung erfahren. Tiermotive an der großen Glasfront laden Besucherinnen und Besucher ein, einen Blick ins Innere der Fachwerkscheune zu werfen. Dort warten zwei Themenbereiche: Die eine Hälfte der Ausstellung widmet sich den Meerbruchswiesen. Filme, Infotafeln und eine interaktive Bootsshow erklären, welche Zugvögel die Feuchtwiesen am Westufer des Meeres als Rastplatz nutzen und wie Nerz und Laubfrosch die Rückkehr in den Naturpark geschafft haben. Zweites Thema der Ausstellung ist der Wald im Naturpark. Die Frage im Mittelpunkt: Wie wird das Ökosystem mit dem Klimawandel fertig? Hier ist ein zeitgemäßer Lernort entstanden. Und in Sichtweite befindet sich die benachbarte Grundschule Steinhude, die 2022 als erste zertifizierte Naturpark-Schule am Steinhuder Meer ihre Plakette entgegennehmen konnte. Themen wie Landwirtschaft oder die heimische Tierwelt sind seitdem fester Bestandteil des Lehrplans und das Klassenzimmer wird regelmäßig ins Moor oder den Wald verlegt.

teractive exhibition "From peat extraction to climate protection" on the topic of moorland, provides information for all interested visitors and houses the headquarters of the nature park administration. Two rangers are now on site as contact persons – with a particular focus on ensuring that nature conservation and tourism go hand in hand at the inland lake.

The Info Barn Steinhude, the Expo location in the historic barn quarter, also underwent a makeover in 2022. Animal motifs on the large glass front invite visitors to take a look inside the half-timbered barn. There are two themed areas: One half of the exhibition is dedicated to the meadows of the Meerbruchs: Films, information boards and an interactive boat show explain which migratory birds use the wet meadows on the western shore of the lake as a resting place and how the mink and tree frog have managed to return to the nature park. The second theme of the exhibition is the forest in the nature park. The central question is: How can the ecosystem cope with climate change?

A contemporary learning centre has been created here. And within sight is the neighbouring Steinhude primary school, which was the first certified nature park school on Lake Steinhuder Meer to receive its plaque in 2022. Since then, topics such as agriculture and the local wildlife have been an integral part of the curriculum and the classroom is regularly moved to the moor or the forest.

Lake Steinhude Nature Park is also "Active for climate protection in German tourism", which is the subtitle of the partner project "Katzensprung 2.0" initiated by the Federal Associa-

S. 14–15 Lebensraumvielfalt am Steinhuder Meer: An das westliche Ufer des Sees grenzen urige Bruchwälder, nasse Hochmoore und nicht zuletzt die extensiv genutzten und besonders artenreichen Wiesen und Weiden im streng geschützten Naturschutzgebiet Meerbruchswiesen.

P. 14–15 Habitat diversity at the Steinhuder Meer: the shores of the lake are bordered by rustic swamp forests, wet raised bogs and, last but not least, the extensively used and particularly species-rich meadows and pastures in the strictly protected Meerbruchswiesen nature reserve.

↑ Schafe und andere Weidetiere sind wichtige Landschaftspfleger in den Naturschutzgebieten am Steinhuder Meer – und „fast natürlich".

↑ Sheep and other grazing animals are important landscape conservationists in the Lake Steinhuder Meer nature reserves – and "almost natural".

„Aktiv für den Klimaschutz im Deutschlandtourismus", so der Untertitel des vom Bundesverbandes der Naturparke initiierten Partnerprojektes „Katzensprung 2.0", ist der Naturpark Steinhuder Meer ebenfalls. Als Modell-Naturpark in Niedersachsen will er sich gemeinsam mit vielen Partnern für einen nachhaltigen Tourismus engagieren, der im Einklang mit Natur und Landschaft steht. Klimaschutz, Klimaanpassungsstrategien und nachhaltige Angebote sind dabei wichtige Bausteine, weil der Klimawandel auch das Steinhuder Meer nicht ausspart. Die Auswirkungen der steigenden Jahresmitteltemperaturen sind in den vergangenen Jahren nicht nur durch sinkende Wasserstände im Meer deutlich sichtbar geworden.

„Klimawandel, Anpassung, Chancen" lautet das entsprechende Motto aktuell und für die Zukunft. Eine jetzt vorliegende Grundlagenuntersuchung ist die Basis für konkrete Schritte zur nachhaltigen Entwicklung von Niedersachsens größtem Binnengewässer.

Dahinter steht auch ein historischer Auftrag: Bereits 1979, fünf Jahre nach Gründung des Naturparks, wurde das Steinhuder Meer als Ramsar-Gebiet, also als Feuchtgebiet von internationaler Bedeutung und europäisches Vogelschutzgebiet, ausgewiesen. Zahlreiche Vogelarten brüten, rasten und überwintern auf der Wasserfläche oder den geschützten Randbereichen wie den Meerbruchswiesen. Diese Gebiete dürfen in ihrer Funktion für den Naturhaushalt und das Landschaftsbild nicht beeinträchtigt werden.

Festgeschrieben ist dies jetzt im „Kodex Steinhuder Meer".

tion of Nature Parks. As a model nature park in Lower Saxony, it wants to work with many partners to promote sustainable tourism that is in harmony with nature and the landscape. Climate protection, climate adaptation strategies and sustainable offers are important building blocks in this endeavour, because climate change is also affecting the Lake Steinhuder Meer. The effects of rising average annual temperatures have become clearly visible in recent years, and not just through falling water levels in the lake.

"Climate change, adaptation, opportunities" is the corresponding motto now and for the future. A fundamental study now available forms the basis for concrete steps towards the sustainable development of Lower Saxony's largest inland waterway.

There is also a historical mission behind this: back in 1979, five years after the nature park was founded, the Lake Steinhuder Meer was designated as a Ramsar site, i.e. a wetland of international importance and a European bird sanctuary. Numerous bird species breed, rest and spend the winter on the water surface or in the protected fringe areas such as the Meerbruchswiesen. These areas must not be impaired in their function for the ecosystem and the landscape.

This is now enshrined in the "Lake Steinhuder Meer Codex". The top priority is to preserve and further develop the Lake Steinhuder Meer as an ecological habitat and recreational area, which also includes taking measures to prevent natural siltation. The signatories of the declaration of principles have thus created the basis for future cooperation around the Lake

↑ Winterliche Landschaft im Westen des Steinhuder Meeres.   ↑ Winter landscape in the west of the Steinhuder Meer.

Oberste Priorität ist es, das Steinhuder Meer als ökologischen Lebensraum und Erholungsgebiet zu erhalten und weiterzuentwickeln, dazu gehört es auch, Maßnahmen gegen die natürliche Verlandung zu ergreifen. Die Unterzeichnerinnen und Unterzeichner der Grundsatzerklärung haben damit die Basis für das künftige Miteinander rund um das Steinhuder Meer und auf dem Wasser geschaffen – ein klares Bekenntnis zu den gemeinsamen Werten und Zielen. Jetzt geht es darum, den Kodex zu leben.

In der Präambel heißt es: „Das Steinhuder Meer und seine Zukunft liegen uns am Herzen. Die Vielfalt von Arten und Lebensräumen ist die Voraussetzung für eine lebenswerte und liebenswerte Umwelt. Wir setzen uns für ihren Erhalt ein und übernehmen dafür auch Verantwortung. Gemeinsam wollen wir dafür sorgen, dass Natur und Menschen im Einklang leben. Deshalb folgen wir diesen Grundsätzen – bitte tun Sie es auch!"

Steinhuder Meer and on the water – a clear commitment to shared values and goals. Now it's about living the code.

The preamble states: "The Lake Steinhuder Meer and its future are close to our hearts. The diversity of species and habitats is the prerequisite for an environment worth living in and loving. We are committed to its preservation and take responsibility for it. Together, we want to ensure that nature and people live in harmony. That's why we follow these principles – please do the same!"

S. 18–19   Faszinierende Eis- und Winterlandschaft, aufgenommen aus einem Flugzeug in einem Jahr, als es viel Eis gab und noch keine Flugeinschränkungen über dem Steinhuder Meer.

P. 18–19   Fascinating ice and winter landscape, taken from an aeroplane in a year when there was a lot of ice and no flight restrictions over the Lake Steinhuder Meer.

↑ Hilfe für das Moor: Mitarbeiterinnen und Mitarbeiter der Ökologischen Schutzstationen Steinhuder Meer (ÖSSM) bemühen sich um den Erhalt und die Vermehrung seltener Torfmoose.

↑ Help for the moor: employees of the Lake Steinhuder Meer Ecological Protection Centre (ÖSSM) are working to preserve and propagate rare peat mosses.

S. 20–21 Einen guten Blick über die Wasserfläche in Richtung Süden ermöglicht der kleine Aussichtsturm in der Nähe der Neuen Moorhütte.

P. 20–21 The small observation tower near the Neue Moorhütte provides a good view of the water surface to the south.

Moor

Peat bogs

Thomas Brandt

Ohne Moos nix los …

Sie sind klein und sie werden kaum wahrgenommen, ihr Effekt auf unser Klima ist jedoch enorm: Torfmoose, von Biologinnen und Biologen ihrem Gattungsnamen entlehnt auch als Sphagnen bezeichnet. Sie sind es, die die Hochmoore aufbauen, jede Menge Feuchtigkeit speichern und über Jahrtausende Kohlenstoff festlegen. Aber Torfmoos ist nicht gleich Torfmoos, wenn sie auch für Laien nur schwer voneinander unterscheidbar sind. Etwa zwanzig Torfmoosarten wachsen in den Mooren im Naturpark. Manche sind heute noch relativ häufig, andere sind echte Raritäten. Die häufigen Torfmoose haben vergleichsweise geringe Ansprüche an ihre Standorte, andere wiederum sind heikel.

Die Geschichte der Torfmoose von Beginn an

Torfmoose haben spezielle Eigenschaften. Einige der Arten besiedeln flache Gewässer und bilden dort eine erhebliche Biomasse. Sie wachsen in die Länge, Richtung Sonne. Nach unten sterben die langen Triebe ab. Diese werden aufgrund der von den Torfmoosen gespeicherten Feuchtigkeit nur wenig zersetzt. Erschwert werden Zersetzungsprozesse dadurch, dass Torfmoose infolge des Austausches von Ionen in die umgebende Flüssigkeit das Wasser ansäuern. Durch Pflanzenzuwachs und geringe Biomassezersetzung baut sich so über Jahrhunderte ein Torfmooskissen auf, das schließlich den Anschluss an das Grundwasser verliert und einen eigenen Wasserhaushalt bildet, der nur aus nährstoffarmem Regenwasser gespeist wird – aus einem Niedermoor mit Grundwas-

Nothing happens without moss …

They are small and hardly noticed, but their effect on our climate is enormous: peat mosses, also known as sphagnum mosses by biologists in honour of their genus name. They are the ones that build up the raised bogs, store lots of moisture and fix carbon over thousands of years. But not all peat mosses are the same, even if they are difficult to distinguish from one another, even for laypeople. Around twenty species of peat moss grow in the bogs in the nature park. Some are still comparatively common today, others are real rarities. The common ones have comparatively low demands on their habitats, while others are tricky.

The history of peat mosses from the beginning

Peat mosses have special characteristics. Some of the species colonise shallow waters and form a considerable biomass. They grow in length, towards the sun. The long shoots die off towards the bottom. Due to the moisture stored by the peat mosses, these are only decomposed to a small extent. Decomposition processes are made more difficult by the fact that peat mosses acidify the water by exchanging ions with the surrounding liquid.
Through plant growth and low biomass decomposition, a peat moss cushion builds up over centuries, which eventually loses its connection to the groundwater and forms its own water balance, which is only fed by nutrient-poor rainwater – in this process, a fen with a groundwater connection becomes a raised bog fed only by rainwater, which gradually changes

↑ Eine Arche für seltene Moorpflanzen. Auf diesem Versuchsfeld im Moor werden von der ÖSSM seltene Hochmoorpflanzen unter natürlichen Bedingungen vermehrt.

↑ An ark for rare bog plants. Rare raised bog plants are propagated under natural conditions on this experimental field in the bog by the ÖSSM.

serverbindung wird in diesem Prozess ein nur noch von Regenwasser gespeistes Hochmoor, das sich über Jahrhunderte nach und nach so sehr verändert, dass Vegetation und Tierwelt der beiden Moortypen kaum noch Ähnlichkeit haben. Die treibenden Kräfte der Entwicklung sind Torfmoose. Es sind jedoch verschiedene Arten, meist aufeinanderfolgend, selten zeitgleich. Zunächst wachsen die, die noch viel Wasser und Nährstoffe vertragen oder sogar brauchen, dann die, die ein saures Milieu vertragen und schließlich die, die es trockener mögen, lichthungrig sind und auf den Schichten der anderen wachsen können. Letztere sind oft rötlich gefärbt und bilden kleine Hügel, Bulten genannt, aus, wie zum Beispiel das Magellans Torfmoos *Sphagnum magellanicum*.

In den Senken zwischen diesen Torfmoosbulten, in den sogenannten Schlenken, wachsen die oft mehr grünlichen Torfmoosarten. Sie mögen es nasser als die Bulttorfmoose. Ein altes, natürliches Hochmoor zeigt also einen riesigen zusammenhängenden Torfmoosteppich aus Bulten und Schlenken, bestehend aus rund einem Dutzend Torfmoosarten. Auf diesem Teppich gedeihen wenige andere, aber auf das sehr spezielle Milieu angepasste Pflanzen. Dazu zählen das Weiße Schnabelried, die Rosmarinheide, die Glockenheide und – sicherlich bekannter – die fleischfressenden Sonnentaue. Von diesen gibt es im Naturpark Steinhuder Meer zwei Arten, den

over centuries to such an extent that the vegetation and fauna of the two types of bog hardly resemble each other. The driving forces behind the development are peat mosses. However, they are different species, usually following each other, rarely at the same time. The first to grow are those that still tolerate or even need a lot of water and nutrients, then those that tolerate an acidic environment and finally those that like it drier, are light-hungry and can grow on the layers of the others. The latter are often reddish in colour and form small mounds called bulbs, such as the Magellan's peat moss *Sphagnum magellanicum*.

In the hollows between these peat moss bulges, in the so-called bog hollows, the often more greenish-coloured peat moss species grow. They like it wetter than the bulbous peat mosses. An old, natural raised bog therefore has a huge, continuous carpet of peat moss consisting of mounds and swales with around a dozen peat moss species. Few other plants thrive on this carpet, but they are adapted to the very special environment. These include the white beak reed, the rosemary heather, the bell heather and – certainly better known – the carnivorous sundews. There are two species of these in the Lake Steinhude Nature Park, the round-leaved sundew and the middle sundew. Both cover their nutritional requirements by catching insects with their sticky leaves. In the drier fring-

↑ Im Detail – Torfmoose im Versuchsgelände bei ihrer wichtigen Arbeit für das Klima: Sie bilden dicke, Wasser speichernde Polster und sorgen dafür, dass organisches Material im Moor kaum zersetzt, aber als Torf gespeichert wird.

↑ In detail – peat mosses in the experimental area doing their important work for the climate: they form thick, water-storing cushions and ensure that organic material in the bog hardly decomposes, but is stored as peat.

Rundblätttrigen Sonnentau und den Mittleren Sonnntau. Beide decken ihren Nährstoffbedarf, indem sie mit ihren klebrigen Blättern Insekten fangen. In den trockeneren Randbereichen der Hochmoore oder dort, wo der Wasserhaushalt gestört ist, kommen weitere Pflanzen dazu, beispielsweise Rauschbeere, Besenheide und Pfeifengras.

Zwischen all diesen Pflanzen leben auch Spezialisten unter den Tieren, zum Beispiel Kreuzottern, unsere einzigen heimischen Giftschlangen, kurzflügelige Beißschrecken – eine harmlose grünbraune Heuschrecke – und Hochmoormosaikjungfern, die zu den großen Libellen zählen. Ohne Hochmoor können sie alle bei uns nicht existieren.

Das Hochmoor ist aber nicht nur Lebensraum für die Spezialisten unter den Pflanzen und Tieren. Im Laufe der Jahrtausende – das Tote Moor östlich des Steinhuder Meeres ist wie der See selbst ca. 12.000 Jahre alt – haben sie jede Menge Kohlenstoff gespeichert, und zwar erheblich mehr als unsere Wälder. Mit dem Torfabbau in den Hochmooren und auch durch Trockenlegung und landwirtschaftliche Nutzung werden diese allerdings wieder freigesetzt. Hochmoorschutz ist also auch Klimaschutz und in seiner Bedeutung nicht zu unterschätzen. Insofern ist es von immenser Bedeutung, die heute verbliebenen und meist landwirtschaftlich genutzten Hochmoorböden wieder zu vernässen, damit der Torfboden

es of the raised bogs or where the water balance is disturbed, other plants are added, e.g. bog bilberry, heather and moor grass.

Specialist animals also live among all these plants, e.g. adders, our only native venomous snakes, short-winged biting grasshoppers – a harmless green-brown grasshopper, and raised bog mosaic dragonflies, which are large dragonflies. Without raised bogs, none of them could exist here.

However, the raised bog is not just a habitat for specialised plants and animals. Over the millennia – the Dead Moor east of the Lake Steinhuder Meer is around 12,000 years old, just like the lake itself – they have stored a lot of carbon, considerably more than our forests. However, peat extraction in the raised bogs and also drainage and agricultural use release this carbon again. Protecting raised bogs is therefore also climate protection and its importance should not be underestimated. In this respect, it is of immense importance to rewet the remaining raised bog soils, which are mostly used for agriculture, so that the peat soil with its organic matter is not decomposed. The remains of the areas mined for peat extraction must be rewetted shortly afterwards to protect the climate by quickly closing the drainage ditches and allowing revitalisation to begin. Peat mosses must be able to grow again and bind carbon. But where should the peat mosses come from?

↑ Praktikant Malte Dierssen bei der Torfmoosernte auf dem Versuchsfeld.
↑ Trainee Malte Dierssen harvesting peat moss in the trial field.

↑ Corinna Roers, wissenschaftliche Mitarbeiterin der ÖSSM, zeigt die seltenen Torfmoose, die an anderen Stellen im Toten Moor wieder angesiedelt werden sollen.
↑ Corinna Roers, research assistant at the ÖSSM, shows the rare peat mosses that are to be reintroduced in other parts of the Dead Moor.

mit seiner organischen Masse eben nicht zersetzt wird. Die Reste der zur Torfgewinnung abgebauten Flächen müssen ebenfalls für den Klimaschutz schnell vernässt werden, indem die Entwässerungsgräben zügig verschlossen werden und eine Revitalisierung starten kann. Torfmoose müssen wieder wachsen und Kohlenstoff binden können. Nur wo sollen die Torfmoose herkommen? Durch die Jahrzehnte während Übernutzung der Hochmoore – heute sind nur noch etwa fünf Prozent der ursprünglichen Hochmoore Niedersachsens im natürlichen oder naturnahen Zustand erhalten – sind sie sehr selten geworden und regional oft ausgestorben. Die Lösung liegt auf der Hand: die letzten Pflanzen der heute seltenen Torfmoose finden, vermehren und dort wieder ansiedeln, wo sie „gebraucht" werden. Das klingt einfacher, als es tatsächlich ist, denn Torfmoose ähneln sich sehr und können nur von geschulten Botanikerinnen und Botanikern unterschieden werden. Torfmoose zu vermehren, ist bei manchen Arten einfach, bei anderen dafür umso schwieriger, weil die Ansprüche am Standort recht unterschiedlich sind. Der Teufel steckt hier wahrlich im Detail und arbeitet nur allzu gern gegen den Klimaschutz.

Eine Arche für die Torfmoose

Um die Torfmoose zu retten und zu vermehren, bedarf es heute noch eines beträchtlichen Maßes an Forschungsarbeit. Die Ökologische Schutzstation Steinhuder Meer (ÖSSM) hat des-

Due to decades of overexploitation of the raised bogs – today only around 5% of the original raised bogs in Lower Saxony remain in a natural or near-natural state – they have become very rare and have often died out regionally. The solution is obvious: find the last plants of today's rare peat mosses, propagate them and reintroduce them where they are "needed". This sounds easier than it actually is, because peat mosses are very similar and can only be recognised by trained botanists. Propagating peat mosses is easy with some species, but all the more difficult with others, as the demands on the location are quite different. The devil really is in the details here and is only too happy to work against climate protection.

An ark for the peat mosses

A considerable amount of research work is still required to save and propagate peat mosses. The Lake Steinhuder Meer Ecological Protection Station (ÖSSM) has therefore set up two test facilities together with the Neustadt peat works and

↑ Besonders seltene Pflanzenarten werden von der ÖSSM auch unter kontrollierten Bedingungen vermehrt.

↑ Particularly rare plant species are also propagated by the ÖSSM under controlled conditions.

wegen zusammen mit dem Torfwerk Neustadt und mit Unterstützung von LEADER und der Bingo-Umweltstiftung zwei Versuchsanlagen aufgebaut – eine im Freiland und eine auf dem Werksgelände. Hier werden Torfmoose seit 2020 unter verschiedenen Bedingungen und unter den Augen der Wissenschaftlerinnen und Wissenschaftler vermehrt und – wichtig – Knowhow gesammelt. Die ersten Erfolge stellten sich bereits ein und 2022 konnten die ersten Torfmoose auf wiedervernässte Flächen in der freien Natur umgesetzt werden. Bis das Tote Moor und andere Hochmoore wieder wertvolle CO_2-Speicher sind, ist es jedoch noch ein langer Weg. Aber ein Anfang ist gemacht.

with the support of LEADER and the Bingo Environmental Foundation – one in the open and one on the factory premises. Since 2020, peat mosses have been propagated here under various conditions and under the watchful eyes of scientists and – importantly – expertise has been gathered. The first successes have already been achieved and the first peat mosses were transferred to rewetted areas in the wild in 2022. However, there is still a long way to go before the Dead Moor and other raised bogs are once again valuable CO_2 reservoirs. But a start has been made.

↑ Rückkehrer mit exotischem Outfit: ein Wiedehopf. ↑ A returnee with an exotic outfit: a hoopoe.

Tiere
Animals

Thomas Brandt

Comeback der Verschollenen – Von tierischen Rückkehrern

„Hup-hup-hup", eine bei uns weitgehend unbekannte Stimme erklingt aus einem Naturschutzgebiet im Naturpark Steinhuder Meer. Kurz darauf erneut: „Hup-hup-hup". Der Verursacher ist einer der spektakulärsten und auch seltensten Vögel Deutschlands: ein Wiedehopf. Schon sein wissenschaftlicher Name *Upupa* ist dem Klang seiner Stimme entlehnt. Zu sehen ist er nicht. Irgendwo versteckt in einer großen Waldkiefer muss er sitzen. Plötzlich fliegt mit einem leicht krächzenden Ruf ein zweiter Wiedehopf an der knorrigen Kiefer vorbei. Und richtig, fast schon eine „Farbexplosion" und der vorher gut getarnte „Hopf" erhebt sich aus dem Baum und verfolgt seinen Artgenossen. Schwarz-weiße Flügel, ein orangebrauner Körper und ein langer, leicht gebogener Schnabel – die Vögel sind wahrlich unverkennbar. Die beiden landen auf zwei nebeneinanderstehenden, mit Flechten übersäten Zaunpfählen, stellen ihre pompösen Federhauben auf und sind sichtlich aufgeregt. Der Verfolger, das Männchen, beugt sich leicht nach vorn: „Hup-hup-hup-hup-hup" – in der Aufregung singt er mit aufgestellter Haube nun eine längere Strophe. Das Interesse des Weibchens ist dagegen nicht besonders ausgeprägt, es dreht sich einmal zum Männchen um und fliegt ab, das Männchen folgt ihr kurz darauf.

Viele Jahrzehnte, vielleicht sogar mehr als 100 Jahre, waren die hübschen Wiedehopfe in Niedersachsen nicht mehr zu sehen. Bestenfalls tauchte hier und da ein Wiedehopf zur Zugzeit auf, weil er seinen Geburtsort, die wenigen in Deutschland bewohnten Gebiete nicht gefunden hat oder durch starke

Comeback of the missing – Animal returnees

"Hup-hup-hup", a voice largely unknown to us, sounds from a nature reserve in the Lake Steinhude Nature Park. Shortly afterwards again: "Hup-hup-hup". The perpetrator is one of the most spectacular and rarest birds in Germany: a hoopoe. Its scientific name "Upupa" is derived from the sound of its voice. It cannot be seen. It must be hidden somewhere in a large Scots pine. Suddenly, a second hoopoe flies past the gnarled pine tree with a slightly croaking call. And that's right, an almost "explosion of colour" and the previously well-camouflaged hoopoe rises out of the tree and pursues its fellow hoopoe. Black and white wings, an orange-brown body and a long, slightly curved beak – the birds are truly unmistakable. The two land on two lichen-covered fence posts next to each other, put up their pompous feathered caps and are visibly excited. The pursuer, the male, leans slightly forwards: "hup-hup-hup-hup-hup" – in his excitement he now sings a long verse with his bonnet up. The female, on the other hand, is not particularly interested, she turns once to the male and flies off, the male follows her shortly afterwards.

For many decades, perhaps even more than 100 years, the pretty hoopoes were no longer to be seen in Lower Saxony. At best, a hoopoe appeared here and there at migration time because it had not found its birthplace, the few inhabited areas in Germany, or was driven away by strong winds. The birds, which are about the size of a blackbird, had become extinct in Lower Saxony until bird conservationists were able to detect a first brood in 2008. In 2020, biologists from the Ökologische

↑ Mit viel Mühe der Naturschützerinnen und Naturschützer ist auch der recht seltene Fischadler wieder am Steinhuder Meer heimisch.
↑ The rare osprey has also returned to the Lake Steinhuder Meer thanks to the effort of the conservationists.

↑ Löffelenten sind deutschlandweit selten geworden. Eine kleine Population brütet am Steinhuder Meer und nutzt dazu die von den Naturschützerinnen und Naturschützern angelegten Kleingewässer. Das Foto zeigt einen Trupp Männchen in ihrem schmucken Prachtkleid.
↑ Shoveler ducks have become rare throughout Germany. A small population breeds at Lake Steinhuder Meer and uses the small bodies of water created by conservationists. The photo shows a flock of males in their beautiful plumage.

Winde verdriftet wurde. In Niedersachsen waren die etwa amselgroßen Vögel ausgestorben, bis Vogelschützerinnen und Vogelschützer 2008 wieder eine erste Brut feststellen konnten. 2020 schließlich entdeckten Biologinnen und Biologen der ÖSSM die tatsächlich von langer Hand vorbereitete Brutansiedlung im Naturpark Steinhuder Meer – und zwar in einem von ihnen für die seltene Vogelart sieben Jahre zuvor selbst angebrachten Spezialnistkasten.

Ganz so einfach war das Comeback des spektakulären Vogels allerdings nicht einzufädeln. Ganz oben auf ihrem Speisezettel stehen große Insekten und deren Larven und die wiederum sind in der intensiv landwirtschaftlich genutzten und vielerorts zugebauten Landschaft ebenfalls selten geworden. Der Plan der Naturschützerinnen und Naturschützer musste zunächst berücksichtigen, dass die Nahrungsgrundlage wieder herzustellen ist – und zwar dort, wo keine Menschen stören und wo kein Straßenverkehr die Vögel gefährden kann. Große Insekten sind aber häufig ebenfalls anspruchsvoll. Auf Äckern und intensiv genutzten Wiesen finden sie kaum ein Auskommen und auch in monotonen Forsten sind sie nicht zu finden. Die dicksten Käfer, die größten Heuschrecken und längsten Schmetterlingsraupen leben auf extensiv genutzten Weiden und Magerrasen, auf und an Sandwegen und deren Wegrainen, in Heiden, in naturnahen Wäldern – kurzum fast

Schutzstation Lake Steinhuder Meer (ÖSSM – Lake Steinhuder Meer Ecological Protection Centre) finally discovered the breeding settlement in the Lake Steinhude Nature Park, which had actually been prepared for a long time – in a special nesting box they had installed for the rare bird species seven years previously.

However, the spectacular bird's comeback was not quite so easy to organise. At the top of its menu are large insects and their larvae, and these in turn have also become rare in the intensively farmed and in many places built-up landscape. The conservationists' plan first had to take into account that the food base had to be restored – in places where no people would disturb the birds and where no road traffic could endanger them. However, large insects are often also demanding. They can hardly make a living in fields and intensively utilised meadows and are also not to be found in monotonous forests. The fattest beetles, the largest grasshoppers and the longest butterfly caterpillars live on extensively used pastures and rough grassland, on and along sandy paths and their verges, in heaths, in near - natural forests – in short, almost only in protected areas where manure and agricultural chemicals have no place.

Hoopoes are cavity-nesting birds. Although they are reasonably flexible when it comes to nesting cavities, they must be

↑ Graureiher nutzen die fischreichen Gewässer zur Nahrungssuche. Häufig sind sie aber auch auf Wiesen zu sehen, wo sie Mäuse und andere Tiere erbeuten.
↑ Grey herons use the fish-rich waters to search for food. However, they can also often be seen in meadows, where they prey on mice and other animals.

nur noch in geschützten Gebieten, in denen Gülle und Agrarchemikalien nichts verloren haben.

Wiedehopfe sind Höhlenbrüter. Sie sind zwar einigermaßen flexibel, was die Bruthöhle betrifft, aber groß und geräumig muss sie für die bis zu acht Jungvögel schon sein. Und natürlich dürfen geeignete Brutplätze nicht weit von den Nahrungsressourcen entfernt liegen, am besten liegen sie mittendrin.

All die Ansprüche an einen Wiedehopflebensraum zu erfüllen, scheint der Quadratur eines Kreises gleichzukommen. Doch gelang es den Naturschützerinnen und Naturschützern, wichtige Nahrungstiere der Hopfe wieder anzusiedeln und zu vermehren. Eine Schlüsselrolle spielt dabei die Feldgrille. Sie selbst gehört landesweit zu den seltensten Insektenarten, in unserer Region starb sie in den 1970er Jahren aus. Schon allein ihrer selbst willen sind Anstrengungen zu ihrem Schutz wichtig. Und tatsächlich gelang es den Naturschützerinnen und Naturschützern der ÖSSM mit Unterstützung der zuständigen Naturschutzbehörden und dem Land Niedersachsen, die hübsche Grille in geeigneten Lebensräumen, deren Management auf Dauer abgesichert ist, wieder heimisch zu machen. Was hier so einfach klingt, bedurfte wiederum einer sorgfältigen Planung und eines immensen Aufwandes. Einzelne Feldgrillen konnten aus der letzten verbliebenen

large and spacious for the up to eight young birds. And, of course, suitable breeding sites must not be far away from food resources. Ideally they should be right in the middle of them.

Fulfilling all these requirements for a hoopoe habitat seems like squaring a circle. However, conservationists have succeeded in reintroducing and reproducing important food animals for the hoopoes. The field cricket plays a key role in this. It is one of the rarest insect species in the country and became extinct in our region in the 1970s. Efforts to protect them are important for their own sake. And indeed, with the support of the relevant nature conservation authorities and the state of Lower Saxony, the conservationists at ÖSSM have succeeded in reintroducing the pretty cricket to suitable habitats, the management of which has been secured for the long term. What sounds so simple here required careful planning and immense effort. Individual field crickets were taken from the last remaining population in the Hannover region and served as a breeding stock. Only a few years later, the field crickets had reproduced so well that their early summer chirping gave the landscape a Mediterranean flair here and there and thus also attracted the magnificent hoopoes.

However, hoopoes and field crickets are by no means the only animals that have returned to the Lake Steinhuder Meer and its surroundings after a long absence. The crane, white-tailed

S. 32–33 Wer hat den schönsten Sitzplatz? Zwei junge Kormorane streiten sich. Kormorane brüten zwar nicht am Steinhuder Meer, sind hier aber regelmäßig zu sehen.

P. 32–33 Who has the best perch? Two young cormorants arguing. Cormorants may not breed at Lake Steinhuder Meer, but they can be seen here regularly.

↑ Auch Wildkatzen waren in ganz Niedersachsen ausgerottet worden. Mittlerweile haben sie große Landesteile zurückerobert. Unter anderem sind sie auch wieder am Steinhuder Meer heimisch und leben – meist sehr heimlich – in den ungestörten Schutzgebieten und größeren Wäldern.

↑ Wildcats had also been wiped out throughout Lower Saxony. They have now recaptured large parts of the state. They have also returned to the Lake Steinhuder Meer and live – usually very secretly – in the undisturbed protected areas and larger forests.

↑ Die kleinen, nur bis etwa 4,5 cm langen Laubfrösche, sind die einzigen Amphibien, die auf Bäume klettern können. Auch sie waren am Steinhuder Meer ausgerottet worden. Ein gut geplantes und wissenschaftlich betreutes Wiederansiedlungsprojekt der Ökologischen Schutzstation Steinhuder Meer brachte sie wieder hierhin zurück.

↑ The small tree frogs, which are only about 4.5 cm long, are the only amphibians that can climb trees. They too had been wiped out at Lake Steinhuder Meer. A well-planned and scientifically supervised reintroduction project by the Steinhuder Meer Ecological Protection Centre brought them back here.

Population innerhalb der Region Hannover entnommen werden und dienten als Zuchtstamm. Nur wenige Jahre später hatten sich die Feldgrillen so gut vermehrt, dass ihr frühsommerliches Zirpen der Landschaft hier und dort ein mediterranes Flair verschaffte und somit auch die prächtigen Wiedehopfe anlockte.

Wiedehopf und Feldgrille sind aber längst nicht alle Tiere, die nach langer Abwesenheit wieder an das Steinhuder Meer und in sein Umfeld zurückkehren konnten. Kranich, Seeadler, Fischadler, Flussseeschwalbe, Europäischer Nerz, Fischotter, Wildkatze, Europäische Sumpfschildkröte, Laubfrosch und Karausche sind populäre Beispiele. In den meisten Fällen gingen dem Comeback der einzelnen Arten die Bemühungen von Naturschützerinnen und Naturschützern voraus. Seeadler, Fischadler und Kranich würden heute nicht am Steinhuder Meer brüten, gäbe es die geschützten Bereiche mit Betretungsverboten nicht, die so den scheuen Vögeln das ungestörte Aufziehen ihrer Brut ermöglichen. Verbunden mit dem wichtigen Ankauf von Flächen für die Natur wurden in Schutzgebieten die Möglichkeiten geschaffen, Lebensräume so zu gestalten, dass sie für einige ausgerottete Tierarten wieder bewohnbar sind. Die Anlage vieler Tümpel und Teiche auf Naturschutzflächen ermöglicht beispielsweise zahlreichen Amphibien- und Vogelarten, große Räume wieder zurückzuerobern, aus denen sie vorher verdrängt wurden.

eagle, osprey, common tern, European mink, otter, wildcat, European pond turtle, tree frog and crucian carp are popular examples. In most cases, the comeback of the individual species was preceded by the efforts of conservationists. White-tailed eagles, ospreys and cranes would not be breeding at Lake Steinhuder Meer today if it were not for the protected areas with access bans, which allow the shy birds to raise their broods undisturbed. In conjunction with the important purchase of land for nature, opportunities have been created in protected areas to create habitats in such a way that they are once again habitable for some extinct animal species. The creation of numerous ponds and pools on nature conservation areas, for example, has enabled numerous amphibian and bird species to reclaim large areas from which they had previously been displaced.

Back to the Lake Steinhuder Meer in a bucket

For some species, the measures came too late and recolonisation on their own was not possible. The well-prepared recolonisation of the tree frog from 2005 onwards, combined with the construction of numerous spawning waters, only succeeded because conservationists armed with buckets placed spawning balls from other populations in aquariums, reared the tadpoles and released them into newly created waters

S. 34–35 Seeadler sind die unbestrittenen Könige der Lüfte. Im Jahr 2000 brüteten sie nach jahrzehntelanger Abwesenheit erstmals wieder am Steinhuder Meer. Mittlerweile gibt es sogar mehrere Paare.

P. 34–35 White-tailed eagles are the undisputed kings of the skies. In 2000, they bred again at Lake Steinhuder Meer for the first time after decades of absence. There are now even several pairs.

↑ *Anax imperator!* Der wissenschaftliche Name der Großen Königslibelle lässt darauf schließen, dass sie zu den größten Libellenarten gehört. Die eindrucksvolle Art profitiert zusammen mit über 30 anderen Libellenarten von der Anlage neuer Kleingewässer am Steinhuder Meer.

↑ *Anax imperator!* The scientific name of the large king dragonfly suggests that it is one of the largest dragonfly species. Together with over 30 other dragonfly species, this impressive species benefits from the creation of new small bodies of water at Lake Steinhuder Meer.

Im Eimer zurück an das Steinhuder Meer

Für manch eine Tierart kamen die Maßnahmen zu spät und eine Wiederbesiedlung aus eigener Kraft war nicht möglich. Die gut vorbereitete Wiederansiedlung des Laubfrosches ab 2005, verbunden mit dem Bau zahlreicher Laichgewässer, gelang nur, weil mit Eimern bewaffnete Naturschützerinnen und Naturschützer Laichballen aus anderen Populationen in Aquarien setzten, die Kaulquappen aufzogen und kurz vor deren Umwandlung zum fertigen Frosch – Metamorphose genannt – in neu angelegte Gewässer entließen. Die Population, die sich in den Folgejahren in den Naturschutzgebieten am Steinhuder Meer aufbaute, besteht heute aus etwa 20.000 Laubfröschen und ist eine der größten und stabilsten in ganz Niedersachsen. Auch die in und am Steinhuder Meer verschollene Karausche, eine früher häufige und heute in vielen Gebieten ausgestorbene Fischart, kam per Eimer wieder in die Landschaft an Niedersachsens größten See zurück. Nach den vergeblichen Bemühungen, Karauschen im Steinhuder Meer selbst und in den zahlreichen Gräben und Bächen drum herum zu finden, um einen Zuchtstamm aufzubauen, konnten Mitarbeiterinnen und Mitarbeiter der ÖSSM eine Teichwirtschaft finden, die noch Karauschen aus dem Weser-Aller-Leine-Einzugsgebiet in ihrem Besitz hatte. Glücklicherweise ließen sich genetische Abgleiche machen, da sich ein

shortly before their transformation into the finished frog – known as metamorphosis. The population that built up over the following years in the nature reserves around Lake Steinhuder Meer now consists of around 20,000 tree frogs and is one of the largest and most stable in the whole of Lower Saxony. The crucian carp, a formerly common fish species that is now extinct in many areas, also returned to the landscape of Lower Saxony's largest lake thanks to a delivery in buckets. After unsuccessful efforts to find crucian carp in the Lake Steinhuder Meer itself and in the numerous ditches and streams around it in order to establish a breeding stock, ÖSSM employees were able to find a pond farm that still had crucian carp in its possession that originated from the Weser-Aller-Leine catchment area. Fortunately, genetic comparisons could be made, as a doctoral student at the University of London was studying the complicated genetics of the species and was able to analyse the samples from the pond farm. After his "GO", 2,000 fish were released into specially prepared waters at Lake Steinhuder Meer and the foundation was laid for his own breeding stock.

Mobile species, especially those capable of flight, understandably find it easier than others to recolonise previously lost territory. Birds such as the common tern, which migrate back and forth between two continents every year anyway – their wintering grounds are in subtropical Africa – and cover thou-

↑ Die einst am Steinhuder Meer selten gewordenen Schilfrohrsänger sind Zugvögel und treffen Mitte April bei uns ein. Heute leben wieder etwa 30 Paare in den Schutzgebieten am Steinhuder Meer.

↑ The reed warblers, which once became rare at Lake Steinhuder Meer, are migratory birds and arrive here in mid-April. Today, around 30 pairs are once again living in the protected areas around Lake Steinhuder Meer.

↗ Eisvögel gehören zu den seltenen Brutvögeln am Steinhuder Meer.
↗ Kingfishers are among the rare breeding birds at Lake Steinhuder Meer.

→ Die am stärksten gefährdete Tierart am Steinhuder Meer ist der Europäische Nerz. Leider ist die Art heute sogar weltweit vom Aussterben bedroht. Naturschützerinnen und Naturschützer versuchen, die Art am Steinhuder Meer wieder heimisch zu machen.

→ The most endangered animal species at the Lake Steinhuder Meer is the European mink. Unfortunately, the species is now threatened with extinction worldwide. Conservationists are trying to reintroduce the species to the Lake Steinhuder Meer.

Doktorand an der Universität in London mit der komplizierten Genetik der Art beschäftigte und die Proben aus der Teichwirtschaft untersuchen konnte. Nach seinem „GO" wurden 2.000 Fische am Steinhuder Meer in eigens dafür vorbereitete Gewässer freigelassen und der Grundstock für einen eigenen Zuchtstamm war gelegt.

Mobile und vor allem flugfähige Arten haben es verständlicherweise leichter als andere, zuvor verlorenes Terrain wieder zu besiedeln. Vögel wie die Flussseeschwalben, die ohnehin jährlich zwischen zwei Kontinenten hin- und herziehen – ihre Überwinterungsgebiete liegen im subtropischen Afrika – und dabei tausende Kilometer zurücklegen, finden geeignete Brutgebiete mit einer gewissen Wahrscheinlichkeit von selbst. Die Rückbesiedlung von Fischadlern am Steinhuder Meer nach mehr als 100 Jahren wurde erst möglich, weil geeignete Nistplätze geschaffen wurden, die die Vögel in unserer Landschaft heute nicht mehr finden. Heute brüten etwa zehn Paare dieser seltenen Vogelart am Steinhuder Meer und an der Mittelweser – das ist etwa ein Drittel aller Fischadler in Niedersachsen!

sands of kilometres in the process, are more likely to find suitable breeding grounds of their own accord. The recolonisation of ospreys on the Lake Steinhuder Meer after more than 100 years was only possible because suitable nesting sites were created, which the birds can no longer find in our landscape today. Today, around ten pairs of this rare bird species breed on the Lake Steinhuder Meer and Mittelweser – that's around a third of all ospreys in Lower Saxony!

→ Der Charaktervogel des Steinhuder Meeres ist der Haubentaucher, dessen Balzspiele die Besucherinnen und Besucher immer wieder faszinieren. Leider ist der Bestand durch den Verlust von Brutplätzen und durch intensive Fischerei mit Stellnetzen gefährdet.

→ The characteristic bird of the Lake Steinhuder Meer is the great crested grebe, whose courtship displays never fail to fascinate visitors. Unfortunately, the population is endangered due to the loss of breeding grounds and intensive fishing with gillnets.

↑ Nicht jeder gefangene Fisch ist gleich ein Aal – dieser schon! Fischer Ulrich Balzer hat seine Mühe, den Fang zu bändigen – Aale sind kräftig.

↑ Not every fish caught is an eel – but this one is! Fisherman Ulrich Balzer has a hard time taming the catch – eels are strong.

↑ Bevor die Aale dem Fischer ins Netz gehen, steht noch viel Arbeit an.

↑ There is still a lot of work to be done before the eels go into the fisherman's net.

↑ Heinz Schweer mit geräucherten Aalen.

↑ Heinz Schweer with smoked eels.

Aale

Eels

Thomas Brandt

„Kommen die Aale wirklich aus dem Steinhuder Meer?"

Das ist eine der häufigsten Fragen, die in Steinhude an der Strandpromenade gestellt werden. „Jein" heißt die Antwort. Ein kleiner Teil der rund um das Steinhuder Meer verkauften Aale kommt zwar tatsächlich aus dem Steinhuder Meer, ist aber nicht auf natürlichem Wege dorthin gelangt. Aale laichen nur in der Sargassosee im Westatlantik vor der Küste Nordamerikas ab. Der Nachwuchs wird dann über den Golfstrom an die europäischen Küsten gespült und verwandelt sich hier in durchsichtige Glasaale. Ein Teil wandert anschließend die Flüsse hinauf. Heute hindern allerdings Kraftwerke und Wehre die Fische daran, bis ins Steinhuder Meer zu gelangen. Stattdessen werden die etwa sechs Zentimeter messenden Glasaale bereits an den europäischen Küsten gefangen und danach direkt – oder zu „Satzaalen" herangezogen – im Steinhuder Meer ausgesetzt. Einige Jahre später werden sie dann gefangen und verarbeitet. Die meisten Aale jedoch, die über die Ladentheke gereicht werden, werden schon im „verkaufsfähigen" Alter angeliefert. Einige Händlerinnen und Händler kaufen sogar sämtliche Aale zum Weiterverkauf ein. Der verkaufte Aal heißt allerdings auch nicht „Steinhuder-Meer-Aal", sondern „Steinhuder Rauchaal"! Eben weil die Aale dort geräuchert und nicht gefangen werden. Leider ist der Aal aufgrund der viel zu hohen Fangmengen und anderer unnatürlicher Verluste heutzutage im Bestand stark gefährdet – was den Genuss beim Verzehr schmälern dürfte.

"Do the eels really come from the Lake Steinhuder Meer?"

This is one of the most frequently asked questions on the beach promenade in Steinhude. "Yes and no" is the answer. A small proportion of the eels sold around the Lake Steinhuder Meer do indeed come from the Lake Steinhuder Meer, but they did not get there naturally. Eels only spawn in the Sargasso Sea in the western Atlantic off the coast of North America. The offspring are then washed up on the European coasts via the Gulf Stream, where they turn into transparent glass eels. Some then migrate up the rivers. Today, however, power stations and weirs prevent the fish from reaching the Lake Steinhuder Meer. Instead, the glass eels, which measure around six centimetres, are caught on the European coasts and then released into the Lake Steinhuder Meer either directly or as "set eels". They are then caught and processed a few years later. However, most of the eels that are sold over the counter are delivered at a "saleable" age. Some retailers even buy all the eels for resale. However, the eel sold is not called "Lake Steinhuder Meer eel", but "Steinhuder smoked eel"! Precisely because the eels are smoked there and not caught. Unfortunately, the eel population is now highly endangered due to excessive catches and other unnatural losses – which is likely to reduce the enjoyment of eating it.

Bringt er nun die Kinder oder nicht? Auf jeden Fall hat der Bestand des Weißstorches rund um das Steinhuder Meer stark zugenommen. →
Does it bring the children or not? In any case, the population of white storks around the Lake Steinhuder Meer has increased significantly. →

Störche

Storks

Thomas Brandt

Es klappert vom Dach und neuerdings auch aus dem Baum – Weißstörche im Naturpark

Wohl kaum ein Vogel ist bekannter als der Weißstorch. Das liegt sicherlich zum einen daran, dass die Vögel eine durchaus imposante Erscheinung sind, immerhin haben sie eine Flügelspannweite von knapp zwei Metern, aber auch daran, dass sie sich dem Menschen eng angeschlossen haben und „Tür an Nest" mit ihm zusammenleben. Dementsprechend haben Weißstörche in unzähligen Sagen und Geschichten Berücksichtigung gefunden – meist übrigens als Glücksvögel.

Schicksal mit unerwarteter Wendung

Die Nähe zum Menschen und die Beliebtheit der Weißstörche haben sie dennoch spätestens ab den 1950er Jahren nicht davor bewahrt, immer seltener zu werden. Auch in der Kulisse des heutigen Naturparks Steinhuder Meer waren sie fast komplett verschwunden, so durchschlagend war die Vernichtung ihrer Lebensgrundlagen, zum Beispiel durch die Entwässerung der Landschaft und den Verlust der Nahrungsgrundlagen. Übrig blieben wenige. Zu Beginn der 1990er Jahre war ein Tiefststand erreicht. Neben den Brutplätzen in Neustadt auf dem Standesamt, auf der Polizeistation in Rehburg oder auf dem Blumengeschäft in Auhagen waren kaum noch Nester besetzt. Und in jedem Frühling bangten Storchenfreundinnen und -freunde, dass die Zugvögel wieder aus ihren südlichen Winterquartieren zurückkommen – was oft genug nicht passierte.

Doch plötzlich und unerwartet setzte eine Wende ein. Ab

Clattering sounds from the roof and recently also from the tree – White storks in the nature park

Hardly any bird is better known than the white stork. On the one hand, this is certainly due to the fact that the birds are quite an imposing sight, after all they have a wingspan of almost two metres, but also because they have become closely attached to humans and live "door to nest" with them. Accordingly, white storks have featured in countless legends and stories – mostly as lucky birds, by the way.

Fate with an unexpected twist

However, the proximity to humans and the popularity of white storks have not prevented them from becoming increasingly rare since the 1950s at the latest. Even in the setting of today's Lake Steinhude Nature Park, they had almost completely disappeared, so drastic was the destruction of their habitat, e.g. due to the drainage of the landscape and the loss of food sources. Only a few remained. A low point was reached at the beginning of the 1990s. Apart from the breeding sites in Neustadt on the registry office, on the police station in Rehburg or on the flower shop in Auhagen, there were hardly any nests left. And every spring, stork enthusiasts worried that the migratory birds would return from their southern wintering grounds – which often enough did not happen.

However, there was a sudden and unexpected turnaround. From the end of the 1990s, the bird population increased again. At first, new individual pairs settled here and there: in 1999 in Winzlar, then in Steinhude and in Sachsenhagen. Even

← Auf der Polizeistation in Rehburg, der ehemaligen Gemeindeschule, haben es sich die Störche gut eingerichtet. Auf den nahe liegenden Wiesen, neben den Bächen, finden die Störche auch genügend Nahrung für ihren Nachwuchs.

← The storks have made themselves at home at the police station in Rehburg, the former municipal school. In the nearby meadows, next to the streams, the storks also find enough food for their offspring.

↑ Bei der Fütterung in einem Nest in Steinhude gibt es zwischen den fast flüggen Jungstörchen oft Gerangel im Nest. Der Altvogel ist an dem roten Schnabel gut zu erkennen.

↑ When feeding in a nest in Steinhude, there is often a tussle between the fledgeling young storks in the nest. The adult bird can be easily recognised by its red beak.

Ende der 1990er Jahren nahm der Bestand der Vögel wieder zu. Zunächst siedelten sich hier und dort neue einzelne Paare an: 1999 in Winzlar, dann in Steinhude und in Sachsenhagen. Selbst zu diesem Zeitpunkt hätte wohl niemand auf eine für Großvögel ungewöhnlich stürmische Bestandsentwicklung ab etwa 2020 gewettet. Allein in Rehburg brüteten 2023 zwölf Weißstorchpaare, im kleinen Ortsteil Winzlar fünf und in Steinhude drei.

Innerhalb von nur zwei Jahrzehnten verzehntfachte sich somit der Bestand der einstigen Sorgenvögel. Und plötzlich zeigten die Störche, was sie im Naturpark Steinhuder Meer jahrzehntelang nicht taten und bauten Nester in Bäumen: 2022 in Münchehagen, 2023 inmitten von Rehburg und knapp außerhalb der Naturparkgrenzen in Mesmerode entstand gleich eine ganze Kolonie von Baumbrütern.

Was hat Reisanbau in Portugal oder Spanien mit unseren Störchen zu tun?

Über die Gründe des Weißstorchbooms wird viel spekuliert. Was ist passiert? Zunächst muss man wissen, dass es unter den mitteleuropäischen Weißstörchen mehrere Überwinterungsstrategien gibt. Einige von ihnen, die sogenannten Westzieher, schlagen auf dem Weg in die Winterquartiere eine südwestliche Route ein, überqueren Frankreich und gelangen nach Spanien. Von dort aus ziehen sie über die Meerenge bei Gibraltar nach Marokko, überqueren Teile der Sahara, um in die nahrungsreichen Winterquartiere des Sahels und weiter südlich zu gelangen. Richtigerweise muss man sagen: Sie zo-

at that time, nobody would have bet on an unusually rapid population development for large birds from around 2020. In 2023, twelve pairs of white storks were breeding in Rehburg alone, five in the small district of Winzlar and three in Steinhude.

Within just two decades, the population of the once problematic birds has thus increased tenfold. And suddenly the storks showed what they had not done for decades in the Lake Steinhude Nature Park and built nests in trees: in 2022 in Münchehagen, in 2023 in the centre of Rehburg and just outside the nature park boundaries in Mesmerode, a whole colony of tree-nesting storks emerged.

What does rice cultivation in Portugal or Spain have to do with our storks?

There is much speculation about the reasons for the white stork boom. What has happened? Firstly, it is important to realise that there are several wintering strategies among Central European white storks. Some, the so-called western migrants, take a south-westerly route on their way to their wintering grounds, crossing France and reaching Spain. From there, they migrate across the strait at Gibraltar to Morocco, crossing parts of the Sahara to reach the food-rich wintering grounds of the Sahel and further south. It is correct to say that they migrated, as most westward-migrating storks now stay in Spain and Portugal and live off the food provided by rice paddies and (increasingly fewer) rubbish dumps. The journey to their wintering grounds is therefore at best half as long, less

↑ Nahrungsflüge führen die Störche vom Nest in die Umgebung – manchmal mehrere Kilometer weit. In diesem Falle bei Pollhagen.

↑ Foraging flights take the storks from the nest to the surrounding area – sometimes several kilometres away. In this case near Pollhagen.

gen, denn die meisten westziehenden Störche bleiben heute in Spanien und Portugal und leben von der Nahrung, die Reisfelder und (zunehmend weniger) Mülldeponien bereithalten. Der Weg in ihre Winterquartiere ist also heute bestenfalls halb so lang, weniger gefährlich und weniger energieaufwendig. Folgerichtig treffen sie auch im nächsten Jahr etwa drei bis vier Wochen früher an den Brutplätzen ein, oft schon im Februar, und starten früher mit der Brut. Durch den geringeren Energieaufwand legen sie vielleicht auch mehr Eier, das ist aber noch nicht bewiesen. Auf jeden Fall aber haben sie es leichter, Nahrung zu finden, denn die Vegetation ist in den Brutgebieten bei ihrer frühen Ankunft noch nicht so hoch und die noch vom Winter feuchten Böden machen die Hauptnahrung der frisch geschlüpften Störche – Regenwürmer – erreichbarer. Die früh im Jahr geschlüpften Störche werden schließlich früher selbstständig und sind bei ihrem Abflug in den Süden fitter und erfahrener und brüten häufiger bereits im übernächsten Jahr und nicht erst im Alter von drei oder vier Jahren.

dangerous and less energy-intensive. Consequently, they also arrive at their breeding sites around three to four weeks earlier the following year, often as early as February, and start breeding earlier. The lower energy expenditure may also mean that they lay more eggs, but this has not yet been proven. In any case, it is easier for them to find food, as the vegetation in the breeding areas is not yet so high when they arrive early and the soil is still moist from the winter, making the main food of the newly hatched storks – earthworms! – more accessible. Storks that hatch early in the year eventually become independent earlier and are fitter and more experienced when they fly south, breeding more frequently the year after next rather than at the age of three or four.

The storks living in the eastern half of Germany, unlike their west-migrating conspecifics, migrate south-eastwards, crossing the Bosporus, Lebanon and Israel, flying along the Arabian Peninsula to East Africa and sometimes even further south. Their migration route is much longer and more dangerous – not only because they can perish in storms or in the countless

↑ Die Störche in Sachsenhagen haben sich schon vor einigen Jahren auf diesem Schornstein eingerichtet. Das Nest ist mittlerweile zu einem stattlichen Bauwerk angewachsen.

↑ The storks in Sachsenhagen settled on this chimney a few years ago. The nest has now grown into a stately structure.

Die in der östlichen Hälfte Deutschlands lebenden Störche ziehen, anders als ihre westziehenden Artgenossen, nach Südosten ab, überqueren den Bosporus, Libanon und Israel, fliegen entlang der arabischen Halbinsel bis nach Ostafrika und teilweise noch weiter südlich. Ihr Zugweg ist viel länger und gefährlicher – nicht nur, weil sie durch Unwetter oder in den unzähligen ungesicherten Stromleitungen umkommen können, sondern weil sie auf der Strecke heute wie früher bejagt oder einfach nur aus Spaß abgeschossen werden. Ostziehende Störche, die erst im April und damit etwa fünf Wochen nach den Westziehern bei uns eintreffen, müssten also den verlustreichen Zug in ihre Winterquartiere mit einer größeren Zahl an Nachkommen kompensieren, um den Bestand zu halten. Das gelingt ihnen auch heute nur schwer.

Tatsächlich brüten Vögel beider Zugrouten im Naturpark. Der Anteil der westziehenden Störche ist in unserer Gegend aus den oben genannten Gründen in den letzten Jahren deutlich gestiegen, der der Ostzieher nicht. Er ist bestenfalls gleichgeblieben. Der Grund für den überraschenden Anstieg des Weißstorchbestandes ist also weitgehend den verbesserten Überwinterungsbedingungen auf der Iberischen Halbinsel zu verdanken.

unsecured power lines, but also because they are hunted on the route today as in the past or simply shot for fun. East-migrating storks, which only arrive in April and thus around five weeks after the west-migrating storks, would therefore have to compensate for the dangerous migration to their winter quarters with a larger number of offspring in order to maintain the population. Even today, they have difficulty doing this.

In fact, birds from both migration routes breed in the nature park. The proportion of west-migrating storks in our area has increased significantly in recent years for the reasons mentioned above, but that of east-migrating storks has not. At best, they have remained the same. The reason for the surprising increase in the white stork population is therefore largely due to the improved wintering conditions on the Iberian Peninsula.

S. 48–49 Im Spätsommer sammeln sich die Störche. In diesem Fall bei Sachsenhagen. Es geht in den Süden! Die meisten der Störche, die am Steinhuder Meer leben, überwintern vermutlich in Spanien.

P. 48–49 The storks gather in late summer. In this case near Sachsenhagen. They are heading south! Most of the storks that live at Lake Steinhuder Meer probably spend the winter in Spain.

↑ Ein Regattafeld von 15er-Jollenkreuzern, auch P-Booten genannt, läuft unter Spinnaker auf die Wendemarke in Lee zu. Diese Bootsklasse ist auf den Binnenseen in Deutschland weit verbreitet und erfreut sich großer Beliebtheit unter den Seglerinnen und Seglern.

↑ A regatta field of 15-metre dinghy cruisers, also known as P-boats, approaches the turning mark downwind under spinnaker. This boat class is widespread on inland lakes in Germany and is very popular among sailors.

Wassersport
Water sports

Stefan Ibold

Wassersport auf dem Steinhuder Meer

Das Steinhuder Meer ist mit ca. 32 km² das größte Binnenrevier Norddeutschlands und hat schon früh Wassersportlerinnen und Wassersportler in seinen Bann gezogen.

Es begann damit, dass Boote gebaut wurden, um zunächst den Torf aus den Hochmooren abzubauen und vor allem abzutransportieren. Es entstanden die noch heute in nahezu gleicher Form gebauten Torfkähne – siehe dazu auch den Text über Torfkähne.

Zu Beginn des 20. Jahrhunderts kamen mehr und mehr „moderne" Segelboote auf das Steinhuder Meer. Schließlich wurden die ersten Segelvereine gegründet. Der Hagenburger Yacht-Club, aus dem später der Hannoversche Yacht-Club hervorging, wurde im Jahr 1906 gegründet und stellt bis heute einen der größten Vereine am Steinhuder Meer dar. Zwei Jahre später kam der „Seglerverein Steinhude" hinzu, der anlässlich der Einweihung seines Clubhauses im Jahr 1914 in „Fürstlich Schaumburg-Lippischer Seglerverein Steinhude" umbenannt wurde.

Im Jahr 1955 wurde die Wettfahrtvereinigung Steinhuder Meer (WVStM) als Zusammenschluss der Vereine Hannoverscher Yacht-Club, Schaumburg-Lippischer Seglerverein, Segel-Club Steinhuder Meer und Akademischer Seglerverein zu Hannover etabliert. Seit 1964 ist diese Interessenvereinigung als gemeinnütziger Verein eingetragen und zählt heute 22 Mitgliedsvereine.

Die WVStM ist verantwortlich für die Organisation der Regatten hinsichtlich der Terminplanung und vertritt die Interessen der Mitgliedsvereine gegenüber nationalen und internationalen Verbänden, Behörden und sonstigen Einrichtungen.

Water sports on the Lake Steinhuder Meer

At around 32 km², the Lake Steinhuder Meer is the largest inland area in northern Germany and has fascinated water sports enthusiasts from an early age.

It all began when boats were built to extract peat from the raised bogs and, above all, to transport it away. The peat barges that are still built in almost the same form today were created – see also the text on peat barges.

At the beginning of the 20th century, more and more "modern" sailing boats came to the Lake Steinhuder Meer. Eventually, the first sailing clubs were founded. The Hagenburg Yacht Club, which later became the Hannover Yacht Club, was founded in 1906 and is still one of the largest clubs on Lake Steinhuder Meer today. Two years later, the "Seglerverein Steinhude" was added, which was renamed the "Fürstlich Schaumburg-Lippischer Seglerverein Steinhude" on the occasion of the inauguration of its clubhouse in 1914.

In 1955, the Wettfahrtvereinigung Steinhuder Meer was established as a merger of the clubs Hannoverscher Yacht-Club, Schaumburg-Lippischer Seglerverein, Segel-Club Steinhuder Meer and Akademischer Segler-Verein zu Hannover. This interest group has been registered as a non-profit association since 1964 and today has 22 member clubs.

The WVStM is responsible for organizing the regattas in terms of scheduling and represents the interests of the member clubs vis-à-vis national and international associations, authorities and other institutions.

It also represents and supports the clubs vis-à-vis the planning authorities in matters of nature, landscape and environmental law.

← Ein Flying Dutchman – gehört offensichtlich zu den schnellsten Segeljollen – unter Spinnaker kurz vor einer Kenterung nach Luv.

← A Flying Dutchman – obviously one of the the fastest sailing dinghies – under Spinnaker shortly before capsizing to windward.

Weiterhin vertritt und unterstützt sie die Vereine gegenüber den Planungsträgern bei Fragen des Natur-, Landschafts- und Umweltrechts.

Zunächst konzentrierten sich die Segelvereine auf den Bereich des Südufers, also auf der Steinhuder Seite. Erst Anfang der 1960er Jahre bildeten sich am Nordufer, der Mardorfer Seite, ebenfalls Vereinigungen, die einen Wassersport am Steinhuder Meer ausüben wollten. Im Jahr 1962 wurde der Segelclub Mardorf gegründet, dem 1964 der Kanu- und Segelklub Minden, der später in den Segelklub Minden umbenannt wurde, folgte.

Die wachsende Zahl der Mitglieder in den einzelnen Vereinen sowie die stark zunehmende Zahl der Regatten, die im Rahmen der WVStM durchgeführt wurden, führte dazu, dass auf Initiative der WVStM eine öffentlich-rechtliche Wasserrettungsvereinbarung mit dem damaligen Landkreis Hannover (der heutigen Region Hannover) geschlossen wurde.

Die Kooperation zwischen der Wasserrettung Steinhuder Meer und der Region Hannover sowie die zwischen der Wasserrettung Steinhuder Meer und der Feuerwehr macht das Steinhuder Meer zu einem der sichersten Wassersportreviere weltweit und sorgt dafür, dass bei den Regatten und auch an Wochenenden immer eine ausreichende Anzahl an Motorbooten zur Verfügung steht, um Wassersportlerinnen und Wassersportlern in Not helfen zu können.

Die zunehmende Anzahl und Qualität der Regatten brachte immer mehr herausragende Seglerinnen und Segler vom Steinhuder Meer hervor. Olympiaseglerinnen und Olympiasegler und zum Beispiel America's-Cup-Teilnehmende vom Steinhuder Meer sind in der Welt keine Seltenheit und machten das Revier weltweit bekannt.

Die zunehmende Internationalität führte gerade in der jüngeren Vergangenheit dazu, dass neben den Deutschen und Internationalen Deutschen Meisterschaften, die der Deutsche Segler-Verband (DSV) ausrichtet und bei dem die Vereine rund um das Steinhuder Meer mit der Durchführung der Regatten betraut werden, Europameisterschaften und Weltmeisterschaften ausgetragen wurden.

2016 wurde beim Hannoverschen Yacht-Club die Weltmeisterschaft der Flying-Dutchman-Klasse (FD), einer ehemaligen

Initially, the sailing clubs concentrated on the southern shore, i.e. the Steinhude side. It was not until the early 1960s that associations also formed on the northern shore, the Mardorf side, which wanted to practice water sports on the Lake Steinhuder Meer. The Mardorf Sailing Club was founded in 1962, followed by the Minden Canoe and Sailing Club in 1964, which was later renamed the Minden Sailing Club.

The growing number of members in the individual clubs, as well as the rapidly increasing number of regattas that were being held within the framework of the Lake Steinhuder Meer Racing Association, led to the conclusion of a public-law water rescue agreement with the then district of Hannover (now the Hannover region) on the initiative of the Lake Steinhuder Meer Racing Association.

The cooperation between the Lake Steinhuder Meer Water Rescue Association and the Hannover region, as well as between the Lake Steinhuder Meer Water Rescue Association and the fire department, makes the Lake Steinhuder Meer one of the safest water sports areas in the world and ensures that a sufficient number of motorboats are always available during regattas and at weekends to help water sports enthusiasts in distress.

The increasing number and quality of regattas has produced more and more outstanding sailors from Lake Steinhuder Meer. Olympic sailors and, for example, America's Cup competitors from Lake Steinhuder Meer are not uncommon in the world and have made the area famous worldwide.

In the recent past, the increasing internationality has led to European and World Championships being held in addition to the German and international German championships, which are organized by the German Sailing Association (DSV) and where the clubs around the Lake Steinhuder Meer are entrusted with organizing the regattas.

In 2016, the World Championship of the Flying Dutchman class (FD), a former Olympic two-man boat class, was held at the Hannoverscher Yacht-Club. With over 110 boats and participants from fifteen nations, including New Zealand, Mexico and Australia, one of the biggest events in sailing took place on the Lake Steinhuder Meer.

This was followed by the 2023 Raceboard World Champion-

↑ Raceboards an der Leebahnmarke. 2023 wurde die Weltmeisterschaft auf dem Steinhuder Meer ausgetragen.

↑ Raceboards at the leeward mark. In 2023, the world championship was held on the Lake Steinhuder Meer.

olympischen Zweimann-Bootsklasse, durchgeführt. Mit über 110 Booten und Teilnehmenden aus fünfzehn Nationen, darunter Neuseeland, Mexiko und Australien, fand eines der größten Ereignisse des Segelsports auf dem Steinhuder Meer statt.

Daran anschließen konnte, mit rund 170 Teilnehmenden aus aller Welt, die Raceboard-Weltmeisterschaft, die 2023 beim Yacht-Club Niedersachsen am Nordufer durchgeführt wurde. Erste Surfbretter wurden in den 1970er Jahren auf dem Steinhuder Meer gesehen.

Die Entwicklung der Segel-Surfbretter ging von da an stetig voran und damit nahm auch deren Geschwindigkeit zu. Über die sogenannten Funboards, später Kitesurfer – statt des üblichen Segels nutzen die Kitesurfer Schirme, die denen eines Gleitschirms bei Fallschirmspringen sehr ähneln – kam es zu

ship, which was held at the Yacht-Club Niedersachsen on the northern shore with around 170 participants from all over the world. The first surfboards were seen on Lake Steinhuder Meer in the 1970s.

From then on, the development of sail surfboards progressed steadily and their speed also increased. The so-called fun boards, later kite surfers – instead of the usual sail, kite surfers use chutes that are very similar to those used by parachutists – led to the currently frequently used foil boards, where the board no longer glides directly over the water, but on a modified fin. In the meantime, another development is becoming more and more popular – wingfoiling, in which the surfer has contact with his feet via footstraps on the board and holds the wingsail with his arms. The athlete's body is the connection between the sail and the board.

S. 54–55 Dieter und Andreas Bröer (Letzterer im Foto) kurz vor der Wendemarke auf ihrem 15er-Jollenkreuzer PHANTOM, während der Herbstwettfahrten des YSTM 2020.

P. 54–55 Dieter and Andreas Bröer (the latter in the photo) shortly before the turning mark on their 15 dinghy cruiser PHANTOM, during the autumn races of the YSTM 2020.

→ Die Steganlagen bei Mardorf aus der Luft betrachtet.
→ The jetties at Mardorf seen from the air.

← 15er-Jollenkreuzer kurz nach dem Start.
← 15sqm dinghy cruiser shortly after the start.

↙ Optimistenkinder beim Üben. Im Segler-Verein Großenheidorn wird die Kinder- und Jugendarbeit großgeschrieben.
↙ Optimist children practising. The Großenheidorn Sailing Club emphasize training children and teenagers.

↑ Kitesurfen mit einem Foilboard – abgehoben!
↑ Kitesurfing with a foil board – airborn!

↑ Wingfoilen ist eigentlich Windsurfen – nur ohne Mast.
↑ Wingfoiling is actually windsurfing – only without a mast.

den aktuell häufig genutzten Foilboards, bei denen das Brett nicht mehr unmittelbar über das Wasser gleitet, sondern auf einer modifizierten Finne. Inzwischen gewinnt eine weitere Entwicklung mehr und mehr Zuspruch – das Wingfoilen, bei dem die Surferin bzw. der Surfer über Schlaufen am Board mit den Füßen Kontakt hat und mit den Armen das Wingsail hält. Der Körper der Sportlerin bzw. des Sportlers ist die Verbindung zwischen Segel und Board.

Das Steinhuder Meer bietet nicht nur in den Sommermonaten viele Möglichkeiten, einen Wassersport auszuüben. Wenn das Meer zufriert, dann werden von den den Sportlerinnen und Sportlern die Eisschlitten ausgepackt und vorbereitet.

Innerhalb kürzester Zeit wird von erfahrenen Seglerinnen und Seglern ermittelt, ob die Eisfläche ausreichend tragend ist, um sicher mit den Eisschlitten befahren werden zu können. Dann werden umfangreiche Vernetzungen der Sportlerinnen und Sportler untereinander aktiviert und Seglerinnen und Seglern aus aller Welt reisen an, um an einer der begehrten Regatten auf dem Steinhuder Meer teilnehmen zu können.

The Lake Steinhuder Meer offers many opportunities for water sports, and not just in the summer months. When the lake freezes over, the ice sleds are unpacked and prepared by the athletes.

Within a very short time, experienced sailors determine whether the ice surface is sufficiently stable to be safely navigated with the ice sleds. Extensive networking between the athletes is then activated and sailors from all over the world travel to take part in one of the coveted regattas on the Lake Steinhuder Meer.

↑ DN-Eisschlitten in voller Fahrt hoch am Wind. Sie erreichen Geschwindigkeiten von über 100 km/h. Bei diesen Geschwindigkeiten ist es klar, dass bei einem Sturz Wasser hart sein kann ...

↑ DN ice sledges at full speed sailing close to the wind. They reach speeds of over 100 km/h. At these speeds, it is clear that water can be hard in the event of a fall ...

S. 60–61 Schlittschuhvergnügen vor Steinhude bei besten Eis- und Wetterbedingungen.

P. 60–61 Skating fun in front of Steinhude in the best ice and weather conditions.

↑ Schöner kann der Ausblick kaum sein: die Sicht auf den Kanal vor dem Clubgelände der Baltischen Segler-Vereinigung.

↑ The view could hardly be more beautiful: The view of the canal in front of the Baltische Segler Vereinigung club premises.

Baltische Segler-Vereinigung
Baltic Sailing Association

Frank Ludowig

Kindheitserinnerungen und Leidenschaft für das Segeln

Das Steinhuder Meer hat mein Leben auf vielfältige Weise geprägt. Als ich noch ein Kind war, hatte ich nur einen begrenzten Bezug zu diesem idyllischen Ort. Mein Onkel, der Notar Martin Ludowig, besaß ein Segelboot, auf das wir nur bei schönem Wetter zum sogenannten Kaffeesegeln eingeladen wurden. Meine lebhafteste Erinnerung an jene Tage ist der Sturm, der uns einmal überraschte. In großer Aufregung packten wir alle mit an, um Boot und Mannschaft sicher in den Hafen zu bringen. Was ich damals als Kind als Sturm empfand, wäre für eine erfahrene Seglerin bzw. einen erfahrenen Segler heute wohl etwas weniger Aufregendes.

Unsere Kindheit war geprägt von einer anderen Zeit, einer Zeit, in der unsere Eltern Teil des Wirtschaftswunders waren und zugleich selbstständige Handwerksmeister mit einem mittelständischen Unternehmen. Für Hobbys blieb da wenig Raum. Fleiß und Strebsamkeit wurden uns stattdessen in die Wiege gelegt und vorbildhaft vorgelebt. So blieb es bei Kontakt mit dem Wassersport ohne eigenes Boot.

Es ist ja bekannt, dass einige Fernsehberühmtheiten aus Fleischerfamilien stammen, darunter auch meine Schwester Frauke. Für Zufall halte ich das nicht. Das Leben in einer Handwerksfamilie prägt nun mal. Und unser Beruf erfordert von uns beiden ständigen Einsatz und stetiges Engagement.

Ich hingegen blieb dem Handwerk treu, was sich letztendlich als meine wahre Bestimmung erwies.

Mein Leben nahm dann eine entscheidende Wendung – nicht am Steinhuder Meer, sondern in Griechenland auf der Insel Kos, dabei spielte das Wasser erneut eine wichtige Rolle. Dort lernte ich meine heutige Ehefrau Monika kennen und wir verbrachten somit die erste gemeinsame Zeit am Strand.

Zehn Jahre später schickten wir unsere Kinder in den Ferien zum Segelcamp ans Steinhuder Meer, um die Sommerzeit bestmöglich zu nutzen. Es war meine Frau, die daraufhin auf den Gedanken kam, dass jemand, der so nah am Wasser lebt,

From childhood memories to a passion for sailing

The Lake Steinhuder Meer has shaped my life in many ways. When I was a child, I only had a limited connection to this idyllic place. My uncle, the notary Martin Ludowig, owned a sailing boat, which we were only invited on when the weather was fine for so-called coffee sailing. My most vivid memory of those days is the storm that surprised us once. In great excitement, we all pitched in to bring the boat and crew safely into the harbor. What I perceived as a storm as a child would probably be less exciting for an experienced sailor today.

Our childhood was shaped by a different time, a time when our parents were part of the economic miracle and at the same time self-employed master craftsmen with a medium-sized company. There was little room for hobbies. Instead, diligence and ambition were instilled in us and exemplified. So we remained in contact with water sports without our own boat.

It is well known that some TV celebrities come from butcher families, including my sister Frauke. I don't think that's a coincidence. Life in a family of craftspeople has a formative influence. And our profession requires constant commitment and dedication from both of us.

I, on the other hand, remained true to my craft, which ultimately proved to be my true destiny.

My life then took a decisive turn – not at Steinhuder Meer, but in Greece on the island of Kos, where water once again played an important role. It was there that I met my current wife Monika and we spent our first time together on the beach.

Ten years later, we sent our children to a sailing camp on the Lake Steinhuder Meer during the vacations to make the most of the summer. It was my wife who then came up with the idea that someone who lives so close to the water should also sail and use the water. She gave me a sailing license for my fortieth birthday.

I still remember my first sailing lesson in heavy weather and

↑ Die Terrasse der BSV lädt zum Verweilen ein.
↑ The BSV terrace invites you to stay and linger a while.

auch segeln sollte und das Wasser nutzen sollte. Zu meinem 40. Geburtstag schenkte sie mir einen Segelschein.

Ich erinnere mich noch gut an meine erste Segelstunde bei heftigem Wetter und wie sehr mir das Segeln trotz der Anstrengungen Spaß machte – im Gegensatz zu meinem Segellehrer. Daraufhin wechselte ich die Segelschule und setzte meine Ausbildung bei Peter Günther fort, dem wohl bekanntesten Segellehrer hier vor Ort, dem ich bis heute dankbar bin. Unter seiner Anleitung erwarb ich schnell nacheinander alle notwendigen Seescheine, auch für die Hochsee. Von da an waren alle Urlaube Segelreisen auf Charteryachten – zunächst an der Ostsee, später im Mittelmeer.

Dennoch bleibt das Steinhuder Meer mein Heimathafen, ein sicherer Hafen für Nachmittage und Abende, an denen ich einfach mal auf meine Miniyacht oder den Katamaran springen kann. Jeder Besuch dort fühlt sich wie ein kleiner Urlaub vom Alltag an und ist von unschätzbarem Wert. Neben meiner schnellen und leichten *Jantar 21* teile ich mir mit meinem Freund Jörn einen olympischen Tornado. Dabei schließt sich der Kreis zu früheren Zeiten, denn auch Jörns Vater war ein Handwerksmeister und enger Freund meines Vaters.

Das Steinhuder Meer hat nicht nur meine Kindheitserinnerungen geprägt, sondern auch meine Leidenschaft für das Segeln entfacht. Es ist ein Ort, an dem ich meine Sorgen hinter mir lassen kann und meine Seele im Rhythmus der Wellen baumeln lassen kann. Die Verbindung zum Wasser und zu diesem wunderschönen Fleckchen Erde werde ich immer in meinem Herzen tragen.

Heute ist es eine schöne Tradition geworden, dass meine Schwester, die berufsbedingt mit ihrer Familie in Köln lebt, uns regelmäßig besucht. Dabei führt uns unser gemeinsamer Weg immer zum Steinhuder Meer, sei es zum Essen in der Clubgastronomie der Baltischen Segler-Vereinigung (BSV) oder für einen erfrischenden Badeausflug auf dem Wasser. Dann packen wir unsere Badehosen und Bikinis ein und befestigen die Badeleiter an unserer *Jantar 21*. Das Steinhuder Meer ist für uns also auch zu einem Ort der Erholung, des gemeinsamen Genusses und der kostbaren Familienzeit geworden.

how much I enjoyed sailing despite the effort – unlike my sailing instructor. I then changed sailing school and continued my training with Peter Günther, probably the best-known sailing instructor in the area, to whom I am still grateful today. Under his guidance, I quickly acquired all the necessary sailing licenses, including for the open sea. From then on, all my vacations were sailing trips on charter yachts – first in the Baltic Sea and later in the Mediterranean.

Nevertheless, the Lake Steinhuder Meer remains my home port, a safe haven for afternoons and evenings when I can simply jump on my mini yacht or catamaran. Every visit there feels like a little vacation from everyday life and is invaluable. In addition to my fast and light *Jantar 21*, I share an Olympic Tornado with my friend Jörn. This brings us full circle to earlier times, as Jörn's father was also a master craftsman and close friend of my father.

The Lake Steinhuder Meer not only shaped my childhood memories, but also sparked my passion for sailing. It's a place where I can leave my worries behind and let my mind wander to the rhythm of the waves. I will always carry the connection to the water and this beautiful spot in my heart.

Today, it has become a nice tradition for my sister, who lives in Cologne with her family for work reasons, to visit us regularly. Our journey together always takes us to the Lake Steinhuder Meer, whether for a meal in the club restaurant of the Baltic Sailing Association or for a refreshing swim on the water. Then we pack our swimming trunks and bikinis and attach the bathing ladder to our *Jantar 21*. The Lake Steinhuder Meer has also become a place of relaxation, shared enjoyment and precious family time for us.

Das ist die BSV

Die Baltische Segler-Vereinigung wurde 1878 und erneut 1940 gegründet. Heute hat der Verein insgesamt ca. 860 Mitglieder, davon hat der Hauptsitz Steinhude ca. 470 Mitglieder. Der Verein verfügt über ein 16.000 m² großes Gelände mit einem Hafen für 86 Boote. Hinzukommen ca. 70 Landliegeplätze für kleinere Sportboote. Mittlerweile hat sich auch eine aktive Surf- und SUP-Gemeinschaft entwickelt. Das Clubhaus, das 1968 in Eigenregie gebaut und bis in die 1990er Jahre ständig erweitert wurde, wurde in den letzten Jahren aufwendig renoviert und ist mittlerweile barrierefrei zu erreichen.

Die BSV führt regelmäßig überregionale Regatten durch. Die regelmäßige Teilnahme und Durchführung des ehrenamtlichen Rettungsdienstes am Steinhuder Meer gehört ebenfalls zu den Aufgaben. Ein Höhepunkt ist die jährliche Jugendsegelfreizeit, an der mittlerweile über 30 Kinder eine Woche ihrer Sommerferien bei uns verbringen und segeln lernen. Dabei werden sie von unseren Mitgliedern und älteren Jugendlichen betreut.

Viele erfolgreiche Seglerinnen und Segler haben ihre Heimat in der BSV. Besonders zu nennen sind aktuelle Olympiateilnehmerinnen und Olympiateilnehmer, Welt- und Europameisterinnen bzw. Welt- und Europameister in verschiedenen Bootsklassen.

This is the BSV

The Baltic Sailing Association was founded in 1878 and again in 1940. Today the club has a total of approx. 860 members, of which the Steinhude headquarters has approx. 470 members. The association has a 16,000m² site with a marina for 86 boats. There are also approx. 70 land moorings for smaller pleasure craft. In the meantime, an active surfing and SUP community has also developed. The clubhouse, which was built by the club itself in 1968 and continuously expanded until the 1990s, has been extensively renovated in recent years and is now barrier-free.

The BSV regularly organises supra-regional regattas. The regular participation and organisation of the voluntary rescue service on the Lake Steinhuder Meer is also part of the tasks. A highlight is the annual youth sailing camp, when over 30 children now spend a week of their summer holidays with us and learn to sail. They are supervised by our members and older young people.

Many successful sailors have their home in the BSV. Particularly noteworthy are current Olympic participants, world and European champions in various boat classes.

↑ Das Clubhaus der BSV aus der Luft gesehen. ↑ The BSV clubhouse seen from the air.

↑ Kurt „Kurti" Prenzler in seinem geliebten Flying Dutchman während einer der Wettfahrten zur Weltmeisterschaft 2016.

↑ Kurt "Kurti" Prenzler in his beloved Flying Dutchman during one of the races for the 2016 World Championship.

Hannoverscher Yacht-Club
Hannover Yacht Club

Heinrich K.-M. Hecht

Kurt Prenzler – Beispiel eines weit gereisten Seglers, der sich am wohlsten am Steinhuder Meer fühlt

Für Kurti, wie er liebevoll in seinen Kreisen genannt wird, gibt es kaum etwas Schöneres, als seine Zeit am Steinhuder Meer und im Hannoverschen Yacht-Club (HYC) zu verbringen. Jeder, der am Steinhuder Meer ambitioniert segelt, kennt Kurt Prenzler. Jahrzehntelang leitete der studierte Diplom-Kaufmann mit viel Charme und straffer Hand eine der ältesten und größten Parfümerien Deutschlands, aber wenn das Segeln zu einer Regatta oder zum Training rief, ließ Kurti Büro – das eh nie wirklich aufgeräumt war – Büro sein, und eilte nach Steinhude.

Seine Eltern hatten eigentlich so gar nichts mit Segeln am Hut, aber Kurti hatte das Segelvirus während eines Spaziergangs mit seiner Mutter am Maschsee in Hannover gepackt und es ließ ihn nie wieder los: „Schau mal, Mama, das Segelboot dort drüben, das segelt ja von ganz alleine!"

Kurti trat 1957 im Alter von dreizehn Jahren in den HYC ein, der für ihn ein zweites Zuhause wurde und ihm die Unterstützung bot, die Kurti zum erfolgreichen Segler werden ließ. Bereits 1961 wird Kurti, gemeinsam mit seiner Vorschoterin Christel Gollert, Niedersächsischer Jugendmeister im Pirat. Später stieg Kurti, nach einem kurzen Gastspiel in der Korsarenklasse, in den olympischen FD um und wurde rasch zum ernsten Gegner der etablierten Seglerinnen und Segler dieser Klasse. Nach Hamburg umgezogen gewinnt er bereits 1966 den Senatspreis und düpiert seine Hamburger Konkurrenz.

Bei den Ausscheidungen 1972 zu den Olympischen Spielen

Kurt Prenzler – Example of a well-traveled sailor who feels most at home on the Lake Steinhuder Meer

For Kurti, as he is affectionately known in his circles, there is hardly anything better than spending time on the Lake Steinhuder Meer and at the Hannover Yacht Club (HYC). Anyone who sails ambitiously on the Lake Steinhuder Meer knows Kurt "Kurti" Prenzler. For decades, the business graduate managed one of the oldest and largest perfumeries in Germany with a lot of charm and a firm hand, but when sailing called for a regatta or training, Kurti left the office – which was never really tidy anyway – and hurried to Steinhude.

His parents weren't really into sailing at all, but Kurti caught the sailing bug during a walk with his mother on the Maschsee in Hannover and never let it go: "Look, mom, that sailboat over there, it sails all by itself!"

Kurti joined the HYC in 1957 at the age of thirteen, which became a second home for him and offered him the support that enabled Kurti to become a successful sailor.

As early as 1961, Kurti, together with his foresailor Christel Gollert, became Lower Saxony's youth champion in the Pirat. Later, after a brief guest appearance in the Corsair class, Kurti switched to the Olympic Flying Dutchman (FD) and quickly became a serious rival to the established sailors in this class. Moving to Hamburg, he won the Senate Prize as early as 1966 and outdid his Hamburg rivals.

In the 1972 qualifiers for the Olympic Games, there is a tough neck-and-neck race with the later two-time Olympic medal winner Ulrich "Ulli" Libor, to whom he generously handed

↑ Kurt Prenzler Sen. begrüßt seinen Sohn Kurt „Kurti" und dessen Vorschoterin Christel Gollert anlässlich der Deutschen Jugendmeisterschaft im Pirat, Pfingsten 1961 am Dümmer. Die beiden wurden Erste in der Regatta und somit Deutsche Jugendmeister.

↑ Kurt Prenzler Sen. welcomes his son Kurt "Kurti" and his foresailor Christel Gollert on the occasion of the German Youth Championship in the Pirat, Whitsun 1961 at the Dümmer. The two of them came first in the regatta and thus became German youth champions.

gibt es ein hartes Kopf-an-Kopf-Rennen mit dem späteren zweifachen Olympiamedaillengewinner Ulrich „Ulli" Libor, dem er großzügig, nachdem klar war, dass es für Kurti keine Olympischen Spiele geben wird, seinen damaligen Vorschoter Peter Naumann überließ. Libor und Naumann, den alle wegen seiner Locken nur „Lumumba" nennen, gewinnen in Kiel die Silbermedaille.

Kurt Prenzler bleibt bis heute in der anspruchsvollen FD-Klasse und wird unter anderem 1973 Deutscher Meister. Im Jahr 2016 veranstaltet sein Verein, der HYC, die FD-Weltmeisterschaft mit 113 teilnehmenden Booten aus fünfzehn Nationen. Keine Frage, dass Kurti auch an dieser Regatta als „Oldie" noch teilnimmt – und segelt so manchem Favoriten besonders beim Start davon.

Insgesamt besaß Kurti 27 FDs und segelt inzwischen mit seiner „persönlichen" Segelnummer 66 auf dem Steinhuder Meer und verbringt so viel Zeit wie möglich im Hannoverschen Yacht-Club.

over his then foreship Peter Naumann after it became clear that there would be no Olympic Games for Kurti. Libor and Naumann, who everyone called "Lumumba" because of his curly hair, won the silver medal in Kiel.

Kurt Prenzler remains in the demanding FD class to this day and becomes German champion in 1973. In 2016, his club, the HYC, organizes the FD World Championship with 113 participating boats from fifteen nations. There's no question that Kurti still takes part in this regatta as an "oldie" and sails away from many a favorite, especially at the start.

To date, Kurti has owned 27 FDs and now sails with his "personal" sail number 66 on the Lake Steinhuder Meer and spends as much time as possible at the Hannover Yacht Club.

Das Clubhaus des HYCs am Südufer des Steinhuder Meeres. →

The clubhouse of the HYC on the southern shore of the Lake Steinhuder Meer. →

Das Boot GER 66 gehört Kurt Prenzler (HYC). FD beim Start zu einer Wettfahrt der Weltmeisterschaft 2016, die federführend durch den HYC durchgeführt wurde. →

The boat GER 66 is Kurt Prenzler (HYC). FD at the start of a race at the 2016 World Championship, which was organised by the HYC. →

↑ Das Clubhaus des Segel-Clubs Mardorf am Nordufer. Der SCMa ist einer der ältesten Vereine am Nordufer des Steinhuder Meeres.

↑ The clubhouse of the Mardorf Sailing Club on the northern shore. The SCMa is one of the oldest clubs on the north bank of the Lake Steinhuder Meer.

Segel-Club Mardorf
Mardorf Sailing Club

Heinrich K.-M. Hecht

Was hat ein Seglerverein in Mardorf mit gutem Essen zu tun?

Das Erste, was mir zum Segel-Club Mardorf (SCMa) einfällt, ist gutes Essen! Und das ist nicht böse gemeint …
Vor einigen Jahren heuerte im SCMa der Koch eines ehemaligen Sternerestaurants aus Hannover an und beglückte die Seglerinnen und Segler und einkehrenden Gäste mit ausgezeichneten Speisen. Selbst die Seglerinnen und Segler der zahlreichen Vereine des Südufers nahmen den Weg gerne auf sich und legten am SCMa an, um Abwechslung von den Speisen der eigenen Vereine zu bekommen. Irgendwann zog der begnadete Koch weiter. Aktuell hat der SCMa das „Glück", dass ein Restaurant in Schneeren abbrannte und sein Wirt ein neues Zuhause im SCMa fand und nun ebenfalls die Gäste mit außergewöhnlich gutem Essen versorgt. Die Besonderheit des SCMa ist ferner, dass er direkt am Spazierweg des Nordufers liegt und auch Menschen, die keine Seglerinnen und Segler oder Wassersportlerinnen und Wassersportler sind, dort einkehren können und sich verwöhnen lassen.
Gute Seglerinnen und Segler setzt man eigentlich am Steinhuder Meer voraus, so dass es nicht verwundert, dass der SCMa, 1962 gegründet, mehrfach Deutsche Meister und Europacup-Gewinner zu seinen Mitgliedern zählt. Regatten richtet der Club in einigen Klassen aus, darunter auch die German Open der Microcupper – kleine Regattayachten mit einer kleinen Kajüte.
Heute hat der SCMa 260 Mitglieder, davon 45 Kinder und Jugendliche, die durch eine zielgerichtete Jugendarbeit im Segeln unterstützt werden. Die Steganlage ist behindertengerecht und verfügt zurzeit über 80 Liegeplätze.

What does a sailing club in Mardorf have to do with good food?

The first thing that comes to mind when I think of the Mardorf Sailing Club (SCMa) is good food! And I don't mean that in a bad way …
A few years ago, a chef from a former Michelin-starred restaurant in Hannover was hired by the SCMa and delighted the sailors and guests with excellent food. Even the sailors from the numerous clubs on the south bank were happy to make the journey and moor at the SCMa to get a change from the food served by their own clubs. At some point, the gifted chef moved on. Currently, the SCMa was "lucky" that a restaurant in Schneeren burned down and its landlord found a new home in the SCMa and now also delights guests with exceptionally good food. Another special feature of the SCMa is that it is located directly on the footpath along the north bank and people who are not sailors or water sports enthusiasts can also drop in and enjoy a meal there.
Good sailors are a given on the Lake Steinhuder Meer, so it is not surprising that the SCMa, founded in 1962, has several German champions and European Cup winners among its members. The club organizes regattas in several classes, including the German Open of the Micro Cupper – small regatta yachts with a small cabin.
Today, the Mardorf Sailing Club has 260 members, 45 of whom are children and young people who are supported in their sailing through youth work. The jetty is handicapped accessible and currently has 80 berths.

↑ Starboote am Steinhuder Meer beim Start zu einer Wettfahrt. Stare am Steinhuder Meer zu segeln, geht nur dann, wenn das Meer gut mit Wasser gefüllt ist.

↑ Star boats on the Lake Steinhuder Meer at the start of a race. Sailing a Stare on the Lake Steinhuder Meer is only possible when the lake is well filled with water.

Schaumburg-Lippischer Seglerverein
Schaumburg-Lippe Sailing Club

Heinrich K.-M. Hecht

Der fürstliche Seglerverein und seine „Stare"

Der Schaumburg-Lippische Seglerverein (SLSV), gerne auch der Fürstliche genannt – weil offiziell Fürst zu Schaumburg-Lippe qua Geburt Mitglied ist – ist immer für eine Überraschung gut!

Gediegen mit Kamin und edlem Porzellan ist die Atmosphäre im Inneren des Clubhauses, sportlich auf dem Wasser. So könnte man den Club in kurzen Worten beschreiben, der sich 1908 als dritter Segelverein am Steinhuder Meer etablierte.

Um auf die Probleme mit dem niedrigen Wasserstand am Steinhuder Meer hinzuweisen, organisierte der Sportwart des SLSVs, Niels Hentschel, eine Regatta mit Starbooten und 2.4ern. Normalerweise können diese Boote aufgrund ihrer festen Kiele und des Tiefgangs nicht auf dem Steinhuder Meer segeln, aber in begrenztem Maße ist es durchaus möglich, wenn man die richtigen Bereiche nutzt, die der niedrige Wasserstand zulässt. Insgesamt kamen 85 Boote aus sieben Nationen zusammen, darunter die international bedeutende Bootsklasse der „Stare", die mit einer Segelfläche von 27 m² und einem Tiefgang von 1,02 Metern etwas Besonderes darstellt. Dazu gesellte sich die inklusive Bootsklasse 2.4er, die infolge ihrer ebenfalls festen Kiele gut zu den Staren passt.

Ergiebige Regenfälle vor der Regatta und ein annehmbarer Wasserstand ließen die Regatta zu. Niels Hentschel: „Bei nur 10 cm weniger Wasser im Meer hätten wir dieses Event kurzfristig absagen müssen. Eine Absage wäre für die Teilnehmer aus den Niederlanden, Schweden, dem Vereinigten Königreich, Dänemark und Deutschland sowohl logistisch als auch in der Wahrnehmung des Steinhuder Meers äußerst schwierig gewesen."

Example of a well-traveled sailor who feels most at home on Lake Steinhuder Meer

The Schaumburg-Lippe Sailing Club (SLSV), also known as the Princely Club – because Prince of Schaumburg-Lippe is officially a member by birth – is always good for a surprise! The atmosphere inside the clubhouse is dignified with a fireplace and fine china, and sporty on the water. This is a brief description of the club, which was established in 1908 as the third sailing club on Lake Steinhuder Meer.

To draw attention to the problems with the low water level at Lake Steinhuder Meer, the SLSV's sports manager, Niels Hentschel, organized a regatta with starting boats and 2.4s. Normally, these boats cannot sail on the Lake Steinhuder Meer due to their fixed keels and draught, but to a limited extent it is perfectly possible if you use the right areas that the low water level allows. A total of 85 boats from seven nations came together, including the internationally important "Star" boat class, which is something special with a sail area of 27 square meters and a draft of 1.02 meters. They were joined by the inclusive 2.4 boat class, which is also a good match for the Stars due to its fixed keels.

Abundant rainfall before the regatta and an acceptable water level allowed the regatta to take place. Niels Hentschel: "With only 10 cm less water in the lake, we would have had to cancel this event at short notice. Cancellation would have been extremely difficult for the participants from the Netherlands, Sweden, the United Kingdom, Denmark and Germany, both logistically and in terms of the perception of the Lake Steinhuder Meer".

Nevertheless, it was only possible to sail on Saturday due to a storm on Friday and a calm on Sunday. The sailors took it in

↑ Die großzügige Hafenanlage des SLSVs.   ↑ The spacious marina facilities of the SLSV.

Trotzdem konnte bedingt durch Sturm am Freitag und Flaute am Sonntag, nur am Samstag gesegelt werden. Die Seglerinnen und Segler nahmen es mit Humor und geselligem Verhalten bei Speis und Trank auf dem Clubgelände des SLSVs. Alle Beteiligten waren begeistert von der Regatta, dem Clubgelände und dem drum herum organisierten geselligen Teil. Die Sieger waren eigentlich Nebensache, und trotzdem aus chronistischem Grund erwähnt: Sieger im Starboot, der alle drei ausgeschriebenen Preise gewann, war Hubert Merkelbach mit seinem dänischen Vorschoter Jan Eli Gravad, und im 2.4er gewann Karl „Kalle" Dehler.

good humor and socialized over food and drink on the SLSV club grounds.
Everyone involved was delighted with the regatta, the club grounds and the social part organized around it. The winning were actually a minor matter, but nevertheless mentioned for archival reasons: the winner in the Star boat, which won all three prizes on offer:
Hubert Merkelbach with his Danish foreskipper Jan Eli Gravad. The 2.4 category was won by Karl "Kalle" Dehler.

↑ Die 2.4er-Boote sind insbesondere für Seglerinnen und Segler mit Einschränkungen gedacht. Inzwischen findet die Klasse zunehmend auch Freunde bei den Seglerinnen und Seglern ohne Einschränkungen. Die Boote ähneln in ihrem Design großen Yachten, die früher beim America's Cup gesegelt wurden.

↑ The 2.4 square metre boats are designed especially for sailors with disabilities. The class is now becoming increasingly popular with sailors without disabilities. The boats are similar in design to the large yachts that used to be sailed in the America's Cup.

↑ Der mehrfache Deutsche Meister im P-Boot, Uwe Lätzsch, Mitglied im Yachtclub Steinhuder Meer (YSTM) seit Geburt an, mit Vorschoter Marc Romberg, auf einem Raumschotkurs unter Spinnaker. In dieser Regatta erkämpften sich die zwei ihren ersten Deutschen Meistertitel im P-Boot.

↑ The multiple German P-Boat champion, Uwe Lätzsch, a member of the Steinhuder Meer Yacht Club (YSTM) since birth, with foredeck Marc Romberg, on a sailing broad reach under spinaker. In this regatta, the two won their first German championship title in the P-Boat.

Yachtclub Steinhuder Meer

Steinhuder Meer Yacht Club

Henning Windhagen

Warum segeln wir?

Fragen Sie das mal eine Seglerin oder einen Segler am Steinhuder Meer! Weil es einfach eine Sucht ist, da draußen zu sein. Aber fragen Sie auch mal Nicht-Seglerinnen und Nicht-Segler – viele Menschen fühlen eine Attraktion zum Wasser und zu Booten, obwohl sie aktiv gar nicht dabei sind. Hunderttausende radeln ums Steinhuder Meer und schauen auf die schönen Boote.

Mich hat es in der Jugend zusammen mit meinem Bruder zum Segeln gebracht, von Eltern, die nichts, aber auch gar nichts mit dem Segeln zu tun hatten. Retrospektiv fragt man sich, warum die nicht segelnde Mutter ihre Kinder permanent an den Dümmer fuhr, und nicht ins nächstgelegene Schwimmbad. Offensichtlich verband sie eine besondere Faszination mit dem Segeln, unbewusst und nicht erlebt, und wollte das für ihre Kinder.

Wenn die Nicht-Seglerin bzw. der Nicht-Segler auf maritime Fotos und plüschige Bilder mit viel Sonne, leichtem Wind, blauem Wasser, elegantem Holz und weißen Segeln schaut, kommt sie hoch, die gesamte Segelromantik mit all ihren Reisen, den fernen Ländern und den Abenteuern unterm Sternenhimmel. Der Traum des sesshaften, diskret saturiert-frustrierten Menschen: alles hinter sich lassen, Boot besteigen, lossegeln in den Sonnenuntergang, die Routine hinter sich lassen. Auch wenn es für uns Steinhuder-Meer-Seglerinnen und -Segler nur bis zum Wilhelmstein geht – ein Boot, leichter Wind, Sonne und ein entspannter Drink – unser limbisches System im Gehirn lässt uns keine Chance.

Why do we sail?

Ask a sailor on the Lake Steinhuder Meer! Because it's simply an addiction to be out there. But ask non-sailors too – many people feel an attraction to the water and to boats, even though they are not actively involved. Hundreds of thousands of people cycle around Lake Steinhuder Meer and watch the beautiful boats.

My brother and I were introduced to sailing in our youth by parents who had nothing, absolutely nothing, to do with sailing. In retrospect, you wonder why the non-sailing mother constantly drove her children to the Dümmer and not to the nearest swimming pool. Obviously she had a special fascination with sailing, unconsciously and not experienced, and wanted that for her children.

When the non-sailor looks at maritime photos and fluffy pictures with lots of sun, light wind, blue water, elegant wood and white sails, it brings up the whole romance of sailing with all its travels, faraway countries and adventures under the stars. The dream of the sedentary, discreetly saturated and frustrated person: leave everything behind, board the boat, sail off into the sunset, leave the routine behind. Even if it only goes as far as Wilhelmstein for us Lake Steinhuder Meer sailors – a boat, light wind, sun and a relaxed drink – the limbic system in our brains won't let us leave anything behind.

The real sailors have also earned the romance of sailing. After all, every sailor knows the hardships: a broken boat, bad wind, wet and cold, seasickness and perhaps money worries. It's mostly the laws of nature – sailing is a game with the elements and, to a certain extent, is also grounding.

↑ Das seit 1927 bestehende Clubhaus des YSTM aus Holz.
↑ The wooden clubhouse of the YSTM, which has existed since 1927.

↗ Eine Besonderheit am Steinhuder Meer: die Aussichtsplattform am Flaggenmast im YSTM – hier schmeckt bei Sonnenuntergang der Rosé am besten!
↗ A special feature at Lake Steinhuder Meer: the viewing platform at the flagpole at the YSTM – this is where the rosé tastes best at sunset!

→ Der Autor mit einem Teil seiner Familie in seiner H-Jolle (Bj. 1959), die er seit 1984 segelt. Heinrich K.-M. Hecht ist Mitglied im YSTM.
→ The author with part of his family in his H dinghy (built in 1959), which he has sailed since 1984. Heinrich K.-M. Hecht is a member of the YSTM.

Die echten Seglerinnen und Segler haben sich die Segelromantik auch verdient. Denn die Mühen kennt auch jede Seglerin bzw. jeder Segler: kaputtes Boot, schlechten Wind, Nässe und Kälte, Seekrankheit, dazu vielleicht Geldsorgen. Eben meist Naturgesetze – Segeln ist das Spiel mit den Elementen und erdet gewissermaßen auch.

Für manche ist der Kampf mit den Elementen Herausforderung, im Sturm zu bestehen. Wanten pfeifen, überfliegende Gischt und einstellige Lufttemperaturen. Die Gewalten erleben. Auch am Steinhuder Meer. Nur wer es selbst erlebt hat, kann verstehen, wie sich 30 km² Wasserfläche vom lieblichen Teich in eine feindliche Landschaft verändern.

Segeln kann auch zum Rausch werden, der Rausch der Geschwindigkeit. Etwa unter Spinnaker, auf Katamaranen, beim Windsurfen oder unter dem Kite. Die technische Entwicklung kennt keine Grenzen, jetzt wird gefoilt und damit schon halb geflogen. Und der Wettbewerb, Regattasegeln, zutiefst in der Psyche der menschlichen Natur – das Sich-Messen und der seglerische Wettbewerb: Wie sagt man so schön – zwei Boote gleich eine Regatta.

Und dann die Boote. Die Segelnden und ihr Boot. Manche segeln gar nicht, sie haben ein Boot. Sie suchen eine Beschäftigung. Am Boot gibt's immer was zu tun, wenigstens muss es immer geputzt werden. Ganze Lebensgeschichten sind von

For some, the battle with the elements is a challenge in a storm. Whistling shrouds, flying spray and single-digit air temperatures. Experience the forces. Even on the Lake Steinhuder Meer. Only those who have experienced it for themselves can understand how 30 km2 of water can change from a lovely pond into a hostile landscape.

Sailing can also be a thrill, the thrill of speed. For example, under spinnaker, on catamarans, windsurfing or under a kite. Technical development knows no bounds, people are now foiling and half-flying. And the competition. Regatta sailing. Deep in the psyche of human nature – competing and sailing competition. As the saying goes – two boats equal a regatta.

And then the boats. The sailor and his boat. Some don't sail at all, they have a boat. Are you looking for an occupation? There's always something to do on the boat, at least it always has to be cleaned. Entire life stories are filled with people who have spent thousands of hours building boats.

Boats embody aesthetics and elegance. Speed is important, but beauty is much more important. Posters with photographs of classic sailors are ubiquitous. A special human affinity for water, mahogany wood, waves and "fast lines" seems to be deeply rooted in our evolutionary biology.

You can sail as a loner or as a gregarious person. Some sail non-stop around the world alone. Others are not looking for

↑ Das Sommerfest im YSTM ist mit untergehender Sonne ein besonderes Erlebnis für alle Mitglieder.

↑ Summer party at the YSTM with the setting sun is always a special experience for all members.

Menschen gefüllt, die Boote in tausenden von Stunden gebastelt haben.

Boote verkörpern Ästhetik und Eleganz. Schnell ist wichtig, schön aber viel wichtiger. Poster mit Fotografien klassischer Segler sind allgegenwärtig. Eine besondere Sympathie des Menschen zu Wasser, Mahagoniholz, Wellen und „schnellen Linien" scheint evolutionsbiologisch tief in uns drin zu stecken. Segeln kann man als Einzelgängerin und Einzelgänger oder als Beziehungsmensch. Die einen fahren alleine Nonstop um die Welt. Die anderen suchen keine Ruhe, sondern Gemeinschaft am Steinhuder Meer. Das Allerbeste am Segeln ist, dass ja beides geht, je nach Lust oder Laune. Viele gehen dazu in einen der Steinhuder Segelclubs.

Segelclubs sind für einige überhaupt der Grund, zu segeln. Bei einigen, so auch bei unserem, gibt es maritime Traditionen und einen gesellschaftlichen Anspruch. Manchmal als elitär verspottet sind gerade Stunden in einem Club mit zuvorkommendem, zivilem Umgang, Rücksichtnahme, und Gemeinschaftssinn eine Wohltat in einer Welt mit zunehmender Gleichgültigkeit und Selbstzentriertheit. Engagement für die Jugend und Naturschutz sind dann der wahre Luxus.

Segeln ist ein Sport, der eine Lebenseinstellung ist, der physische und mentale Kraft gibt und im nächsten Sturm sogar eine sinnvolle Portion menschliche Demut lehrt.

peace and quiet, but for company on the Lake Steinhuder Meer. The best thing about sailing is that you can do both, depending on your mood. Many people go to one of the Lake Steinhuder Meer sailing clubs.

For some, sailing clubs are the reason for sailing in the first place. Some, like ours, have maritime traditions and social aspirations. Sometimes derided as elitist, hours spent in a club with courteous, civil interaction, consideration and a sense of community are a blessing in a world of increasing indifference and self-centredness. Commitment to youth and nature conservation are the true luxury.

Sailing is a sport that is a way of life, that gives physical and mental strength and even teaches a meaningful portion of human humility in the next storm.

Holzboote

Wooden boats

Torfkähne

Peat barges

Klaus Fesche

Neben dem Wilhelmstein und dem Aal ist der Torfkahn ein Wahrzeichen des Steinhuder Meeres. Vielerorts verwenden Traditionspflege oder Fremdenverkehrswerbung sein Bild oder ausrangierte Exemplare dieses besonderen Bootstyps zur Wiedererkennung, um Interesse zu wecken und Besucherinnen und Besucher anzulocken. Ein stilisierter Torfkahn bildet das Logo der Ortsgemeinschaft Seeprovinz im Schaumburg-Lippischen Heimatverein; ausgemusterte Torfkähne stehen an prominenten Orten in Steinhude und Hagenburg, und ein Exemplar wird im Steinhuder Fischer- und Webermuseum aufbewahrt. Ein Boot wie den Torfkahn des Steinhuder Meeres findet man sonst nirgendwo. Was macht ihn so einzigartig?

Vielleicht lässt sich das Besondere des Kahns in folgender Formel zusammenfassen: Es lässt sich kein Wasserfahrzeug vorstellen, das so einfach gebaut ist und das sich gleichzeitig so perfekt für seine verschiedenen Einsatzzwecke an genau diesem Ort – dem Flachsee Steinhuder Meer – eignet. Noch kürzer: minimaler konstruktiver Aufwand für maximale Zweckmäßigkeit. Der Steinhuder Torfkahn besteht nur aus einer Handvoll Elementen: einem kastenartigen Rumpf, der durch ein Schott geteilt ist, zwei Segeln samt den sie tragenden Masten, und dem „Firrer", also dem Steuer(ruder). Unverzichtbares Zubehör sind zwei lange Holzstangen zum Staken; Ruder zur Vorwärtsbewegung gehören nicht zur Ausstattung. Zur Besonderheit der Konstruktion gehört auch, dass das etwa mittschiffs angebrachte Hauptsegel – mit sieben bis acht qm Fläche etwa drei qm größer als das Vorsegel – je nach Windrichtung back- oder steuerbords aufgestellt werden kann. Entsprechend dieser Aufstellung wird auch der Firrer

Alongside the Wilhelmstein and the eel, the peat barge is a symbol of the Lake Steinhuder Meer. Many places use its image or discarded examples of this special type of boat to promote tradition and tourist advertising in order to arouse interest and attract visitors. A stylised peat barge forms the logo of the local community Seeprovinz in the Schaumburg-Lippe Heritage Association; decommissioned peat barges can be found in prominent locations in Steinhude and Hagenburg, and one example is kept in the Steinhude Fishermen's and Weavers' Museum. You won't find a boat like the Steinhude peat barge anywhere else. What makes it so unique?

Perhaps the special nature of the barge can be summarised in the following formula: It is impossible to imagine a watercraft that is so simply built and at the same time so perfectly suited to its various uses at this very location – the shallow Lake Steinhuder Meer. In a nutshell: minimum design effort for maximum practicality. The Steinhuder Torfkahn consists of just a handful of elements: A box-like hull divided by a bulkhead, two sails, together with the masts supporting them, and the "Firrer", i.e. the steering (rudder). Two long wooden poles for punting are essential accessories; oars for forward movement are not part of the equipment. Another special feature of the design is that the main sail, which is positioned roughly amidships and has a surface area of seven to eight square metres – around three square metres larger than the foresail – can be positioned on the port or starboard side depending on the wind direction. Depending on this position, the rudder is also attached to the left or right of the ship – i.e. to leeward. The hull is also practical: probably developed directly from the dugout canoe, it is traditionally made of old oak.

↖ Noch heute prägen die historischen Torfkähne das Bild des Steinhuder Meeres.

↖ The historic peat barges still characterise the image of the Lake Steinhuder Meer today.

↑ Die namensgebende Verwendung der Torfkähne war der Transport des Torfs von den Torfstichen des Toten Moores nach Steinhude.

↑ The peat barges were used to transport peat from the peat pits of the Toten Moor to Steinhude.

links oder rechts am Schiff – also in Lee – angebracht. Zweckmäßig auch der Rumpf: Wohl direkt aus dem Einbaum entwickelt, besteht er traditionell aus altem Eichenholz. Die starken Bordwände sind leicht nach innen geneigt, so dass die im Kahn stehende Schifferin bzw. der im Kahn stehende Schiffer bei der Arbeit gut abgestützt ist. Der noch stärkere Boden hat keinen Kiel, der Kahn kann so überall an den flachen Ufern des Meeres anlanden.

Und welches sind nun die Einsatzzwecke? Die Bezeichnung Torfkahn verrät schon einen – nämlich den Torftransport aus dem ans Steinhuder Meer grenzenden Moor. Torf, früher verbreitetes Heizmaterial, wurde von der Bevölkerung Steinhudes auf dem Markt in Hannover verkauft. Aber auch alle anderen Lasten ließen sich mit dem Torfkahn transportieren, angefangen beim Baumaterial für den Wilhelmstein – möglicherweise hat die Konstruktion des Torfkahns hier ihren Ursprung. Und bestens geeignet ist der Torfkahn natürlich auch für den Fischfang, für die Arbeit der Steinhuder Fischerinnen und Fischer an den Aalreusen und Stellnetzen.

Im späten 20. Jahrhundert kam schließlich noch ein Verwendungszweck hinzu: Seit 1978 die Fischerkreidage in Steinhude wieder ins Leben gerufen wurden, werden zur Gaudi der Schiffseignerinnen und Schiffseigner sowie des Publikums Torfkahnregatten gefahren – und siehe da: Der Torfkahn ist obendrein auch recht flott! Übrigens: Ein Fragment eines fast 6.000 Jahre alten Einbaums, das 1935 am Steinhuder Meer gefunden wurde, kann in der Festung auf dem Wilhelmstein besichtigt werden.

The strong sides are slightly inclined inwards so that the skipper standing in the boat is well supported while working. The even stronger bottom has no keel, so the barge can land anywhere on the shallow shores of the sea.

And what are its purposes? The name Torfkahn (peat barge) already gives one away – namely the transport of peat from the moor bordering the Lake Steinhuder Meer. Peat, once a common heating material, was sold by the people of Steinhude at the market in Hannover. But all other loads could also be transported by peat barge, starting with building materials for the Wilhelmstein – the construction of the peat barge may have originated here. And the peat barge is of course also ideally suited for fishing, for the work of the Steinhude fishermen on the eel traps and gillnets.

In the late 20th century, another purpose was finally added: since the Fischerkreidage in Steinhude was brought back to life in 1978, peat barge races have been held for the enjoyment of the boat owners and the public – and lo and behold, the peat barge is also quite fast!

By the way: a fragment of an almost 6,000-year-old dugout tree, which was found on the Lake Steinhuder Meer in 1935, can be viewed in the fortress on the Wilhelmstein.

↑ Mit mehreren miteinander verbundenen Torfkähnen ließen sich sogar Strandhäuser transportieren.
↑ Even beach houses could be transported with several interconnected peat barges.

↑ Die Silhouette des Torfkahns wird geprägt durch die beiden fast quadratischen Segel am Bug und mittschiffs.
↑ The silhouette of the peat barge is characterised by the two almost square sails at the bow and amidships.

↑ Im Fischer- und Webermuseum in Steinhude lässt sich ein gut erhaltener Torfkahn besichtigen.
↑ A well-preserved peat barge can be viewed in the fishing and weaving museum in Steinhude.

↑ Wenn es die Kapitäne wollen, kann auch mit Auswanderern eine kleine Regattasituation entstehen – sofern der Wind passt.

↑ If the skippers want it, a small regatta situation can also be created with emigrants – provided the wind is favourable.

↖ Eigentlich ist ja in einem Auswanderer schon der Weg das Ziel, aber die Insel Wilhelmstein lockt jung und alt!

↖ In emigrant boats, the journey is the destination, but the island of Wilhelmstein attracts young and old!

← Einer der traditionsreichen Auswandererkapitäne: Udo Töffel.
← One of the traditional emigrant captains: Udo Töffel.

Auswanderer

Emigrants

Heinrich K.-M. Hecht

Ein Bootsname, der, als er entstand, gewissermaßen ein Trend war

Auswanderer? Was für ein Name für eine wohl zumindest in Europa einzigartige Art Boot. Schon als Kind hatte ich mich über diesen ungewöhnlichen Namen gewundert. Wenn es stimmt, was berichtet wird, gibt es in ganz Europa keine ähnliche Bootsklasse.

Der Auswanderer ist ein Holzboot, gaffelgetakelt, zwischen acht und elf Meter lang, um die zweieinhalb bis drei Meter breit und bietet rund 25 bis 30 Personen Platz. Bei passendem Wetter wird gesegelt und ansonsten hilft ein kleiner Motor.

Der Name stammt aus einer Zeit, in der sowohl der Tourismus entstand, als auch zahlreiche Menschen ein besseres Schicksal in Übersee suchten. Die Ufer des Steinhuder Meeres, die teilweise noch zum Fürstentum Schaumburg-Lippe als auch zum preußisch-hannoverschem „Ausland" gehörten, bildeten auch damals den Ausgangspunkt der Auswandererboote. Startete ein Boot zum Beispiel von Hagenburg aus und fuhr nach Mardorf, sprach man halt von Ausland. Manche Überlieferung berichtet auch von frisch vermählten Paaren, die mitsamt ihrem Hausstand zum angrenzenden Ausland „auswanderten".

Heute fahren meist Touristinnen und Touristen mit einem Auswanderer von Steinhude aus zur Insel Wilhelmstein oder nach Mardorf. Die rund 30 Auswandererkapitäne sind in der Steinhuder Personenschifffahrt organisiert und führen so eine wunderbare Tradition fort. Und trifft man sie auf dem Wilhelmstein in einer ruhigen Minute, erzählt der eine oder andere Kapitän sicherlich gerne die eine oder andere Geschichte …

A boat name that was somewhat of a trend when it was created

Emigrant? What a name for what is probably a unique type of boat, at least in Europe. Even as a child I had wondered about this unusual name. If what is reported is true, there is no similar class of boat in the whole of Europe.

The Auswanderer is a wooden boat, gaff-rigged, between eight and eleven metres long, around two and a half to three metres wide and can accommodate around 25–30 people. It is sailed when the weather is suitable and is otherwise powered by a small motor.

The name comes from a time when tourism was developing and many people were seeking a better fate overseas. The shores of the Lake Steinhuder Meer, some of which still belonged to the Principality of Schaumburg-Lippe as well as to the Prussian-Hanoverian "foreign country", were also the starting point for emigrant boats at that time. If a boat started from Hagenburg, for example, and travelled to Mardorf, it was referred to as a "foreign country". Some traditions also tell of newlywed couples who "emigrated" to foreign countries together with their pets.

Today, tourists usually travel with an emigrant from Steinhude to the island of Wilhelmstein or to Mardorf. The 30 or so emigrant captains are organised in the Steinhude Passenger Shipping Association and thus continue a wonderful tradition. And if you meet them on the Wilhelmstein in a quiet moment, one or other of the captains will certainly be happy to tell you a story or two …

← Eine recht seltene 20er-Rennjolle, auch Z-Boot genannt. Liebevoll sagt man auch segelndes Streichholz.
← A very rare 20s racing dinghy, also known as a Z-boat. It is also affectionately known as a sailing matchstick.

Auf der Planke rund ums Steinhuder Meer
On the plank around Steinhuder Meer

Jürgen Engelmann

Holzbootregatta im Segler-Verein Großenheidorn

Auf dem Steinhuder Meer hat sich der Segelsport relativ spät etabliert. Die ersten Segelclubs wurden um 1905 gegründet, und die eigentliche Regattatätigkeit begann nach dem Krieg in den 1920er und 1930er Jahren. Man segelte unter anderem 22er-, 15er-, 10er-Rennjollen, Weserjollen und ab ca. 1930 die schönsten, die 20er-Rennjollen – auch Z-Boote genannt. Alles sehr elegante Jollen, natürlich aus wertvollem Holz und in bester Bootsbautechnik geplankt.

Einige dieser Boote haben auch den Zweiten Weltkrieg überstanden, manche wurden von den englischen Besatzern beschlagnahmt und später zurückgegeben.

Bei den Holzbootregatten des Segler-Vereins Großenheidorn (SVG) sind noch ein paar von ihnen dabei. Seit 1998 veranstaltet der SVG diese Holzbootregatta für ältere Holzboote.

Vorausgehend ab 1982 gab es das Pfingsttreffen der Z-Boote am Steinhuder Meer.

Die Boote werden mit Drei-Mann-Besatzung sowie mit Spinnaker und Trapez gesegelt. Die Besatzungsmitglieder setzen sich aus allen Altersgruppen zusammen.

Seit den 1980er Jahren hat die Bootsklasse hier Freunde gefunden und wird seitdem auf dem Steinhuder Meer vom Segler-Verein Großenheidorn betreut. Der Verein veranstaltete bisher zahlreiche Ranglistenregatten, aber auch drei Internationale Deutsche Klassenmeisterschaften. Es kamen drei bis vier Boote vom Steinhuder Meer, meist sechs bis acht Boote vom Ratzeburger See und einige sogar vom Mondsee aus Österreich und von den süddeutschen Seen.

Wooden boat regatta at the Großenheidorn Sailing Club

Sailing was established relatively late on the Lake Steinhuder Meer. The first sailing clubs were founded around 1905, and the actual regatta activity began after the war in the 1920s and 1930s. The boats sailed included 22s, 15s, 10s racing dinghies, Weser dinghies and, from around 1930, the most beautiful, the 20 m² racing dinghies – also known as Z-boats. All very elegant dinghies, naturally made of valuable wood and planked using the best boatbuilding techniques.

Some of these boats survived the Second World War, some were confiscated by the British occupying forces and later returned.

A few of them can still be seen at the wooden boat regattas organised by the Großenheidorn Sailing Club (SVG). The SVG has been organising this wooden boat regatta for older wooden boats since 1998.

It was preceded in 1982 by the Whitsun meeting of the Z-boats at Lake Steinhuder Meer.

The boats are sailed with a crew of three as well as a spinnaker and harness. The crew members come from all age groups.

The boat class has found friends here since the 1980s and has been organised by the Großenheidorn Sailing Club on the Lake Steinhuder Meer since then. The club has organised numerous ranking list regattas, as well as three international German class championships. There were three to four boats from Lake Steinhuder Meer, mostly six to eight boats from Ratzeburger See and some even from Mondsee in Austria and the southern German lakes.

← Zwei R-Boote, ein P-Boot und eine wunderschöne Weserjolle (mit Holzlatten im Segel) während einer der Regatten vom SVG.

← Two R-boats, a P-boat and a beautiful Weser dinghy (with wooden battens in the sail) in one of the regattas organised by the SVG.

↑ Wenn der Wind und das Wetter passen, macht eine Regatta richtig Spaß! In diesem Fall auf einem R-Boot: Martina Stichnoth, Tobias Stichnoth, Robert Muthmann und Skipper und Eigner Dirk Stichnoth.

↑ When the wind and weather are right, a regatta is great fun! In this case on an R-boat: Martina Stichnoth, Tobias Stichnoth, Robert Muthmann and skipper and owner Dirk Stichnoth.

↑ Bis ein altes Holzboot – nach zu wenig Pflege vom Vorbesitzer – wieder regattatauglich ist, geht viel Zeit ins Land – das wird mit einer zünftigen Bootstaufe gerne gefeiert. Hier im SLSV mit dem P-Boot IDEYA von Jakob Kasel, Maximllian Lippold und Falk Blase.

↑ It takes a long time for an old wooden boat – after too little care – to become regatta-capable again – and this is often celebrated with a proper boat christening. Here at the SLSV with the P-boat IDEYA from Jakob Kasel, Maximllian Lippold and Falk Blase.

Das erste Treffen der Z-Boote fand 1982 im Verein der Wandersegler in Steinhude statt, weil es da zwei Z-Boote gab, die Niobe von Dr. Rolf Brinkmann und Undine von Jo Bald. Im Jahr darauf übernahm der SVG diese Z-Boot-Treffen und -Regatten. Karl Heinz-Schade, Großenheidorner und lange Vorsitzender vom SVG, hat sie über Jahre bis zur letzten Z-Boot-Bestenermittlung 2009 mit mir organisiert und meist auch die Wettfahrten geleitet. Diese letzte Z-Boot-Meisterschaft hat Jo Bald mit seiner Undine Z 419 mit Bernd Rintelmann am Ruder gegen starke Konkurrenz vom Ratzeburger See und vom Chiemsee gewonnen.

Ende der 1990er Jahre, einige der Akteure waren verstorben und einige Boote mangels Pflege nicht mehr seetüchtig, kamen nur noch wenige dieser schönen Schiffe zusammen. Wir erinnerten uns, dass es außer den Z-Jollen noch andere Holzbootklassen gab und luden alle Eignerinnen und Eigner für einen Sonntag zu einer Holzbootregatta „auf der Planke rund ums Steinhuder Meer", ein. Ursprünglich sollte das Baujahr vor 1975 sein, später sprachen wir von mindestens 25 Jahren und es können außer den geplankten Booten auch solche mit formverleimten Rümpfen dabei sein.

Inzwischen nehmen meist ca. 30 Boote teil, davon viele Jollenkreuzer, H-Jollen und weitere Klassen. Von den ältesten ist immer die Weserjolle von Bernd Metz von 1943 dabei, genauso wie die O-Jolle von Dr. Peter Spreter von 1935 und aus Elmshorn die M-Jolle (15er-Rennjolle) von Manfred Möller von 1930, und ferner zwei P-Boote aus den 1930er Jahren. Segelnde Antiquitäten und ein Augenschmaus für die Zuschauenden.

Die Wertung der Holzbootregatta erfolgt nach Yardstick, also mit einem Berechnungsfaktor für die jeweilige Klasse. So können die Platzierungen einigermaßen gerecht aus der gesegelten Zeit berechnet werden.

Den Wanderpreis „Holzplanke" habe ich zusammen mit Jo Bald auf der Z 419 als Erster gewonnen – daran erinnert man sich besonders gerne als Akteur und Autor. Eine weitere „Planke", gestiftet von Oliver Berking (Robbe & Berking) aus Flensburg, kam für die Siegerinnen und Sieger dazu und vier Halbmodelle, von Helmut Stille gefertigt und gestiftet, dazu eine Silberschale von 1928 für die R-Boote und ein H-Jollenpreis, gestiftet von Heinrich K.-M. Hecht. Bei allen Wanderpreisen wird der Platz nach vielen Jahren für weitere Siegergravuren mittlerweile knapp. Inzwischen treffen sich die meisten Holzbootseglerinnen und Holzbootsegler bereits am Samstag im SVG zu einem „Open Ship" oder zu einer Geschwaderfahrt, um ihre Holzbootschätze zu zeigen und miteinander über die besten Restaurationsmethoden zu sprechen, was am Abend noch lange dauern kann.

The first Z-boat meeting took place in 1982 at the Wandersegler club in Steinhude because there were two Z-boats there, Dr Rolf Brinkmann's Niobe and Jo Bald's Undine. The following year, the SVG took over these Z-boat meetings and regattas. Karl Heinz-Schade, from Großenheidorn and long-time chairman of the SVG, organised them with me for many years until the last Z-Boat Championship in 2009 and usually also led the races. Jo Bald won this last Z-Boat Championship with his Undine Z 419 with Bernd Rintelmann at the helm against strong competition from Ratzeburger See and Chiemsee.

By the end of the 1990s, some of the participants had passed away and some of the boats were no longer "seaworthy" due to lack of care, so only a few of these beautiful boats were left. We remembered that there were other wooden boat classes apart from the Z dinghies and invited all owners to a wooden boat regatta "on the plank around Lake Steinhuder Meer" on a Sunday. Originally the year of construction was supposed to be before 1975, later we talked about at least 25 years, and in addition to the planked boats, those with cold moulded hulls can also take part.

There are now usually around 30 boats taking part, including many dinghy cruisers, H-dinghies and other classes. Of the oldest, Bernd Metz's Weser dinghy from 1943 is always there, as is Dr Peter Spreter's O-dinghy from 1935 and Manfred Möller's M 15 racing O-dinghy from 1930 from Elmshorn, as well as two P-boats from the 1930s. Sailing antiques and a feast for the eyes of the spectators.

The wooden boat regatta is scored according to yardstick, i.e. with a calculation factor for the respective class. This allows the placings to be calculated fairly on the basis of the time sailed.

I was the first to win the "wooden plank" challenge prize together with Jo Bald on the Z 419 – this is particularly fondly remembered as a participant and author. Another "plank" donated by Oliver Berking (Robbe & Berking) from Flensburg was added for the winners and four half models, made and donated by Helmut Stille, plus a silver bowl from 1928 for the R-boats and an H-dinghy prize donated by Heinrich K.-M. Hecht. After many years, there is now not enough space for further engravings on all the travelling prizes. In the meantime, most wooden boat sailors meet on Saturday at the SVG for an "Open Ship" or a squadron trip to show off their wooden boat treasures and talk to each other about the best restoration methods, which can go on for a long time in the evening.

↑ Für die Feinheiten an einem Holzboot legt der Chef, Christian Dietrich, gerne auch einmal selber Hand an.

↑ The boss, Christian Dietrich, is also happy to do the finishing touches to a wooden boat himself.

Bootswerft Bopp & Dietrich

Boatyard Bopp & Dietrich

Heinrich K.-M. Hecht

Wer am Steinhuder Meer oder irgendwo im deutschsprachigen Raum in der Binnen-Segelszene über Holzboote und gute Qualität spricht, kommt um Christian Dietrich und seine Werft in Steinhude nicht umhin.

Egal ob es um einen Neubau, eine Restaurierung, einen Cruiser zum gemütlichen Dahingleiten, oder um ein rasantes Regattaboot geht, mit dem jemand eine Meisterschaft gewinnen will – Christian Dietrich mit seiner Werft ist eine gute Adresse dafür und Beispiel exzellenter Handwerksarbeit.

Gegründet 1985, um Holzzugvögel zu bauen, etablierte sich die Werft bereits nur ein Jahr später mit dem Bau eines Regatta-20er-Jollenkreuzers mit dem passenden Namen *Raserati*, bei der Deutschen Meisterschaft mit einem ersten Platz in der Liste der bekannten und bevorzugten Werften. In den 1980er Jahren gewann der heute international bekannte America's-Cup-Segler, Karol Jablonski, alleine dreimal den Titel des Deutschen Meisters auf einem 20er-Jollenkreuzer von der Werft Bopp & Dietrich. In der Klasse der 15er war auf den Booten der Werft besonders der Steinhuder Wilfried Schweer erfolgreich. Christian Dietrich selber am Ruder ließ die Konkurrenz 1987 sein Heck sehen und wurde ebenfalls Deutscher Meister. So ging es stetig aufwärts und weiter. Bis heute wurden bereits 31 Deutsche Meisterschaften mit Bopp-& -Dietrich-Booten gewonnen.

Das Tagesgeschäft neben den hochgezüchteten Regattabooten sind aber Jollenkreuzer der Klassen 15er und 20er, auch P- und R-Boote genannt, die meist von Freizeitkapitänen über die Binnenseen gesteuert werden. Für den Winter kann man einen Eisschlitten ordern, damit nach dem Sommer keine Langeweile aufkommt – es ist ein am Steinhuder Meer in der

Anyone who talks about wooden boats and good quality on the Lake Steinhuder Meer or anywhere in the German-speaking world in the inland sailing scene cannot fail to mention Christian Dietrich and his shipyard in Steinhude.

Whether it's a new build, a restoration, a cruiser for cosy cruising or a fast regatta boat with which someone wants to win a championship – Christian Dietrich and his shipyard are a good address for this and an example of excellent craftsmanship.

Founded in 1985 to build wooden Zugvogel boats, the shipyard established itself just one year later with the construction of a racing 20-dinghy cruiser with the fitting name *Raserati*, which took first place in the list of well-known and favoured shipyards at the German Championships. In the 1980s, the now internationally renowned America's Cup sailor, Karol Jablonski, won the title of German Champion three times alone on a 20-dinghy cruiser from the Bopp & Dietrich shipyard. Steinhude's Wilfried Schweer was particularly successful in the 15cc class on the shipyard's boats. Christian Dietrich himself at the helm had the competition watching his stern in 1987 and also became German champion. And so it went on and on, until today 31 German championships have already been won with Bopp & Dietrich boats.

The day-to-day business alongside the high-powered regatta boats, however, are dinghy cruisers in the 15 and 20 class, also known as P- and R-boats, which are mostly steered by recreational skippers on the inland lakes. For the winter, you can order an ice sledge so that you don't get bored after the summer – gliding over the ice at speeds of 100 km/h and more is a popular pastime on *Black Ice* at Lake Steinhuder Meer in the

↑ Mit und am Holz zu arbeiten, ist immer etwas Besonderes.
↑ Working with and on wood is always something special.

↖ In dieser Werkstatt gibt es immer etwas zu tun.
↖ There is always something to do in this workshop.

← Alle Eignerinnen und Eigner, die ein solches Boot aus der Werft als Neubau oder Reparatur bekommen, können sich über das Ergebnis freuen.

← Every owner who receives such a boat from the shipyard as a new build or repair can be delighted with the result. Several coats of varnish give the boat a flawless appearance.

eiskalten Jahreszeit auf *Black Ice* gerne betriebener Zeitvertreib, mit Geschwindigkeiten von 100 km/h und mehr über das Eis zu gleiten. Im Jahr 1992 war zwischendurch noch Zeit für ein wesentlich größeres Boot, eine 42-Fuß-Segelyacht mit dem Namen *Milonga*, die im Auftrag des Akademischen Segler-Vereins zu Hannover entstand. Erst kürzlich war die Yacht wieder am Steinhuder Meer, nachdem ein Havarieschaden, der in den schwedischen Schären passierte, repariert werden musste.

2002 vergab einer der renommiertesten Bootsbauer in Deutschland, Markus Glas vom Starnberger See, einen Auftrag für die Rumpfschale eines L-Bootes. Daraus ergab sich eine jahrelange Zusammenarbeit, die bis heute Bestand hat und inzwischen fast 100 Rumpfschalen entstehen ließ. 2003 übernimmt Christian Dietrich die Werft als alleiniger Inhaber und weitet das Geschäft mit dem Bau von hochwertigen Holzbooten, aus.

Bis heute kann sich Christian Dietrich nicht über mangelnde Arbeit mit seiner Mannschaft beklagen und ist auch in den Vereinen rund um das Steinhuder Meer immer ein gern gesehener Gast mit seiner ruhigen, sachlichen und kompetenten Art.

freezing cold season. In 1992, there was still time in between for a much larger boat, a 42-foot sailing yacht called *Milonga*, which was commissioned by the Academic Sailing Club of Hannover. The yacht was only recently in for repairs at the Lake Steinhuder Meer after an accident in the Swedish archipelago.

In 2002, one of the most renowned boat builders in Germany, Markus Glas from Lake Starnberg, placed an order for the hull shell of an L-boat. This resulted in years of co-operation, which continues to this day and has since resulted in almost 100 hulls. In 2003, Christian Dietrich took over the shipyard as sole owner and expanded the business to include the construction of high-quality wooden boats.

To this day, Christian Dietrich cannot complain about a lack of work with his team and is always a welcome guest in the clubs around the Lake Steinhuder Meer with his calm, matter-of-fact and competent manner.

↑ Es darf auch mal an Bord ein gut gekühltes Glas Rosé im Sonnenuntergang sein – natürlich nicht für den Skipper bzw. die Skipperin.
↑ A well-chilled glass of rosé in the sunset is also allowed on board – not for the skipper, of course.

← Immer mehr Seglerinnen und Segler am Steinhuder Meer wünschen sich ein stilvolles E-Boot, um auch bei Flaute eine Ausfahrt zu genießen. Das Boot auf diesem Foto dürfte aufgrund seiner Ausführung und der vielen Details wie zum Beispiel Kühlschrank, Hi-Fi-Anlage und Gasgrill einmalig sein.
← Increasing numbers of sailors on the Lake Steinhuder Meer are looking for a stylish e-boat to enjoy a trip even in calm conditions. The boat in this photo is probably unique due to its design and the many details such as the refrigerator, hi-fi system and gas grill.

E-Boot E-Tender

Eine Art Krönung seines umfassenden Könnens bewies Christian Dietrich vor einigen Jahren mit dem Bau eines viel beachteten E-Bootes, das jedes Mal, wenn es mit rauschender Bugwelle durch das Wasser des Steinhuder Meeres gleitet, zahlreiche bewundernde Blicke auf sich zieht.

Die besonderen Details ergeben sich aber erst während einer genaueren Begutachtung am Steg oder einer Kaimauer – oder noch besser – als Gast an Bord. Denn an Bord befindet sich nicht nur ein Kühlschrank, der immer gekühlte Getränke sicherstellt, sondern auch ein Holzkohlegrill. Daneben bietet das Boot – *E-Tender* genannt – eine große Liegefläche, die das so ungesunde Sonnenbaden zum Vergnügen werden lässt. Im Wasser zu baden und zu schwimmen, erleichtert die eingebaute Badeplattform, die sich runterklappen lässt. Erstaunlich ist die Tatsache, dass trotz relativ hoher Geschwindigkeit und ebensolchen Gewichts, die im Boot verbauten Akkus für einen ganzen Tag lang Vergnügen mit dieser besonderen Art von Freizeitboot garantieren. Der Autor dieser Zeilen kam während einiger seiner Aufnahmen durch die Großenheidorner Kanäle oder auf der Fahrt zur Insel Wilhelmstein in diesen unvergleichlichen Genuss. Dabei immer umgeben von edelsten Hölzern und Edelstahl.

E-boat E-Tender

A few years ago, Christian Dietrich crowned his extensive skills with the construction of a much-noticed e-boat, which attracts many admiring glances every time it glides through the waters of the Lake Steinhuder Meer with a rushing bow wave.

However, the special details only become apparent during a closer inspection on the jetty or quay wall – or even better, as a guest on board. This is because there is not only a refrigerator on board, which ensures that drinks are always chilled, but also a charcoal grill. The boat – called an *e-tender* – also has a large sunbathing area, which makes sunbathing, which is so unhealthy, a pleasure. Bathing and swimming in the water is made easier by the built-in bathing platform, which can be folded down. It is astonishing that despite its relatively high speed and weight, the batteries installed in the boat guarantee a whole day of fun on this special type of leisure boat. The author of these lines enjoyed this incomparable pleasure during some of his photo shootings through the Großenheidorn canals or on a trip to the island of Wilhelmstein. Always surrounded by the finest woods and stainless steel.

↑ Gehört auch zu Großenheidorn: der Großenheidorngraben, der „Klein Venedig" mit dem offenen „Meer" verbindet.

↑ Also part of Großenheidorn: the Großenheidorngraben, which connects "Little Venice" with the open "sea" (as the lake is called in its German name).

Großenheidorn

Jürgen Engelmann

Großenheidorn und seine Geschichte

2024 wird das Jubiläum 777 Jahre Großenheidorn begangen. Das ist wie immer in Großenheidorn ein guter Grund, gemeinsam zu feiern. Bei vielen Gelegenheiten ist deutlich geworden, dass es in Großenheidorn eine intakte Dorfgemeinschaft gibt. Der sehr große Sportverein MTV mit vielen aktiven und erfolgreichen Handballmannschaften, die Feuerwehr, die Schützen, die „Bürgers", die Laienspielgruppe und die Segel- und Anglervereine am Strand, nicht zuletzt die Kirchengemeinde schaffen es immer wieder, gemeinsam Märkte und Feste zu organisieren.

Als Gründungsjahr des Ortes ist in einer Urkunde 1247 genannt. Eine Besiedlung zwischen dem Südwestrand des Moores im Südosten des Steinhuder Meeres und dem Wald im Süden hat es bereits ab 1220 gegeben. Die Grafen von Roden ließen ein Hagenhufendorf durch Rodung des Waldes errichten, in dem es erhebliche Vorkommen von Weiß- und Schwarzdornbüschen gab. Der Name „Heithorn" später „Heidorn" leitet sich daraus ab. Die Grafen von Roden mussten schon in der Urkunde von 1247 den Ort an den Bischof von Minden abtreten. Schließlich gelang es den Grafen von Holstein-Schaumburg, diesen Ort und Steinhude zu übernehmen. Im 15. Jahrhundert wurden dann die schaumburgischen Siedlungen Großenheidorn und Steinhude in das Amt Hagenburg eingegliedert.

Schaumburger, später Schaumburg-Lipper, sind die Großenheidorner wie die Steinhuder bis zur Gebiets- und Verwaltungsreform 1974 geblieben. In der Reform wurden es Ortsteile von Wunstorf in der Region Hannover.

Großenheidorn and its history

2024 marks the 777th anniversary of Großenheidorn. As always in the case of an anniversary, this is a good reason to celebrate together in Großenheidorn. It has become clear on many occasions that there is an intact village community in Großenheidorn. The very large sports club MTV with many active and successful handball teams, the fire brigade, the marksmen's club, the "Bürgers", the amateur dramatics group and the sailing and fishing clubs on the beach, not to mention the church community, always manage to organise markets and festivals together.

The year the village was founded is mentioned in a document from 1247. Settlement between the south-western edge of the moor to the south-east of the Lake Steinhuder Meer and the forest to the south dates back to 1220. The Counts of Roden had a "Hagenhufendorf" village built by clearing the forest, in which there were considerable deposits of hawthorn and blackthorn bushes. The name "Heithorn", later "Heidorn", is derived from this. The Counts of Roden had to cede the site to the Bishop of Minden in the document of 1247. Eventually, the Counts of Holstein-Schaumburg succeeded in taking over the village and Steinhude. In the 15th century, the Schaumburg settlements of Großenheidorn and Steinhude were incorporated into the Hagenburg district.

The people of Großenheidorn and Steinhude remained Schaumburgers, later Schaumburg-Lippers, until the regional and administrative reform of 1974. During the reform, the areas became districts of Wunstorf in the Hannover region.

When the village was settled, a path or road was laid out on

↑ MTV-Großenheidorn: Torwart Lars Wagner vor – wie üblich – voller Hütte.   ↑ MTV-Großenheidorn: Goalkeeper Lars Wagner in front of – as usual – a full house.

Bei der Besiedlung wurde ein Weg oder eine Straße auf der Grenze der Bodenerhebung im Süden zur Meerniederung angelegt. Die Bebauung im Ort vollzog sich wie bei Hagenhufen üblich an der Nordseite des Weges mit den Wiesen hinter den Häusern und den Ackerflächen auf der anderen Seite der Straße. Später wurde auch die Südseite bebaut, dazu dehnte sich der Ort in Richtung Steinhude aus.

Bis heute hat sich der Ort kontinuierlich mit fließenden Übergängen bis an Steinhude heran entwickelt und in weiteren Schritten ist die Bebauung weiter nach Norden erfolgt. Dort sind vor allen Dingen in den 1950er Jahren Siedlungen entstanden, die durch den Flüchtlingszuzug notwendig wurden.

Hinter den bäuerlichen Anwesen an der Dorfstraße, die zum Teil noch heute bestehen, ist dabei eine große parkähnliche Wiesenlandschaft frei geblieben und unter Schutz gestellt. Es gibt alte große Bäume, die dem „Eichenkamp" seinen Namen geben.

Ein Baurecht im Süden des Ortes gibt es nicht, weil dort die Einflugschneise zum Fliegerhorst Wunstorf liegt. Im Osten schließt sich schon der Fliegerhorst mit einem aktuellen Neubau einer großen Wartungshalle der Firma Airbus an. Mit dem Fluglärm und dem Heranrücken des Fliegerhorstes und der Wartungsfirma an den Ort können sich die meisten

the border of the land elevation in the south towards the sea lowlands. As was usual with Hagenhufen villages, the buildings were constructed on the north side of the road with the meadows behind the houses and the farmland on the other side of the road. Later, the south side was also developed and the village expanded in the direction of Steinhude.

To this day, the village has developed continuously with gradual transitions extending up to Steinhude and further development has taken place further north. It was mainly in the 1950s that housing estates were built there as a result of the influx of refugees.

Behind the farming estates on the village road, some of which still exist today, a large park-like meadow landscape has been preserved and placed under protection. There are large old trees that give the "Eichenkamp" its name.

There are no building rights in the south of the village because the flight path to the Wunstorf airbase is located there. In the east, the air base is already adjacent, with a new large maintenance hangar being built by Airbus. Most people in Großenheidorn can put up with the aircraft noise and the proximity of the air base and the maintenance company to the village because there are around 2,000 jobs with qualified training there. Several craft businesses have established themselves in the village, as well as a large civil engineering company, a

← Egal ob Damen oder Herren, es war und ist beim MTV in Großenheidorn an Erfolgen fast alles dabei – Regionalliga, Oberliga und Landesliga. Auf diesem Foto ging es in einem Vorbereitungsspiel gegen den Bundesligisten Burgdorf: Gerrit Otte setzt zum Sprung an, am Kreis Jonas Borgmann, beide im weißen Trikot.

← Whether it's men's or women's handball, the MTV sports club in Großenheidorn has enjoyed almost every kind of success – regional league, upper league and state league. In this photo, it was a preparation game against the Bundesliga team Burgdorf: Gerrit Otte starts to jump, with Jonas Borgmann at the circle on the court, both in white jerseys.

↖↑ Wundervoll sanierte Bauernhäuser aus dem 17. Jahrhundert wechseln sich zuweilen mit grünen Wiesen in Großenheidorn ab.

↖↑ Beautifully renovated farmhouses from the 17th century alternate with green meadows in Großenheidorn.

Großenheidornerinnen und Großenheidorner abfinden, weil es dort ca. 2.000 Arbeitsplätze mit qualifizierter Ausbildung gibt. Im Ort haben sich einige Handwerksbetriebe etabliert, dazu eine größere Tiefbaufirma, eine Firma für Werkzeugbau und einen Kunststoff verarbeitenden Betrieb mit ganz besonderem Schwerpunkt bei großen Formteilen. Viele Ortsansässige müssen zu ihren Arbeitsplätzen nach Wunstorf oder Hannover fahren.

Um von und nach Großenheidorn zu gelangen, gab es von 1898 die Steinhuder Meerbahn, eine Schmalspurbahn von Wunstorf über Steinhude nach Rehburg, die leider 1960 den Betrieb eingestellt hat. Jetzt gib es recht gute Busverbindungen mit der Weiterfahrt von Wunstorf aus mit der Bahn.

toolmaking company and a plastics processing company with a particular focus on large moulded parts. Many residents of the village have to travel to their workplaces in Wunstorf or Hannover.

To get to and from Großenheidorn, there was the Steinhuder Meerbahn from 1898 onwards, a narrow-gauge railway from Wunstorf via Steinhude to Rehburg, which unfortunately ceased operation in 1960. Nowadays, there are quite good bus connections with the possibility of continuing the journey by train from Wunstorf.

↑ Das ehemalige Strandhotel von Großenheidorn, eröffnet 1927 – dient heute dem Yachtclub Steinhuder Meer als Clubhaus, siehe auch Seite 78.

↑ The former beach hotel in Großenheidorn, opened in 1927, now serves as a clubhouse for the Lake Steinhuder Meer Yacht Club, see also page 78.

Großenheidorn Strand – Manche sagen auch Klein Venedig

Von der Hauptstraße beträgt die Entfernung zum Steinhuder Meer in der Luftlinie etwa eineinhalb Kilometer. Die Wiesen nördlich der Bebauung erstreckten sich bis ans Meer heran. Offensichtlich gab es über die Jahre kein Interesse, an das Meer zu kommen. Vielleicht hätte die Bevölkerung von Großenheidorn gern Fische gefangen, aber das war nur den Steinhuder Fischerinnen und Fischern erlaubt. Direkt am Meer waren es mehr nasse Wiesen, die nicht immer betreten werden konnten. Vor dem Ufer breiteten sich Schilfinseln aus. Baden oder Spazierengehen war dort kaum möglich.

In Steinhude gab es nach dem Bau der Steinhuder Meerbahn schon ab 1900 erhebliche Besucherinnen- und Besucherströme und in Mardorf entwickelte sich am Nordufer ein Wander- und Badetourismus. Westlich von den Heidorner Wiesen konnte man auf die ersten Besiedlungen mit Wochenendhäusern am Steinhuder Ostenmeer blicken.

Erst nach dem Krieg 1920 gab es erste Planungen für ein Strandbad am Großenheidorner Ufer. Das Projekt wurde von der gegründeten Großenheidorner Strandbad GmbH betrieben, an der die Gemeinde Großenheidorn, einige Hannoveranerinnen und Hannoveraner und der Architekt Flügel beteiligt waren. Schon 1926 entstanden die ersten Häuser am „Flügelhorst", eine Besiedlung mit ca. 40 standardisierten Wochenendhäusern, die von Flügel entworfen waren entlang der Uferlinie von der Strandstraße bis zum „Ostenmeer" in Steinhude. Von den besonderen Häusern, die giebelständig zum erschließenden Weg und zum Meer hin standen, sind noch

Großenheidorn beach – some call it Little Venice

As the crow flies, the distance from the main road to Lake Steinhuder Meer is about 1.5 kilometres. The meadows to the north of the development stretched all the way to the sea. Obviously there has been no interest in getting to the lake over the years. Perhaps the people of Großenheidorn would have liked to catch fish, but only the Steinhude fishermen were allowed to do so. Directly by the lake, there were more wet meadows that could not always be walked on. Reed islands spread out in front of the shore. Swimming or walking was hardly possible there.

After the construction of the Steinhuder Meerbahn railway, there was a considerable influx of visitors from 1900 onwards in Steinhude and hiking and bathing tourism developed on the northern shore in Mardorf. To the west of the Heidorn meadows, the first settlements with weekend houses could be seen on the eastern shore of Lake Steinhuder Meer (Ostenmeer).

It was not until after the war in 1920 that the first plans were made for a lido on the Großenheidorn shore. The project was run by the specially founded company Großenheidorner Strandbad GmbH, in which the municipality of Großenheidorn, some Hanoverians and the architect Flügel were involved. As early as 1926, the first houses were built on the "Flügelhorst", a settlement of around 40 standardised weekend houses designed by Flügel along the shoreline from Strandstrasse to the "Ostenmeer" in Steinhude. Some of the special houses, which stood with their gable ends facing to the

Unweit von Großenheidorn Strand führt dieser Weg zu einem Vogelbeobachtungsturm. →

Not far from Großenheidorn Strand district, this path leads to a bird-watching tower. →

↑ Von der Insel Sonneck geht der Blick auf diese Wasserfläche, auf der man wunderbar die Natur genießen kann.

↑ From the island of Sonneck, the view is of this expanse of water where you can enjoy nature to the full.

heute einige erhalten und in der ursprünglichen Form gepflegt.

Die Pachtenden oder späteren Besitzerinnen und Besitzer waren waren meist mittelständische Hannoveraner, die hier ihre Freizeit mit Baden und Segeln verbrachten. Probleme gab es zu der Zeit mit Verschlammungen und Versandung. Um aufs Meer zu gelangen, wurden Schneisen durch das Schilf gebuddelt oder Stege hindurchgebaut, was die Verlandung der Schilfinseln forcierte. Erst in den 1980er Jahren wurden die Schilfinseln „Wulves Kuhlen" unter besonderen Schutz gestellt und breite Wasserzufahrten vor den Ufern so gebaut, dass alle Grundstücke erreichbar waren. In den letzten Jahren konnte auch in dem Bereich das Gebüsch mit Genehmigung der Naturschutzbehörde entfernt werden, so dass die weitere Verlandung reduziert wird.

Zeitgleich mit der Besiedlung „Flügelhorst" wurde das Strandbad gebaut und 1927 in Betrieb genommen. Es ist ein großes Gebäude mit Hotel, Restauration, Tanz und Theatersaal sowie einem großen Sandstrand. Der Betrieb lief zunächst hervorragend, mit Ausflüglerinnen und Ausflüglern, die mit dem Bus oder mit der Meerbahn und zu Fuß bis zum Strand kamen, um im Restaurant zu sitzen, zu baden und zu tanzen. Trotz erheblicher Krisen konnte das Strandbad seinen Betrieb aufrechterhalten und nach mehr oder weniger guten Jahren wurde das Gelände 1961 verkauft und der Yachtclub Steinhu-

access road and the sea, are still preserved today and maintained in their original form.

The tenants or later owners were mostly middle-class Hanoverians who spent their leisure time here swimming and sailing. At the time, there were problems with siltation and sand buildups. To get to the sea, paths were dug through the reeds or footbridges built through them, which accelerated the silting up of the reed islands. It was not until the 1980s that the reed islands "Wulves Kuhlen" were placed under special protection and wide water access roads were built in front of the shores so that all properties could be reached. In recent years, it has also been possible to remove the bushes in this area with the authorisation of the nature conservation authority, thus reducing further sedimentation.

The lido was built at the same time as the "Flügelhorst" settlement and opened in 1927. It is a large building with a hotel,

↑ Teepavillon auf der Ecke des Endgrundstücks der Insel Sonneck. Eine schöne Lage.

↑ Tea pavilion on the corner of the end plot of the Sonneck island. A lovely location.

der Meer (YSTM) nutzt das große Gelände bis heute für den Segelsport und seine Vereinsaktivitäten.

Neben dem Gelände hatte die Gemeinde Großenheidorn noch ein Grundstück, das an die Bucht angrenzte, an einer Landzunge ins Meer. 1951 baute der Nachbar Feldheim dort eine „Stranddiele", also ein Gasthaus, von dem aus auch ein Strandbad betrieben wurde.

1959 gründeten viele Strandanliegerinnen und Strandanlieger und einige andere dort den Segler-Verein Großenheidorn (SVG). Sie taten sich zusammen, um gemeinsam Lösungen für ihre Bootsliegeplätze zu finden, gerade weil in dem Jahr extrem niedriger Wasserstand war und die Boote vor den Kanälen und vor der Bucht an Bojen festgemacht werden mussten. Um mit Booten zu fahren und anzulegen, wurden in der Bucht 1962, zusammen mit anderen Anwohnenden und dem YSTM, erhebliche Sandmengen zum Teil mit einer Raupe bewegt und auf der Landzunge oder den Uferbereichen abgelagert. Die Landzunge ist für die Öffentlichkeit zugänglich.

Der SVG hat in den Folgejahren das Haus und das Grundstück übernehmen können und hat mit sehr viel Eigeninitiative eine komfortable Segelsportanlage mit neuem Clubhaus für seine jetzt ca. 240 Mitglieder geschaffen. Bekannt ist der SVG durch seine herausragende Jugendarbeit und Regattatätigkeit. Einige nationale und internationale Erfolge sind zu verbuchen und der Verein hat viele Regatten durchgeführt, auch nationale und internationale Meisterschaften.

Anschließend an das Strandbad entwickelte sich Bebauung auf

restaurant and a dance and theatre hall, as well as a large sandy beach. Business was excellent at first, with day-trippers coming by bus or Meerbahn railway and on foot to the beach to sit in the restaurant, swim and dance. Despite considerable crises, the lido was able to maintain its operations and after more or less good years, the site was sold in 1961 and the Lake Steinhuder Meer Yacht Club (YSTM) still uses the large site today for sailing and its club activities.

In addition to the site, the municipality of Großenheidorn also had a plot of land adjacent to the bay on a spit of land into the sea. In 1951, the neighbour Feldheim built a "Stranddiele", a guesthouse from which a lido was also operated.

In 1959, a number of waterfront residents and a few others founded the Großenheidorn Sailing Club (SVG). They got together to find solutions for their boat moorings, especially because the water level was extremely low that year and the boats had to be moored to buoys in front of the canals and the bay. In 1962, together with other residents and the YSTM, considerable quantities of sand were moved in the bay, in part with a bulldozer, and deposited on the headland or the shore areas in order to allow boats to sail and moor. The headland is accessible to the public.

The SVG was able to take over the house and the land in the following years and, with a great deal of initiative, created a comfortable sailing sport facility with a new clubhouse for its now approx. 240 members. The SVG is known for its youth work and regatta activities. The club has achieved several na-

↑ Glücklich, wer ein Wassergrundstück in Großenheidorn Strand hat, der hat sein Boot direkt vor der Haustür.

↑ If you have a waterfront property in Großenheidorn Strand, you are lucky to have your boat right on your doorstep.

„Anlandungsflächen" nördlich und nordöstlich, zunächst auf der Insel Sonneck, dann auf der Insel Bärbel und an der Strandallee. „Anlandungsflächen" bedeutet, dass sie im Steinhuder Meer hier am Ostufer durch Versandung und Verschlammung entstanden sind. Die Gemeinde Großenheidorn und Bauwillige mussten sie vom Meereseigentümer erwerben. Das waren in den 1920er Jahren der schaumburg-lippische Staat und das Fürstenhaus Schaumburg-Lippe. Zu den Grundstücken gab es Gräben und später Kanäle, die zunächst von der Gemeinde Großenheidorn freigehalten werden mussten. Sie hatte extra dafür einen Schaufelbagger angeschafft. Mit dem Sand wurden die Grundstücke aufgefüllt. Die Grundstückseinfassungen mit Spundwänden zum Wasser mussten die Grundstücksbesitzerinnen und Grundstücksbesitzer erstellen.

Jetzt müssen die Kanäle durch neue Verträge von der Region Hannover oder vom Land Niedersachsen freigehalten werden, so dass die Anwohnenden eine Zufahrt zum Meer haben. Ein Kanal östlich der Insel Sonneck wurde in den 1930er Jahren noch vom Reichsarbeitsdienst errichtet, der auch die Wiesen trockengelegt hat. In dem Bereich gab es in den 1970er Jahren den Plan, eine weitere Wochenendsiedlung mit Kanälen zu den Grundstücken zu bauen. Die Pläne wurden verworfen. Heute ist dort ein Schlammpolder für die immer wieder notwendigen Baggerarbeiten auch vor dem Großenheidorner Strand.

Die Kanäle vor der Strandallee und vor dem Flügelhorst wurden vor einigen Jahren verbreitert, um eine günstigere

tional and international successes and has organised many regattas, including national and international championships.

Following the development of the lido, construction expanded onto "accretion areas" to the north and northeast, initially on Sonneck Island, then on Bärbel Island and along the Strandallee avenue. "Accretion areas" means that they were formed here on the eastern shore of Lake Steinhuder Meer through sedimentation and silting. The municipality of Großenheidorn and those wishing to build had to acquire them from the owner of the lake. In the 1920s, this was the Schaumburg-Lippe state and the Princely House of Schaumburg-Lippe. There were ditches and later canals leading to the land, which initially had to be kept clear by the municipality of Großenheidorn. It had purchased a shovel excavator especially for this purpose. The land plots were filled with sand. The landowners had to build the property enclosures with sheet pile walls facing the water.

The canals now have to be kept clear by the Region Hannover administration or the State of Lower Saxony government through new contracts, so that the residents have access to the lake. A canal to the east of Sonneck Island was built in the 1930s by the Reich Labour Service, which also drained the meadows. In the 1970s, there were plans to build another settlement with weekend homes in the area with canals to the properties. The plans were cancelled. Today, there is a mud polder there for the repeatedly necessary dredging works, including in front of Großenheidorn Strand.

↑ Das Clubhaus des SVG in der lauschigen Abendstimmung.
↑ The SVG clubhouse in the balmy evening atmosphere.

↑ Der SVG hat vom Clubhaus aus einen sehr schönen Blick über die Stege auf das Steinhuder Meer.
↑ The SVG has a beautiful view from the clubhouse over the jetties to the Lake Steinhuder Meer.

Strömung herzustellen. Mit mäßigem Erfolg, besonders vor Flügelhorst und in der Bucht musste wieder ausgebaggert werden.

Durch die Bebauung am Flügelhorst und der Anlandungsflächen mit den Kanälen dazwischen ist eine Ansiedlung mit ganz besonderem Reiz entstanden. Man kann mit dem Boot vom Meer her kommend bei der Baltischen Segler-Vereinigung am Ostenmeer in den Wasserweg vor dem Flügelhorst einbiegen, dort vor den Häusern längst bis in die Bucht mit den Steganlagen vom YSTM und dem SVG wieder aufs Meer hinausfahren, um dann etwas weiter nördlich in die Zufahrt durch das Schilf zu den anderen Halbinseln in östlicher Richtung einzuschwenken. Von dort erreicht man die Häuserreihen Strandallee und weiter den nächsten Kanal zur Insel Sonneck und noch weiter dann, hinter der Insel Sonneck, gelangt man zu den etwas versteckt liegenden Wiesen. Dabei kommt man an dem mit vielen Seerosen bewachsenen nördlich gelegenen „Antendiek", dem Ententeich vorbei.

Sowohl Flügelhorst als auch die anderen Gebiete sind als Wochenendbebauung geplant und ausgeführt. Das wurde im Krieg ab etwa 1943 und danach anders. Viele Hannoveranerinnen und Hannoveraner waren ausgebombt und mussten Zuflucht in ihren Häuschen am Strand finden.

Erst in den 1950er Jahren blieb der „Strand" wieder überwiegend Wochenend- und Feriensiedlung.

Auch als Wochenendsiedlung war zunächst das Bebauungsgebiet „Am Strand" südöstlich von der bisherigen Baugrenze

The canals in front of Strandallee and Flügelhorst were widened a few years ago to create a more favourable current. With moderate success – dredging had to be carried out again, particularly in front of Flügelhorst and in the bay.

The development of the Flügelhorst and the accretion areas with the canals in between has created a settlement with a very special charm. Coming by boat from the sea, you can turn into the waterway in front of the Flügelhorst at the Baltic Sailing Association on the Ostenmeer. There, in front of the houses, you can continue to the bay with the jetties of the YSTM and the SVG and then head out to sea again. A little further north, you can turn into the access channel through the reeds to the other peninsulas in an easterly direction. From there, you reach the rows of houses on along the Strandallee and continue along the next canal to Sonneck Island and then even further behind Sonneck Island to the meadows. You will also pass the "Antendiek" – the duck pond – located to the north and overgrown with many water lilies.

Both Flügelhorst and the other areas were planned and realised as weekend developments. This changed during the war starting around 1943 and thereafter. Many Hanoverians were bombed out and had to find refuge in their little houses by the beach.

It was not until the 1950s that the "Strand" once again remained predominantly a weekend and holiday development.

The "Am Strand" development area to the south-east of the previous building boundary was also initially planned as a

↑ Eine der zahlreichen Meisterschaften, die der SVG ausrichten durfte: Internationale Deutsche Jugendmeisterschaft der 420er von 2011.

↑ One of the many championships organised by the SVG: International German Youth Championship of the 420 from 2011.

↑ Ein schöner Sonnenuntergang über den Booten vom SVG und dem Nachbarverein YSTM scheint sicher zu sein.

↑ A beautiful sunset over the boats of the SVG and the neighbouring club YSTM seems certain.

mit ca. 50 Grundstücken und neuen Straßen geplant und in den 1980er Jahren fertiggestellt. Inzwischen haben dort wie im ganzen Bereich Großenheidorner Strand viele Ortsansässige ihren festen Wohnsitz. Die Infrastruktur ist im ganzen Gebiet ausgebaut und es gibt eine Busverbindung nach Wunstorf und Steinhude.

Die „Strandies", auch schon mal „Strandbutjer" genannt, war der Bevölkerung Großenheidorns nicht immer geheuer. Inzwischen ist es für die meisten klar, dass sie alle Großenheidornerinnen und Großenheidorner sind und bei der 777-Jahr-Feier wie schon bei der 750-Jahr-Feier dabei sind.

weekend estate with around 50 plots and new roads and was completed in the 1980s. In the meantime, as in the entire Großenheidorner Strand district, many residents have taken up permanent residence there. The infrastructure has been developed throughout the area and there is a bus connection to Wunstorf and Steinhude.

The "Strandies", also known as "Strandbutjer", were not always trusted or accepted by the residents of Großenheidorn. However, over time, it has become clear to most people that they are all part of the Großenheidorn community. They participate in events such as the 777th anniversary celebration, just as they did during the 750th anniversary festivities.

S. 104–105 Abendstimmung im SVG mit Blick auf den Steg und das Steinhuder Meer.

P. 104–105 Evening atmosphere at the SVG with a view of the jetty and the Lake Steinhuder Meer.

↑ Ursprünglich hatte die Kirche im Inneren eine etwas andere Aufteilung, was an einem größeren Umbau in den 1950er Jahren liegt und sich auch durch die links befindliche Empore ausdrückt, die vor dem Umbau auf drei Seiten vorhanden war.

↑ Originally, the interior of the church had a slightly different layout, which is due to a major remodelling in the 1950s and is also expressed by the gallery on the left, which was present on three sides before the remodelling.

St. Thomas Kirche
St. Thomas church

Peter Zenker

Es gab einen Vorgängerbau der Kirche, der vor dem Jahr 1000 entstand. Die ältesten Teile der heutigen Kirche stammen aus dem 15. Jahrhundert. Eine kleine Kapelle, die an gleicher Stelle stand, wurde zwar von 1687 bis 1689 umgebaut, dann aber vom Kirchenvorstand doch als zu klein erachtet und wieder abgetragen. Dafür entstand 1691 die heutige Saalkirche aus Bruchsteinen mit einem dreiseitigen Schluss des Chors im Osten. 1956 wurde der Bau verändert. Nach Süden wurde ein Querarm angebaut. Das Portal im Westen ersetzte das nördliche. Die Strebepfeiler deuten darauf hin, dass der Innenraum überwölbt werden sollte. Aus dem Satteldach des Kirchenschiffs erhebt sich im Westen ein achtseitiger Dachreiter mit Klangarkaden, der einen spitzen Helm trägt. Der kleine Kirchraum wird von einer flachen Decke mit seitlichen Vouten überspannt. Kleine, schmale Emporen befinden sich auf der Eingangsseite und an der nördlichen Längswand. Hinter dem Altar deutet sich der kleine Chor an, dessen zentrales Wandstück mit einem Kruzifix, die seitlichen Wände durch zwei zeitgenössische Wandbilder geschmückt werden.

There was a predecessor to the church, which was built before 1000. The oldest parts of the today's church date back to the 15th century. A small chapel that stood on the same site was rebuilt between 1687 and 1689, but was then deemed too small by the church council and demolished. In 1691, the present-day hall church was built from quarry stone with a three-sided choir closure in the east. The building was altered in 1956. A transept was added to the south. The portal in the west replaced the northern one. The buttresses indicate that the interior was to be vaulted. Rising from the saddle roof of the nave is an octagonal ridge turret with sound arcades topped by a pointed spire. The small church interior is spanned by a flat ceiling with lateral vaults. Small, narrow galleries are located on the entrance side and on the northern longitudinal wall. Behind the altar is the small choir, with a central wall section adorned with a crucifix and the side walls decorated with two contemporary murals.

↑ Statt eines Kirchturmes hat die St.-Thomas-Kirche einen Dachreiter, der sich gut in das Gesamtbild einfügt.

↑ Instead of a church tower, St Thomas's Church has a ridge turret that blends in well with the overall picture.

↑ Die Orgel, im Ursprung von 1914, befindet sich seit dem Umbau in einer Nische zum Süden hin.

↑ The organ, originally from 1914, has been located in a niche facing south since the renovation.

↑ Seit 2014 sind die Airbus-Flugzeuge A400M am Fliegerhorst stationiert – hier vor dem seinerzeit neu entstandenen Ausbildungszentrum.

↑ The Airbus A400M aircraft have been stationed at the airbase since 2014 – here in front of the newly built training centre at the time.

Fliegerhorst Wunstorf

Wunstorf Airbase

Heinrich K.-M. Hecht

Immer wenn ich als Kind an den Zäunen des Fliegerhorstes mit meinen Eltern entlangfuhr, spürte ich einen Hauch von Abenteuer. Sei es, dass ich gerne einmal über den Zaun geklettert wäre, oder weil ich wusste, dass das, was hinter dem Zaun passierte nicht alltäglich war. Und das war es im Sinne des Wortes eigentlich nie ...

Die Gründung des Fliegerhorstes fällt in eine Zeit, die nicht zu den ruhmreichen unseres Landes zählt und wurde, zum Schutz vor den Feinden, unter dem Deckmantel einer Verkehrsfliegerschule ins Leben gerufen. So war vor und nach dem Krieg alles an Maschinen zu sehen, was das Herz eines Luftfahrt-Oldtimer-Freundes höher schlagen ließe: Messerschmitt, Junkers, Heinkel und natürlich Dornier.

Ruhmreicher als die Kriegszeit war sicherlich die Zeit danach, die der Berliner Luftbrücke, als regelmäßig Maschinen vom Typ DC 3 und Avro York vom Fliegerhorst aus starteten, um die Versorgung der Berliner Bevölkerung mit dem Notwendigsten zu sichern. Dies alles unter dem Kommando der Royal Air Force, den Luftstreitkräften des Vereinigten Königreichs, die seit Ende des Kriegs den Fliegerhorst nutzten. Nach der Luftbrücke wurde der Fliegerhorst wieder zum Stützpunkt der britischen Staffel Wing 123, die größtenteils aus Spitfire-Maschinen bestand.

Ab 1958 übernahm die Luftwaffe der Bundeswehr den Standort unter dem Begriff Flugzeugführerschule „S" – ab 1978 Lufttransportgeschwader 62 – und schulte ihre Piloten auf Noratlas- und Transall-Flugzeugen. Beide Maschinen sind über dem Luftraum des Steinhuder Meeres über 50 Jahre lang ein gewohnter Anblick gewesen – bis im Jahre 2014 der moderne Airbus A400M eingeführt wurde.

Whenever I drove along the fences of the airbase with my parents as a child, I felt a sense of adventure. Whether it was because I would have liked to climb over the fence or because I knew that what happened behind the fence was not an everyday occurrence. And it never was, in the true sense of the word ...

The airbase was founded at a time that was not one of our country's most glorious and it was done to protect us from the enemy under the guise of being a commercial flying school. Before and after the war, everything that would make the heart of a vintage aviation enthusiast beat faster was on display: Messerschmitt, Junkers, Heinkel and, of course, Dornier. More glorious than the war period was certainly the time after the war, that of the Berlin Airlift, when DC 3 and Avro York aircraft regularly took off from the airbase to ensure that the Berlin population was supplied with essentials. All this took place under the command of the United Kingdom's Royal Air Force, which had been using the airbase since the end of the war. After the airlift, the airbase once again became the base of the British Wing 123 squadron, which consisted mainly of Spitfire aircraft.

In 1958, the German Air Force took over the site under the name "S" Aircraft Pilot School – from 1978 Air Transport Wing 62 – and trained its pilots on Noratlas and Trans-all aircraft. Both aircraft were a familiar sight over the airspace of Lake Steinhuder Meer for over fifty years – until the modern Airbus A400M was introduced in 2014.

The Airbus A400M also led to the construction by Airbus of an extensive maintenance centre for its aircraft at the base, which will go into operation in 2027. This is a very extensive project that will also create new jobs. The aim of the collaboration

↑ Auf dem Fliegerhorst geparkte A400M von Airbus. ↑ Airbus A400M parked at the airbase.

Der Airbus A400M führte auch dazu, dass auf dem Stützpunkt ein umfangreiches Wartungszentrum von Airbus für seine Maschinen entsteht, das 2027 in Betrieb geht. Ein recht umfangreiches Projekt, das auch neue Arbeitsplätze schaffen wird. Als Ziel der Zusammenarbeit der Luftwaffe und Airbus steht hier die reibungslose Wartung und Einsatzbereitschaft der A400M-Flotte, „die für die Sicherung des Landes und für Hilfstransporte in Katastrophengebiete stehen soll", so der Ministerpräsident von Niedersachsen, Stephan Weil, anlässlich des Spatenstichs für das Wartungszentrum.

Wie wichtig der Fliegerhorst insgesamt ist, wurde sicherlich auch deutlich, als im Jahr 2023 eine von Deutschland initiierte multinationale Übung stattfand. „Air Defender 23", in der die sogenannte Kaltstartfähigkeit und Schlagkraft verdeutlicht wurde. Der Fliegerhorst diente in diesem Falle als Logistikdrehscheibe, auf der rund 600 ausländische Soldatinnen und Soldaten vor Ort untergebracht wurden. Ferner wurde die Kraftstoffversorgung sichergestellt, wozu auch das Üben der Betankung von Maschinen in der Luft gehörte.

between the German Air Force and Airbus is to ensure the smooth maintenance and operational readiness of the A400M fleet, "which is intended to contribute to the country's security and transport aid to disaster areas", according to the Minister President of Lower Saxony, Stephan Weil, at the ground-breaking ceremony for the maintenance centre.

The importance of the airbase as a whole certainly became clear when a multinational exercise initiated by Germany took place in 2023. This was "Air Defender 23", in which the so-called cold-start capability and striking power were demonstrated. In this exercise, the airbase served as a logistics hub where around 600 foreign soldiers were accommodated on-site. The supply of fuel was also ensured, which included practising the refuelling of aircraft in the air.

↑ Ein Airbus A400M während eines Routinefluges nahe des Lufttransportgeschwaders 62.

↑ An Airbus A400M during a routine flight near the Air Transport Wing 62 home airbase in Wunstorf.

↑ Ein Transportflugzeug A400M AAR betankt zwei Kampfflugzeuge vom Typ Eurofighter (bestückt mit Lenkwaffen) des Taktischen Luftwaffengeschwaders 73 „Steinhoff" aus Laage.

↑ An A400M AAR transport aircraft refuels two Eurofighter combat aircraft (equipped with guided missiles) of the Tactical Air Force Wing 73 "Steinhoff" from Laage.

S. 112–113   Ein A400M gemeinsam mit einem langsam fliegenden Eurofighter. Die besondere Folierung am Heck der Flugzeuge wurde vor Ort im Systemzentrum 23 des LTG 62 gefertigt.

P. 112–113   An A400M together with a slow-flying Eurofighter. The special foiling on the rear of the aircraft was produced on site at Air Transport Wing 62's System Centre 23.

↑ Das neu entstehende Wartungszentrum. ↑ The new maintenance centre.

Mensch und Technik – Nachbarn der Natur

Wie sagte der Bürgermeister von Wunstorf, Carsten Piellusch anlässlich des Spatenstichs, gegen 13 Uhr am 9. Oktober 2023, zum neuen Wartungszentrum des Airbus A400M am Fliegerhorst im Beisein von hochrangigen Politikerinnen und Politikern, Militär und dem Vorstandsvorsitzenden von Airbus für den Bereich Defence and Space, Michael Schöllhorn:
„Ein Erfolg wie der heutige hat viele Väter und Mütter!"
Sehr lange hat es gedauert, von der ersten Idee bis zum Spatenstich, wahrscheinlich auch wesentlich länger als ursprünglich gedacht, aber letztendlich hat es geklappt – und nur das zählt. Gerüchten zufolge soll auch die ehemalige Verteidigungsministerin eine tragende Rolle mit ihrem Wort als Niedersächsin gespielt haben, aber ohne den Durchhaltewillen der örtlichen, in der Politik tätigen Personen, allen voran der ehemalige Bürgermeister der Stadt Wunstorf, Rolf-Axel Eberhardt, würde es den Standort und die Arbeitsplätze wohl nicht mehr geben.
Ohne die Entscheidungen des Bundes, dass das LTG 62 am Standort verbleibt, die Beschaffung vom Airbus A400M – immerhin 53 Stück im Endausbau – sowie die Vergabe der Wartung an Airbus, ohne diese drei Entscheidungen und das Zusammenwirken von Bundesregierung und Airbus, würde es auch keine zusätzlichen rund 300 Stellen vor Ort geben. All diese Menschen werden in den Genuss der Umgebung des Naturparks kommen – sicher auch ein Argument für einen möglichen Ortswechsel der zukünftigen Mitarbeitenden.
Bis alles fertig ist wird ein dreistelliger Millionenbetrag in Gebäude und Infrastruktur investiert worden sein, um die Wartung der Flugzeuge und somit ständige Verfügbarkeit zu garantieren. Dann ist gewährleistet, dass die Maschinen für Bundeswehr und NATO weltweit zum Einsatz kommen können. Erst das Wartungszentrum, zusammen mit dem LTG 62, macht aus logistischer und militärischer Sicht Sinn. So sagte es auch Ministerpräsident Stephan Weil anlässlich des Spatenstichs: „Niedersachsen ist der wichtigste Bundeswehr-Standort!" Und dazu trägt der Fliegerhorst in Zukunft einen noch größeren und wichtigeren Anteil bei – als Nachbar vom Naturpark.

Man and technology – nature's neighbours

"A success like today's has many fathers and mothers!" said Carsten Piellusch, the mayor of Wunstorf, during the ground-breaking ceremony for the new Airbus A400M maintenance centre at the airbase at around 1 p.m. on 9 October 2023 in the presence of high-ranking politicians, the military, and the CEO of Airbus Defence and Space, Michael Schöllhorn.
It took a very long time, from the initial idea to the ground-breaking ceremony, probably much longer than originally thought, but in the end it worked out – and that's what counts. Rumours suggest that the former Minister of Defence, as a native of Lower Saxony, may also have played a significant role with her words, but without the perseverance of the local politicians, above all the former mayor of the town of Wunstorf, Rolf-Axel Eberhardt, the site and the jobs would probably no longer exist. Without the federal government's decisions to keep Air Transport Wing 62 (LTG 62) at the site, to procure of the Airbus A400M – 53 of which will be completed – and to award of the maintenance contract to Airbus, there would be no additional approximately 300 jobs at the location. These three decisions and the cooperation between the federal government and Airbus were crucial for this outcome. All these people will be able to enjoy the surroundings of the nature park – certainly also an argument in favour of any possible relocation of future employees.
By the time everything is ready, a three-digit million sum will have been invested in buildings and infrastructure to guarantee the maintenance of the aircraft and thus constant availability. This will ensure that the aircraft can be deployed worldwide for the German Armed Forces (Bundeswehr) and NATO. Only the maintenance centre, together with the Air Transport Wing 62, makes sense from a logistical and military point of view. As Minister President Stephan Weil said at the ground-breaking ceremony: "Lower Saxony is the most important Bundeswehr location!" And in the future, the airbase will play an even larger and more important role – as a neighbour of the nature park.

← Ein Jaguar E-Type vor Zuschauerinnen und Zuschauern auf dem Fliegerhorst 1985.
← A Jaguar E-Type in front of spectators at the airbase in 1985.

↑ Gewann 1985 in Le Mans in diesem Design: Porsche 956 – ein in Großenheidorn eher selteneres Fahrzeug.

↑ Won Le Mans in 1985 in this design: the Porsche 956 – a somewhat rare vehicle in Großenheidorn.

Eine Besonderheit des Fliegerhorstes, mit größeren Mengen an Zuschauenden, wurde dem Fliegerhorst in den Jahren von 1964 bis 1998 zuteil, als Motorsport dort stattfand, mit bekannten Fahren wie Jochen Mass und Hans-Joachim „Strietzel" Stuck. Sogar die Deutsche Tourenwagen-Meisterschaft (DTM) kam zwischen 1984 und 1993 zu Besuch. Innerhalb der DTM bot der Fliegerhorst die längste Strecke.

Auch ohne Motorsport lohnt jederzeit ein Besuch, sei es um am Zaun zwischen Planespottern zu stehen und das Starten und Landen der mächtigen Transportflugzeuge zu beobachten oder das am Rande des Fliegerhorst stehende Museum der Ju-52 zu besuchen.

A special feature of the airbase, with large crowds of spectators, was the motorsport that took place there from 1964 to 1998, with famous drivers such as Jochen Mass and Hans-Joachim "Strietzel" Stuck. Even the German Touring Car Championship (DTM) came to visit between 1984 and 1993. Within the DTM, the airbase had the longest track to offer.

Even without motorsport events, a visit is worthwhile at any time. You can stand along the fence among plane spotters and observe the takeoff and landing of mighty transport planes, or visit the Ju-52 aircraft museum located on the outskirts of the airbase.

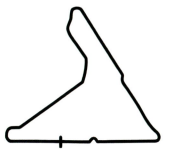

↑ Hans „Strietzel" Stuck – ein gern gesehener Gast auf dem Fliegerhorst, der recht erfolgreich zu seiner aktiven Zeit war.

↑ Hans "Strietzel" Stuck – a welcome guest at the airbase, who was pretty successful during his active career as a race driver..

↑ Der Streckenverlauf des letzten Flugplatzrennens.

↑ The route of the last airfield race.

↑ Steinhude – Stadt am Meer ...

↑ Steinhude – town by the lake ...

Steinhude am Steinhuder Meer

Steinhude on Lake Steinhuder Meer

Jürgen Engelmann

Steinhude am Steinhuder Meer als Ortsteil der Stadt Wunstorf liegt am Westzipfel der Region Hannover. Bis zur Gebietsreform 1974 im Nordostteil des Landkreises Schaumburg-Lippe gelegen, war es eine Gemeinde mit Fleckenrechten.

Der Ort liegt in reizvoller Umgebung am Nordrande des „bergigen Landes", den nördlichen Ausläufern der Mittelgebirge mit Deister, Weserbergland und den Rehburger Bergen. Am Südrand der norddeutschen Tiefebene bettet sich Steinhude ein zwischen den Hügeln nördlich und südlich des Meeres, die als Hinterlassenschaften der Eiszeiten das Landschaftsbild prägen. Das Steinhuder Meer soll auch in der letzten Eiszeit entstanden sein. In Wirklichkeit sind die Vertiefungen die Trittspuren der Riesen, die sich gestritten haben und das Wasser die Tränen der Zwerge, die um ihre von den Riesen verletzten Angehörigen weinten.

Das Leben in Steinhude war und ist geprägt durch die besondere Lage am Meer mit Niedermoor im Westen, Hochmoor im Osten und überwiegend sandigen Hügeln, den Endmoränen der Eiszeiten im Süden. Der See, der wie andere ähnliche Gewässer in Norddeutschland „Meer" (Mare) genannt wurde, gab Möglichkeiten zum Fischen. Das Land um Steinhude herum, die Moorwiesen und das für Ackerbau nur teilweise geeignete Land mit vielen kleinen und großen Findlingen im Süden lies eine karge Landwirtschaft zu, mit der Möglichkeit, aus dem Moor im Osten für den Hausgebrauch Torf zu stechen. Steinhude hat seinen Namen von den Steinen und dem Platz am Wasser (Hude).

Die ohnehin geringen Ackerflächen und darauf befindlichen großen Steine machten es notwendig, sich auf verschiedene Weise den Lebensunterhalt zu sichern.

Steinhude am Steinhuder Meer is a district of the town of Wunstorf at the western tip of the Hannover region. Until the regional reform in 1974, it was located in the north-eastern part of the Schaumburg-Lippe district and was a municipality with local rights.

The town is situated in attractive surroundings on the northern edge of the "mountainous country", the northern foothills of the low mountain ranges with the Deister, Weserbergland and the Rehburg mountains. On the southern edge of the North German Plain, Steinhude is nestled between the hills to the north and south of the sea, which characterise the landscape as a legacy of the ice ages. The Lake Steinhuder Meer is also said to have been formed during the last ice age. In reality, the depressions are the footprints of the giants who fought and the water is the tears of the dwarves who wept for their relatives who had been injured by the giants.

Life in Steinhude was and is characterised by its special location by the sea, with low moorland to the west, high moorland to the east and predominantly sandy hills, the terminal moraines of the ice ages, to the south. The lake, which like other similar bodies of water in northern Germany was called "Meer" (Mare), provided opportunities for fishing. The land around Steinhude, the moor meadows and the fields with their many small and large erratic blocks allowed for sparse farming. In addition, the farmers could cut peat from the moor for domestic use. Steinhude takes its name from the stones and the place by the water (Hude).

The already limited arable land and the large stones on it made it necessary to secure a livelihood in various ways. Weaving developed alongside agriculture and fishing.

↑ Die Promenade wird beidseitig eingerahmt von Wasser. Schöner kann ein Spaziergang kaum sein.

↑ The promenade is framed by water on both sides. A walk could hardly be more beautiful.

↑ Bei entsprechenden Witterungen lockt das Wasser auch an Land.
↑ In suitable weather conditions, the water also attracts visitors onshore.

Neben der Landwirtschaft und der Fischerei entwickelte sich die Weberei. Die älteste Weberei in Deutschland, die Leinenfabrik Seegers, ist als letzte von ehemals sechs mechanischen Webereien in Steinhude noch übrig geblieben.

Besucherinnen und Besucher lockte das Meer, der Wilhelmstein und die reizvolle Umgebung schon länger, aber mit dem Bau der Steinhuder Meerbahn im 19. Jahrhundert gab es einen Aufschwung und der „Tourismus" wurde zum wichtigen Erwerbszweig. Heute gibt es Bestrebungen, die alte Meerbahn zu neuem Leben zu erwecken und eine Verbindung von Hannover aus nach Steinhude zu schaffen – wenn dann die Mittel dafür da sind. Im 20. Jahrhundert wurde Steinhude auch mit vielfältigen Einkaufsmöglichkeiten zum Zentrum in der Meerregion und weit darüber hinaus, zum Beispiel mit seinen Leinenerzeugnissen.

Die besondere Landschaft zieht viele Besuchende, Tagesgäste und Reisende an, die sich sportlich betätigen oder einfach nur an der Natur erfreuen wollen. Mit größeren Parkplätzen, Promenaden am Meer, der Badeinsel und einem Kurpark und Hafenbereich, jeweils mit attraktiven Spielplätzen, ist der Ort auf viele Besucherinnen und Besucher eingestellt. Auch die Ortsansässigen genießen all die Vorzüge und die Möglichkeiten eines attraktiven Wohnortes mit Spiel- und Sportplätzen und der dichten Infrastruktur. An einigen Tagen im Sommer

The oldest weaving mill in Germany, the Seegers linen factory, is the last of the six mechanical weaving mills that once existed in Steinhude.

The lake, the Wilhelmstein and the charming surroundings have attracted visitors for a long time, but the construction of the Steinhuder Meerbahn railway in the 19th century saw an upswing and tourism became an important source of income. Today, efforts are being made to revive the old lake railway and create a connection from Hannover to Steinhude – if the funds are available. In the 20th century, Steinhude also became a centre for shopping in the lakeside region and far beyond, for example with its linen products.

The special landscape attracts many visitors, day trippers and holidaymakers who want to take part in sporting activities or simply enjoy nature. With large car parks, promenades by the lake, the bathing island and a spa park and harbour area, each with attractive playgrounds, the town is well equipped for many visitors. The residents also enjoy all the advantages and opportunities of an attractive residential area with playgrounds and sports grounds and a dense infrastructure. There are also problems on some days in summer and some people from Steinhude would like to close the place due to overcrowding.

Visitors who are not active on the sea and and prefer to be

↑ Einzigartig und bis heute ein Rätsel: das nahtlose Leinenhemd, das im Fischer- und Webermuseum besichtigt werden kann. Im 18. Jahrhundert von Johann Heinrich Bühmann gewebt.

↑ Unique and still a mystery today: the seamless linen shirt, which can be viewed in the Fishermen's and Weavers' Museum. Woven in the 18th century by Johann Heinrich Bühmann.

↑ Im 18. Jahrhundert benötigte man Scheunen am Ortsrand, um dort Stroh und Heu zu lagern. Bereits im darauffolgenden Jahrhundert wurde von Zeit zu Zeit vor den Scheunen gefeiert – was sich bis heute nicht geändert hat.

↑ In the 18th century, barns were needed on the outskirts of the village to store straw and hay. Even in the following century, parties were held in front of the barns from time to time – something that has not changed to this day.

gibt es auch Probleme und manche Steinhuderinnen und Steinhuder würden den Ort gern wegen Überfüllung schließen. Besuchende, die nicht aktiv auf dem Meer sind und sich fahren lassen wollen, werden übers Meer zur Insel Wilhelmstein oder zum Nordufer mit den Auswandererbooten und den Motorbooten der Steinhuder Personenschifffahrt gebracht. Wassersport und die „Landaktivitäten" wie Wandern, Radfahren, Tennis und Golf sind das, was auf und ums Meer herum „angesagt" ist. Die Badeinsel in Steinhude bietet neben dem Platz zum Sonnen und sportlichen Aktivitäten auch Musikevents zum Sonnenuntergang.

Die Steinhuder Museen mit Fischer- und Webermuseum zeigen, wie in Steinhude gelebt und gearbeitet wurde und im Spielzeugmuseum eine reichhaltige Spielzeugsammlung. In der Steinhuder Leinenmangel, die 1855 errichtet wurde, tat bis 1983 eine Kaltmangel ihre Arbeit. Heute wird in dem Industriedenkmal vorgeführt, wie das fertige Leinen unter tonnenschweren Gewichten geglättet und dabei glänzend wurde. In der Windmühle Paula wird an alten Geräten das Korn aufbereitet und gemahlen, ein mühlentechnisches Museum der besonderen Art. Viele Insekten gibt es im Schmetterlingsmuseum zu bestaunen während die Schmetterlinge um die Besuchenden herumfliegen und ihre Betrachterinnen und Betrachter mit ihren fantastischen tropischen Farben begeistern.

taken across the lake to the island of Wilhelmstein or to the north shore with the emigrant boats and the motorboats of the Steinhuder Personenschifffahrt. Water sports and "land activities" such as hiking, cycling, tennis and golf are what is "hip" on and around the lake. The bathing island in Steinhude offers space for sunbathing and sporting activities as well as music events at sunset.

The Steinhude museums, including the fishing and weaving museums, show how people used to live and work in Steinhude. The toy museum has a rich collection of toys. The Steinhude Linen Mangle, which was built in 1855, was used as a cold mangle until 1983. Today, the industrial monument demonstrates how the finished linen was smoothed under weights weighing several tonnes and made shiny in the process. In the Paula windmill, grain is processed and milled using old equipment – a special kind of mill museum. There are many insects to marvel at in the butterfly museum, while butterflies fly around the visitors and delight their onlookers with their fantastic tropical colours.

In the centre of the village and on the Scheunenplatz square, you can see beautiful half-timbered houses with sayings above the archways indicating their origins. In Graf-Wilhelm-Straße, the "Doktorhus", the former vicarage and the "Fischerhus" are particularly striking. This inn also offers a cosy, rustic atmo-

↑ Winterliche Stimmung an der Promenade.

↑ Winter atmosphere on the promenade.

Im Ortskern und auf dem Scheunenplatz sind wunderschöne Fachwerkhäuser anzusehen, die mit den Sprüchen über den Torbögen auf ihre Entstehung hinweisen. In der Graf-Wilhelm-Straße fallen besonders das „Doktorhus", das frühere Pfarrhaus und das „Fischerhus" auf. Dieses Gasthaus bietet auch innen eine gemütliche, rustikale Atmosphäre und wird beworben mit dem Slogan „Haus der berühmten Aale", die es dann unter anderen Gerichten auch in mehreren Variationen zu essen gibt. Die Spezialität „Steinhuder Rauchaal" kann man auch in den Räuchereien direkt aus dem Ofen genießen.

An der Promenade sitzen, aufs Meer sehen und Fischbrötchen oder Eis essen gehört zu den Lieblingsbeschäftigungen der Steinhudefans, dazu gibt es vielleicht den schönsten Sonnenuntergang der Welt, der inzwischen eine so hohe Beliebtheit hat, dass man sich auf der Suche nach dem besten Motiv an den besten Plätzen drängen muss.

sphere inside and is advertised with the slogan "House of the famous eels", which can be eaten in several variations among other dishes. The speciality "Steinhuder Rauchaal" can also be enjoyed in the smokehouses straight from the oven.

Sitting on the promenade, looking out to the lake and eating fish sandwiches or ice cream is one of the favourite pastimes of Steinhude fans, along with perhaps the most beautiful sunset in the world, which is now so popular that you have to jostle for the best spots in search of the best motif.

Fischerhus

Seit 1996 führt Gerrit Schweer in bereits dritter Generation das beliebte Restaurant, „Schweers-Harms Fischerhus", in einem 1751 errichteten Bauernhaus. Von den Schauspielerinnen und Schauspielern angefangen, wie Ingrid Steeger, Horst Janson, Larry Hagman und Gert Fröbe, über Moderator Hans-Joachim Kulenkampff und Bergheld Reinhold Messner bis hin zum Seehelden Felix Graf Luckner, gaben sich diverse Prominente die Klinke in den Jahrzehnten in die Hand.

Die Familie vom heutigen Eigentümer begann zu Beginn des 20. Jahrhunderts mit Landwirtschaft, Fischhandel und später mit der Gastronomie als Nebenerwerb. Erst 1934 wurde von der Gemeinde eine Vollkonzession erteilt und das Restaurant nach und nach ausgebaut.

Das Restaurant beheimatet heute einige kleine Nischenräume, in denen es sich gemütlich speisen und „schnacken" lässt. Ein Besuch lohnt sich schon alleine wegen der interessanten historischen Fotos an den Wänden.

Fischerhus

Since 1996, Gerrit Schweer has been the third generation to run the popular restaurant, "Schweers-Harms Fischerhus", in a farmhouse built in 1751. From actors such as Ingrid Steeger, Horst Janson, Larry Hagman and Gert Fröbe to presenter Hans-Joachim Kulenkampff, mountain hero Reinhold Messner and sea hero Felix Graf Luckner, various celebrities have visited the restaurant over the decades.

At the beginning of the 20th century, the family of the current owner began with farming, fish trading and later catering as a sideline. It was not until 1934 that the municipality granted a full licence and the restaurant was gradually expanded.

Today, the restaurant is home to several small alcoves where you can dine and chat in a cosy atmosphere. The interesting historical photos on the walls alone make a visit worthwhile.

↑ Das Aussehen des Hauses hat sich seit dem 18. Jahrhundert kaum verändert und strahlt eine gewisse Würde aus.
↑ The appearance of the house has hardly changed since the 18th century and exudes a certain dignity.

↑ Kunstvolle Schnitzereien umrahmen den Eingang und geben Auskunft über das Entstehungsjahr.
↑ Artistic carvings frame the entrance and provide information about the year of construction.

↑ Geselligkeit wurde im Fischerhus seit jeher großgeschrieben. Hier tagte zu Beginn des 20. Jahrhunderts der Fischerverein.
↑ Socialising has always been a top priority at the Fischerhus. The fishing club met here at the beginning of the 20th century.

↑ Auch im Innenraum setzt sich die Tradition fort.
↑ The tradition also continues in the interior.

↑ Die Badeinsel vor Steinhude, verbunden durch einen schmalen Steg, lockt nicht nur im Sommer Gäste an.

↑ The bathing island off Steinhude, connected by a narrow footbridge, attracts visitors not only in summer.

Vom Glück des Zurückkehrens
The happiness of returning

Regine Stünkel

Wenn ich an Steinhude denke, dann denke ich an diese unendlich langen Sommer, die gefühlt kein Ende nahmen. An Tage, die unbeschwert und frei daherkamen. An denen ich hundsmüde und mit ein paar Sommersprossen mehr abends nach Hause lief, die Sonne noch auf meiner Haut spürte und den Wind, der sich am liebsten in meinen langen Haaren verfing. Mein Papa hatte ein Boot ganz in der Nähe der Badeinsel liegen. Ein Holzboot aus Mahagoni. Das glänzte immer so verheißungsvoll in der Sonne. Wenn ich an Deck war, dann hörte ich das Wasser glucksen und wie sich der Wind an die Metallmasten der Schiffe im Hafen schmiegte, sie umspielte, bis ein Klangbild entstand, das noch heute in meinen Ohren liegt. Eine Hymne auf die Leichtigkeit des Lebens, orchestriert von der Natur.

In der Schule erzählten sie uns von der Aalwanderung. Nachts, im September, hieß es, machen sich die Aale aus dem Steinhuder Meer auf einen langen Weg. Dorthin zurück, wo sie geboren wurden – in die Sargassosee. Ein Meeresgebiet im Atlantik, östlich von Florida. Es ist ihr letzter Lebenszyklus. Sie hören dann auf zu fressen. Schlängeln sich mit all ihrer verbleibenden Kraft tausende von Kilometern, bis sie ihren Geburtsort erreicht haben. Sie laichen dort und dann sterben sie. Die Geschichte der Aale hatte für mich etwas Tröstliches. Wenn etwas endet, beginnt zugleich etwas Neues. The circle of life.

Als Jugendliche war mir klar, dass auch ich eines Tages wandern muss. Raus aus meiner Heimat, rein in die Welt da draußen, die so verlockend war und nur darauf zu warten schien, von mir entdeckt zu werden. In einem dieser Sommer veranstaltete NDR 2 auf der Badeinsel in Steinhude die Satur-

When I think of Steinhude, I think of those endlessly long summers that felt like they never ended. Days that seemed carefree and free. Days when I would walk home in the evening, dog-tired and with a few more freckles, still feeling the sun on my skin and the wind that loved to get caught in my long hair.

My dad had a boat moored very close to the bathing island. A wooden boat made of mahogany. It always shone so auspiciously in the sun. When I was on deck, I could hear the water gurgling and how the wind nestled against the metal masts of the ships in the harbour, playing around them until a sound emerged that still resonates in my ears today. A hymn to the lightness of life, orchestrated by nature.

At school, they told us about the eel migration. At night, in September, they said, the eels from the Lake Steinhuder Meer set off on a long journey. Back to where they were born – into the Sargasso Sea. A sea area in the Atlantic, east of Florida. It is their last life cycle. They then stop eating. They wriggle thousands of kilometres with all their remaining strength until they reach their birthplace. They spawn there and then they die. The story of the eels had something comforting for me. When something ends, something new begins at the same time. The circle of life.

As a teenager, I realised that one day I too would have to go hiking. Out of my home, into the world out there, which was so enticing and seemed to be just waiting for me to discover it. One summer, NDR 2 organised the Saturday Night Disco on the bathing island in Steinhude. Uwe Bahn was the host. Haddaway sang "what is love". Boats were anchored in front of the bathing island. It was one of those moments when the

↑ Die Autorin Regine Stünkel schwelgt auf der Badeinsel in Erinnerungen.
↑ Author Regine Stünkel reminisces on the bathing island.

↑ Lotte und Philine haben sich als Ziel für ihren Ausflug etwas ganz Besonderes gewählt: Die Posttonne liegt ganz im Osten vom Steinhuder Meer – und das bereits seit 50 Jahren! Die 1964 aus einer Bierlaune und Wette von Mitgliedern des Segelclubs Garbsen heraus entstandene Idee entwickelte sich zu einer Tradition, die viele Seglerinnen und Segler auf dem Steinhuder Meer nicht mehr missen möchten. Der Segelclub Garbsen kümmert sich ebenso lange liebevoll um das Leeren der Posttonne und die Weitergabe der Karten und Briefe an die Post.

↑ Lotte and Philine have chosen something very special as the destination for their excursion: The Posttonne is located in the very east of the Lake Steinhuder Meer – and has been for 50 years! The idea, which originated in 1964 from a beer whim and a bet by members of the Garbsen Sailing Club, developed into a tradition that many sailors on the Lake Steinhuder Meer would no longer want to do without. For just as long, the Garbsen Sailing Club has lovingly organised the emptying of the post bin and the forwarding of cards and letters to the post office.

day Night Disco. Uwe Bahn moderierte. Haddaway sang „What is love". Vor der Badeinsel ankerten Boote. Es war einer der Momente, in dem die Welt ein wenig runder war als sonst. In dem sich alles stimmig anfühlte.

Ich weiß noch genau, wie sich plötzlich vieles fügte. Mir wurde klar, genau so etwas möchtest du auch tun. Menschen etwas erzählen. Ihnen Augenblicke geben, die bleiben. Als der Musiksender VIVA an den Start ging und Moderatorinnen suchte, da wählte ich die Badeinsel, um Fotos zu machen. Der Ort, an dem meine Liebe fürs Moderieren erwachte. Meine Schwester nahm sich den Fotoapparat meiner Eltern und dann starteten wir unser Shooting. Mit den Füßen im Sand und dem Meer um uns herum.

Später kehrte ich als Moderatorin nach Steinhude zurück. Berichtete über den schwimmenden Briefkasten im Meer, der sich nur mit dem Boot erreichen lässt, und von dem aus noch heute Post in alle Welt verschickt wird. Ich besuchte die Spitznamenstraße im Ortskern. Dort hängen an den Türen der Häuser nicht normale Namensschilder, sondern die Spitznamen der Steinhuderinnen und Steinhuder. Und ich machte eine Reportage über den „Steinhuder Hecht", der wohl berühmtesten Erfindung meiner Heimat. Er gilt noch heute als erster deutscher Entwurf eines U-Bootes. Das Boot sieht aus wie ein Hecht und sollte zwölf Minuten lang tauchen

world was a little more rounded than usual. When everything felt right.

I remember exactly how everything suddenly fell into place. I realised that this is exactly what you want to do. Tell people something. Give them moments that stay with them. When the music channel VIVA launched and was looking for presenters, I chose the bathing island to take photos. The place where my love for presenting awoke. My sister took my parents' camera and then we started our shoot. With our feet in the sand and the sea all around us.

Later, I returned to Steinhude as a presenter. I reported on the floating postbox in the sea, which can only be reached by boat and from which post is still sent all over the world today. I visited the nickname street in the town centre. There are not normal nameplates on the doors of the houses, but the nicknames of the people of Steinhude. And I did a report on the "Steinhuder Hecht" (Pike of Steinhude), probably the most famous invention of my home town. It is still regarded today as the first German design for a submarine. The boat looks like a pike and was supposed to be able to dive for twelve minutes. The "Steinhuder Hecht" is even said to have been tested in a canal on the Steinhuder Meer. But nobody really knows how this dive turned out. Perhaps Ulrich Tukur does, when he sings: "And the Lake Steinhuder Meer rustles gently in the

↑ Der Vater von Autorin Regine Stünkel, Werner Stünkel, erhält verdienstvoll seinen Brassenschlag unter dem üblichen Gejohle der Zuschauerinnen und Zuschauer.

↑ The father of author Regine Stünkel, Werner Stünkel, deservedly receives his bream punch to the usual cheers from the audience.

können. Der „Steinhuder Hecht" soll sogar in einem Kanal am Steinhuder Meer ausprobiert worden sein. Wie dieser Tauchvorgang ausging, das weiß aber keiner so recht. Vielleicht ja Ulrich Tukur, wenn er singt: „Und das Steinhuder Meer rauscht sanft in der Nacht. Es singt uns das Lied, das uns glücklich macht."

Das Glück steckt in Steinhude in so vielem. In der Sonne, die das Wasser zum Glitzern bringt. In dem fröhlichen „Guten Morgen", das zum Brötchenkauf fest dazu gehört. In den Ritualen wie dem Brassenschlag, mit dem Steinhuderinnen und Steinhuder, die nicht in dem Ort geboren sind, zum echten Brassen geschlagen werden. Mein Papa ist so ein echter Brasse. Wer in Steinhude groß wird, der wird mit etwas ganz Besonderem groß. Vieles davon inspiriert mich noch heute und fließt in meine Sendungen beim NDR ein.

Wenn ich an meine Heimat denke, dann sind so viele wundervolle Erinnerungen wieder da. Ich rieche den Duft von geräuchertem Aal in den Straßen des Ortes. In meiner Kindheit roch es Weihnachten sogar im Postamt nach Aal. Ich höre die Zugvögel über dem Meer entlangziehen. Ich atme schwere Sommerluft, und ich glaube, ich werde es wie die Aale machen. Eines Tages komme ich zurück. Versprochen.

night. It sings us the song that makes us happy."

There is happiness in so many things in Steinhude. In the sun that makes the water sparkle. In the cheerful "Good morning" that is part and parcel of buying bread rolls. In the rituals such as the bream strike, with which Steinhude people who were not born in the village are beaten to a real bream. My dad is a real bream. If you grow up in Steinhude, you grow up with something very special. Much of this still inspires me today and flows into my programmes at NDR.

When I think of my home, so many wonderful memories come flooding back. I can smell the aroma of smoked eel in the streets of the village. When I was a child, even the post office smelled of eel at Christmas. I can hear the migratory birds flying over the sea. I breathe in the heavy summer air and I think I'm going to do like the eels. I'll be back one day. I promise.

S. 128–129 Drei Highlights der Region auf einem Bild: Badeinsel, Steinhude und die Landmarke Kalimandscharo – wie die Kaliabbauhalde im Volksmund genannt wird – im Hintergrund.

P. 128–129 Three highlights of the region in one picture: bathing island of Steinhude, Steinhude and the landmark Kalimandscharo – as the potash mining tip is popularly known – in the background.

← Bedingt durch die Lage längs der Straße ergab sich eine kleine Allee, die zum Eingang der Kirche führt.

← Due to the location along the road, there was a small alley leading to the entrance of the church.

Petruskirche
St Peter's Church

Peter Zenker

Der Grundstein der im klassizistischen Baustil gebauten Saalkirche aus Natursteinmauerwerk wurde 1804 gelegt. Die Bauzeit betrug bedingt durch Geldmangel 50 Jahre, so dass sie erst 1854 eingeweiht werden konnte.

Das schlichte Kirchenschiff, das nur einfache rechteckige Fenster hat, ist mit einem Satteldach bedeckt, aus dem sich im Westen ein quadratischer Dachturm erhebt, der die Fassade prägt. Das oberste Geschoss des Turmes beherbergt den Glockenstuhl und die Turmuhr, deren Zifferblätter in alle vier Himmelsrichtungen zeigen. Die Klangarkaden sind als gekop-

The foundation stone of the hall church, built in the classicist style from natural stone masonry, was laid in 1804. Due to a lack of funds, it took 50 years to build, so that it could only be consecrated in 1854.

The simple nave, which only has simple rectangular windows, is covered with a gabled roof, from which a square roof tower rises in the west, characterising the façade. The top floor of the tower houses the belfry and the tower clock, whose dials point in all four directions. The sound arcades are designed as coupled windows (biforia). The tower is topped with a spire

↑ Das meiste der Ausstattung der Kirche entstand erst im 20. Jahrhundert. Eines der Fenster stellt den Fischfang Petrus' dar und somit auch eine Verbindung zum Ort, in dem die Kirche steht.

↑ Most of the church's furnishings were not created until the 20th century. One of the windows depicts St. Peter catching fish and thus also has a connection to the place where the church stands.

pelte Fenster (Biforien) gestaltet. Bedeckt ist der Turm mit einem Helm, der von einem quadratischen Ansatz in eine achteckige Spitze übergeht.

Der Innenraum des Kirchenschiffs ist mit einem Tonnengewölbe überspannt. Das Bogenfenster hinter dem Altar, von Kommerzienrat Seegers gestiftet, stellt die Geschichte vom Fischfang des Petrus dar.

Von der klassizistischen Kirchenausstattung sind nur Reste erhalten. Das Kruzifix, die Statue des Johannes hinter dem Taufbecken und die Statuetten an der Kanzel sind zeitgenössische Kunst aus der Hand des Bildhauers Ernst Weber, der 1952 nach Steinhude kam. Ältestes Ausstattungsstück ist ein Opferstock aus dem Jahre 1614.

1996 begann eine umfangreiche Innenrenovierung einschließlich der Neugestaltung der Altarwand. Die oberen Fenster in blauem Glas wie auch die Bilder der zwölf Apostel wurden vom Künstler Oswald Krause-Rischard gestaltet. Der Altar in seiner achteckigen Form nimmt das Profil von Kanzel und Taufstein auf.

that transitions from a square base to an octagonal spire.

The interior of the nave is spanned by a barrel vault. The arched window behind the altar, donated by Kommerzienrat Seegers, depicts the story of St Peter catching fish.

Only remnants of the classicist church furnishings have been preserved. The crucifix, the statue of St John behind the baptismal font and the statuettes on the pulpit are contemporary works by the sculptor Ernst Weber, who came to Steinhude in 1952. The oldest piece of equipment is an offering box from 1614.

In 1996, an extensive interior renovation began, including the redesign of the altar wall. The upper windows in blue glass, as well as the pictures of the twelve apostles, were designed by the artist Oswald Krause-Rischard. The octagonal shape of the altar echoes the profile of the pulpit and baptismal font.

↑ Die Insel ist ein gerne angesteuertes Ziel, sowohl für Tagestouristen als auch für Seglerinnen und Segler: Man hat das Gefühl in einer anderen Welt zu sein.

↑ The island is a popular destination for both day tourists and sailors: you have the feeling of being in another world.

Insel Wilhelmstein

Wilhelmstein Island

Stefan Brüdermann

An einem sehr kalten Wintertag zu Beginn des Jahres 1761 mussten einige Einwohnerinnen und Einwohner des Ortes Steinhude unter strenger Geheimhaltung mit einer Schubkarre einen Stein über das Eis schaffen. An einem genau vorher bestimmten Ort wurde ein Loch ins Eis gehackt und der Stein versenkt – als Grundstein einer Festung und als erster einer großen Menge von Steinen, die in den folgenden Jahren teils mit Schlitten über das Eis, teils mit Lastkähnen an diese Stelle geschafft wurden. Der erste Stein aber trug den Namen des Grafen Wilhelm zu Schaumburg-Lippe.

Graf Wilhelm (1724–1777) war wohl der bekannteste der Regenten Schaumburg-Lippes. Dieses kleine Territorium war 1647 durch die Teilung Schaumburgs entstanden und zog sich von Bückeburg im Westen bis Steinhude im Osten. Aufgrund der Wirrungen seiner Familiengeschichte wurde Graf Wilhelm 1724 in London geboren. Seit Kinderzeiten hatte er unter vielfältigen geistigen Interessen auch eine große Begabung für die militärische Karriere. Er trat 1748 die Regierung Schaumburg-Lippes in seiner Residenz Bückeburg an. Seine Regierungszeit war geprägt von typisch aufklärerischen Wirtschaftsreformen und -projekten und von einer ehrgeizigen Bildungspolitik. Er hatte umfassende geistige Interessen und holte sich zur Unterstützung seiner Politik und auch als Gesprächspartner Gelehrte wie Thomas Abbt und Johann Gottfried Herder an seinen Hof. Vor allem aber bemühte er sich um den Aufbau einer starken Armee, was für den Regenten eines Kleinstaates von kaum 17.000 Einwohnerinnen und Einwohnern ein ehrgeiziges Unterfangen war. Graf Wilhelm sah seinen Kleinstaat bedroht durch seinen Lehnsherrn Hessen-Kassel und vergrößerte sein Heer auf 650 Mann, im Krieg waren es zeitweise dann doppelt so viele. Mit diesen Truppen schloss er sich im Siebenjährigen Krieg der englisch-preußischen Koalition an und hatte großen Anteil am Sieg in der Schlacht von Minden 1759. Legendär wurde sein Ruf, als er 1762 als Oberkommandierender in Portugal eine spanische Offensive abwehrte und später noch eine portugiesische Heeresreform leitete. Allerdings schlug er anders als die meisten seiner Standesgenossen Schlachten nicht um des Ruhmes willen, er wollte vielmehr die Defensive stärken, um den als sinnlose Grausamkeit erkannten Krieg überhaupt zu verhindern.

On a very cold winter's day at the beginning of 1761, some inhabitants of the village of Steinhude had to move a stone across the ice with a wheelbarrow in strict secrecy. A hole was chopped into the ice at a precisely predetermined spot and the stone was sunk – as the foundation stone of a fortress and the first of a large number of stones that were transported to this spot in the following years, some by sledge across the ice and some by barge. The first stone, however, bore the name of Wilhelm, Count of Schaumburg-Lippe.

Count Wilhelm (1724–1777) was probably the most famous of Schaumburg-Lippe's rulers. This small territory was created in 1647 through the division of Schaumburg and stretched from Bückeburg in the west to Steinhude in the east. Due to the complex circumstances of his family history, Count Wilhelm was born in 1724 in London. As a child, he had a wide range of intellectual interests as well as a great talent for a military career. He took up the regency of Schaumburg-Lippe in his residence of Bückeburg in 1748. His reign was characterised by typical Enlightenment economic reforms and projects and an ambitious education policy. He had wide-ranging intellectual interests and brought scholars such as Thomas Abbt and Johann Gottfried Herder to his court to assist him in his policies and as conversation partners.

Above all, however, he endeavoured to build up a strong army, which was an ambitious undertaking for the ruler of a small state with barely 17,000 inhabitants. Count Wilhelm saw his small state threatened by his feudal lord Hesse-Kassel and increased his army to 650 men, at times twice as many during the war. With these troops, he joined the Anglo-Prussian coalition in the Seven Years' War and played a major part in the victory at the Battle of Minden in 1759. His reputation became legendary when, as commander-in-chief in Portugal in 1762, he repelled a Spanish offensive and later spearheaded a reform of the Portuguese army. However, unlike most of his peers, he did not fight battles for the sake of glory, but rather wanted to strengthen the defensive capabilities in order to prevent war, which he recognised as senseless cruelty, from happening in the first place.

The Wilhelmstein fortress was also built with this in mind. For this construction, stones and filling material had to be transported to the centre of the lake for five years, a laborious

← Graf Wilhelm: Namensgeber und Erbauer des Wilhelmsteins und vorausschauender und defensiver militärischer Stratege. Dieses Gemälde hängt im Schloss Bückeburg.

← Count Wilhelm: namesake and builder of the Wilhelmstein and forward-looking and defensive military strategist. This painting hangs in the castle in Bückeburg.

In diesem Sinne wurde auch die Festung Wilhelmstein errichtet. Für diesen Bau mussten fünf Jahre lang Steine und Füllmaterial in die Mitte des Sees geschafft werden, eine Fron, die sogar einmal zu einem Aufstand der Steinhuder Fischer führte. Zwei weitere Jahre wurde an der Festung gebaut, im Sommer 1767 war sie fertig. Ihre Position war so gewählt, dass sie für die Artillerie der Zeit kaum erreichbar war, der Kern der Festung wurde von sechzehn Bastionen geschützt, die als eigenständige Inseln angelegt wurden. Auf den Bastionen waren die Mannschaftsunterkünfte, auf der Mittelinsel Kasematten und ein kleines Schlösschen, das als Wohnung des Kommandanten und der Offiziere diente. Die Form der Inseln entsprach einem geometrischen Ideal, orientiert an der Vermeidung toter Winkel für die Artillerie. Wilhelm ließ eine in der Form ähnliche, aber wesentlich größere Festung in Portugal bei der Stadt Elvas errichten.

Ungeachtet der geringen Größe des Wilhelmsteins waren im Kriegsfall bis zu 800 Mann zu ihrer Besatzung vorgesehen, tatsächlich waren es zu Wilhelms Zeiten maximal 144 Soldaten, später wesentlich weniger. Zur Verteidigung dienten 166 meist kleinkalibrige Geschütze, außerdem standen fünf kleine Kanonenboote zur Verfügung. Der berühmte „Steinhuder Hecht" allerdings existiert nur als Projektzeichnung, gebaut wurde eine kleinere Variante. Graf Wilhelm richtete auf der Festung eine Militärschule ein, an der er selbst unterrichtete. Sein berühmtester Schüler war der spätere preußische General und Militärreformer Gerhard von Scharnhorst. Nach Wil-

drudgery that even led to a revolt by the Steinhude fishermen on one occasion. The fortress was built for a further two years and was completed in the summer of 1767. Its position was chosen in such a way that it could hardly be reached by the artillery of the time; the core of the fortress was protected by sixteen bastions, which were constructed as independent islands. On the bastions were the crew quarters, on the centre island casemates and a small castle that served as the commander's and officers' quarters. The shape of the islands corresponded to a geometric ideal, designed to avoid blind spots for the artillery. Wilhelm had a similar but much larger fortress built in Portugal near the town of Elvas.

Despite the small size of the Wilhelmstein, it was intended to be manned by up to 800 men in the event of war; in fact, there were a maximum of 144 soldiers in Wilhelm's time, and considerably fewer later on. The defence was provided by 166 mostly small-calibre guns and five small gunboats. However, the famous "Steinhuder Hecht" (Steinhude Pike, regarded as the first German submarine) only exists as a project drawing; it was actually built in a smaller version. Count Wilhelm set up a military school at the fortress, where he himself taught. His most famous pupil was the later Prussian general and military reformer Gerhard von Scharnhorst.

After William's death in 1777, the military school was quickly dissolved and the garrison of the fortress reduced. Nevertheless, it passed its only military test in 1787: after the death of Count Philipp Ernst, the Hessian Landgrave attempted to con-

↑ Zwei Auswanderer legen ab vom Wilhelmstein und bringen die Tagestouristinnen und Tagestouristen wieder nach Steinhude. Wer so etwas noch nicht gemacht hat, verpasst etwas.
↑ Two emigrants set sail from Wilhelmstein and bring the day tourists back to Steinhude. Anyone who hasn't done something like this is definitely missing out.

↑ So lässt es sich aushalten. Der Kiosk ist nicht weit weg und wartet mit Speisen und Getränken, um das Wohlbefinden, neben dem Ausblick, noch zu steigern.
↑ It's a great place to stay. The kiosk is not far away and offers food and drinks to make you feel even better, in addition to the view.

helms Tod 1777 wurde die Militärschule schnell aufgelöst, die Besatzung der Festung verringert. Dennoch bestand sie 1787 ihre einzige militärische Bewährungsprobe: Nach dem Tod des Grafen Philipp Ernst versuchte der hessische Landgraf, das schaumburg-lippische Lehen einzuziehen und ließ sein Militär einmarschieren. Nur die Besatzung des Wilhelmsteins widerstand – bis die Nachbarn Intervention androhten und die Hessen abziehen mussten. Bald wurde die Festungsinsel zur Attraktion für Reisende. Schon 1767 gab es erste Einträge in einem Gästebuch, in den ersten Jahren blieb aber die Zahl der Besuchenden aus Gründen der Geheimhaltung sehr beschränkt, ab 1790 besuchten immerhin 200 bis 300 Personen im Jahr die Insel. Aus Gründen der Bauerhaltung mussten bald die kleinen Inselchen miteinander durch Auffüllung der Zwischenräume verbunden werden, bis 1814 hatte der Wilhelmstein seine heutige Gestalt gewonnen.

Die Kasematten wurden inzwischen als Gefängnis für Sträflinge benutzt, meist waren es etwas sechs bis zehn Männer, die langjährige Gefängnisstrafen abzusitzen hatten. Insgesamt verbrachten etwa 300 Gefangene ihre Haftzeit auf dem Wilhelmstein.

1867 schloss Schaumburg-Lippe eine Militärkonvention mit Preußen, es war das Ende des eigenständigen schaumburg-lippischen Militärs. Damit endete auch die Geschichte des Wilhelmsteins als Gefängnis. Fortan war der Wilhelmstein „nur" noch eine Touristinnen- und Touristenattraktion.

fiscate the Schaumburg-Lippe fiefdom and had his military march in. Only the garrison of the Wilhelmstein resisted – until the neighbours threatened to intervene and the Hessians had to withdraw.

The fortress island soon became an attraction for travellers. The first entries were made in a visitors' book as early as 1767, but in the early years the number of visitors remained very limited for reasons of secrecy, with 200–300 people a year then visiting the island from 1790 onwards. To preserve the construction, the small islets soon had to be joined together by filling in the spaces between them, and by 1814 the Wilhelmstein had taken on its present form.

The casemates were now used as a prison for convicts, mostly between six and ten men serving long prison sentences. In total, around 300 prisoners served their time at Wilhelmstein.

In 1867, Schaumburg-Lippe concluded a military convention with Prussia, marking the end of the independent Schaumburg-Lippe military. This also marked the end of Wilhelmstein's history as a prison. From then on, the Wilhelmstein was "only" a tourist attraction.

← Irgendwo auf der Insel gibt es immer einen schönen Platz zum Ausruhen und Beobachten. Diese Bank steht vor dem Inselladen, der so manches schöne Souvenir führt.

← Somewhere on the island there is always a nice place to rest and watch the world go by. This bench is in front of the island shop, which sells many lovely souvenirs.

← Im Inneren der Festung lässt sich nachvollziehen, wie karg das Leben dort vor rund 300 Jahren gewesen sein muss – besonders zur Zeit der Belagerung.

← Inside the fortress, you can see how meagre life must have been there around 300 years ago – especially during the siege.

↑ Aus der Vogelperspektive sieht man gut die Aufteilung der Insel mit der Festung in der Mitte und dem kleinen Strand unten links.

↑ From a bird's-eye view, you can clearly see the layout of the island with the fortress in the centre and the small beach at the bottom left.

↑ Die Winter, in denen das Eis zu Ausflügen zur Insel Wilhelmstein lockte, sind leider rar geworden.

↑ The winters in which the ice lured visitors to the island of Wilhelmstein have unfortunately become rare.

Im Nebel der Erinnerung
In the mist of memory

Alexander Fürst zu Schaumburg-Lippe
Alexander, Prince of Schaumburg-Lippe

Wer mit einem der blitzblank lackierten Segelboote, die man in der Gegend von Steinhude „Auswanderer" nennt – sie heißen so, weil man mit ihnen über das Steinhuder Meer zum benachbarten Königreich Hannover gelangen konnte – auf den Wilhelmstein übersetzt, dort das Festungsbauwerk besucht, das quietschende Drehkreuz am Eingang hinter sich lässt und durch tunnelartige Gewölbe die Treppe hinaufsteigt, kann durch eine moderne Glastür in das einstige Wohnzimmer des Inselkommandeurs blicken und, sofern jemand den Schlüssel dabei hat, die Räume auch betreten.

Dort, auf dem Tisch gegenüber dem Eingang, findet man ein schmales Buch vor, etwas kleiner als ein DIN-A4-Blatt. Sein Einband zeugt von einer Kunst des Buchbinderhandwerks, die es bei uns heute nicht mehr gibt – in der Mitte das große Staats- und Familienwappen Schaumburg-Lippes, versehen noch mit dem vierstrahligen „Fürstenhut", der per Verordnung von 1893 durch die achtstrahlige Herzogskrone ersetzt wurde, mit zwei Engeln unter dem Hermelin zur Rechten und Linken des Wappens, das Ganze goldgeprägt auf blauem Leder, umgeben von prunkvollen Ornamenten im Stil des späten 19. Jahrhunderts.

Das Buch umfasst nur ein paar Dutzend Seiten und die meisten sind nach wie vor leer. Es dürfte sich um eines der ältesten Gästebücher handeln, die nach wie vor in Gebrauch sind, und zugleich um eines der am seltensten benutzten. Zwischen den Einträgen liegen regelmäßig Jahre oder Jahrzehnte, ein- oder zweimal ganze Menschenleben. Die Geländer der Holztreppen, die zum Aussichtsturm der Festung führen, haben viel mehr geschnitzte und geritzte Einträge vorzuweisen als dieses Buch.

If you take one of the spick-and-span sailing boats to Wilhelmstein (the boats are known locally in Steinhude as "emigrants" because they could be used to cross Lake Steinhuder Meer to the neighbouring Kingdom of Hanover), visit the fortress building, leave the squeaky turnstile at the entrance behind you and climb the stairs through tunnel-like vaults, you can look through a modern glass door into the former living room of the island commander and, if someone has the key with them, enter the rooms.

There, on the table opposite the entrance, you will find a narrow book, slightly smaller than an A4-sized sheet. Its cover bears witness to an art of bookbinding that no longer exists today - in the centre is the large state and family coat of arms of Schaumburg-Lippe, still bearing the four-pointed "princely hat", which was replaced by the eight-pointed ducal crown by decree in 1893. It has two angels under the ermine to the right and left of the coat of arms, the whole embossed in gold on blue leather, surrounded by magnificent ornaments in the style of the late 19th century.

The book contains only a few dozen pages, and most of them are still blank. It is probably one of the oldest guest books still in use and also one of the least frequently used. The entries are regularly separated by years or decades, sometimes by entire lifetimes. The banisters of the wooden stairs leading up to the fortress lookout tower have many more carved and engraved entries than this book.

The very first one was made in 1874, on October 4th, by my great-great-grandfather Adolph (Adolf I) Georg, the second reigning Prince of Schaumburg-Lippe. Like his wife Hermine, he used only his first name. Below them, Heinrich XXII Prince

S. 140–141 Die Kommandanturstube: Hier liegt das Tagebuch des Wilhelmsteins mit Einträgen der Fürstenfamilie, beginnend mit dem auslaufenden 19. Jahrhundert.

P. 140–141 The commandant's parlour: here lies the diary of the Wilhelmstein with entries from the Princely Family, starting at the end of the 19th century.

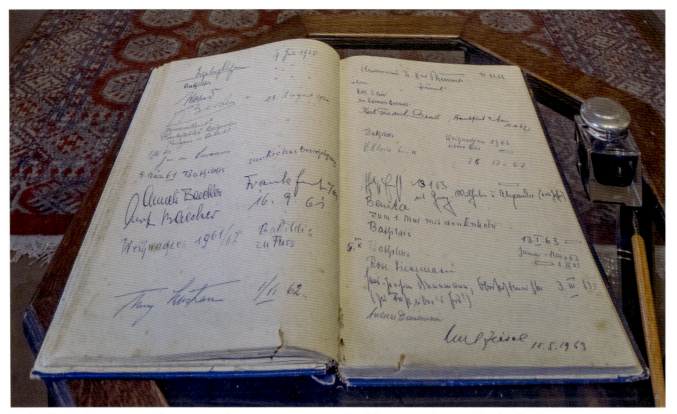

↑ Eine Tagebuchseite mit einem Eintrag vom 19. Januar 1963 – mit einem Hinweis zu einem winterlichen Besuch der Fürstenfamilie.

↑ A diary page with an entry dated 19 January 1963 with a reference to a winter visit by the Princely Family.

Den allerersten fertigte im Jahre 1874, am 4. Oktober, mein Ururgroßvater Adolph (Adolf I.) Georg, der zweite regierende Fürst zu Schaumburg-Lippe an. Er benutzte, ebenso wie seine Gemahlin Hermine, nur seinen Vornamen. Darunter zeichneten Heinrich XXII. Fürst Reuß und Fürstin Ida, eine geborene Prinzessin zu Schaumburg-Lippe, mit ihren vollen Titeln, die Fürstin zusätzlich mit dem Geburtsnamen. Dann folgen die Kinder: Otto, Adolf, Marie, Hermine ... Sie scheinen alle die preußische Verwandtschaft begleitet zu haben. Oder fehlt jemand? Familienausflug kurz vor dem zweiten Hochzeitstag von Heinrich und Ida, die vermutlich in Bückeburg geheiratet hatten.

Als Nächstes, 1882, zeichnete mein Urgroßvater Georg mit seinem Titel als Erbprinz, die Erbprinzessin Marie Anna mit dem ihrigen, dann einige Gäste. Zwei Seiten weiter, 1895, heißt der Erbprinz bereits Adolf und sein Vater Georg ist regierender Fürst. Einige Gäste, die nicht zur Familie gehören, stehen darunter. Wir blättern nur ein paarmal und sind bereits im April 1963, „Bathildis mit Motorboot", meine Großmutter. Ich war dabei, mein Bruder Georg-Wilhelm konnte bereits unterschreiben, mein Name von der Hand meines Vaters darunter. Dann ein Eintrag vom 29. Dezember 1965. „Die Hagenburger vom Schloss wünschen Familie Cichon" – den Inselverwaltern – „ein gutes neues Jahr 1966."

Dieser Ausflug, ich war gerade sieben, scheint mir zu meinen ältesten Erinnerungen zu gehören. War er das wirklich? Ich werde im Gästebuch nicht erwähnt. Aber ich sehe deutlich vor mir den weißen Nebel, der über der Eisfläche des Meeres schwebte. Aus demselben Nebel scheint die Erinnerung aufzusteigen. Wir waren, meine ich, mit Schlittschuhen, Rodelschlitten und Hunden unterwegs, das konnte man damals noch. Start war Schloss Hagenburg, dann ging es den vereisten Kanal hinunter bis ins offene Steinhuder Meer, das ich als gigantische, unermessliche, faszinierende Winterwüste

Reuss and Princess Ida, a born Princess of Schaumburg-Lippe, signed their full titles, the Princess additionally using her maiden name. Then follow the children: Otto, Adolf, Marie, Hermine ... They all seem to have accompanied the Prussian relatives. Or is someone missing? Family outing shortly before the second wedding anniversary of Heinrich and Ida, who had presumably married in Bückeburg.

Next, in 1882, my great-grandfather Georg signed with his title as Hereditary Prince, the Hereditary Princess Marie Anna with hers, and then some guests. Two pages further on, in 1895, the hereditary prince is already called Adolf and his father Georg is the reigning prince. Some guests who are not part of the family are listed below. We only need to turn the pages a few times and we are already in April 1963, "Bathildis with motorboat", my grandmother. I was there, my brother Georg-Wilhelm was already able to sign, my name from my father's hand underneath. Then an entry dated 29 December 1965: "The Hagenburgers from the castle wish the Cichon family" – the island administrators – "a Happy New Year 1966."

This trip, when I was just seven, seems to be one of my oldest memories. Was it really? I'm not mentioned in the guest book. But I can clearly see the white mist hovering over the icy surface of the sea. The memory seems to rise from the same mist. I think we were travelling with skates, toboggans and dogs – you could still do that back then. We started at Hagenburg Castle and then travelled down the icy canal to the open Lake Steinhuder Meer, which I perceived as a gigantic, immense, fascinating winter wasteland. There was a wafer-thin layer of snow on the ice, which was so fine that you could easily skate across it. I remember seeing ice gliders in the distance, graceful, elegant structures that I marvelled at and didn't understand. What was that? At some point, the Wilhelmstein emerged from the depths of the fog. Land in sight! And a cup of hot chocolate.

↑ Einsam im Eis liegt die Insel Wilhelmstein und lockt als kleines Abenteuer zu einem Ausflug mit Schlittschuhen.

↑ Lying alone in the ice, the island of Wilhelmstein is an enticing little adventure for a trip on ice skates.

wahrgenommen habe. Auf der Eisfläche lag eine hauchdünne Schneedecke, die so fein war, dass man sie problemlos mit Schlittschuhen passieren konnte. Ich erinnere mich an Eissegler in der Ferne, graziöse, elegante Gebilde, die ich bestaunte und nicht begriff. Was war das? Irgendwann tauchte aus der Tiefe des Nebels der Wilhelmstein auf. Land in Sicht! Und eine Tasse heiße Schokolade.

In einem Verschlag am Rande des Kanals lag die „Graf Wilhelm", später „Graf Wilhelm II.", ein kleines Motorboot mit Verdeck; mein Vater sprach vom „Bötchen". Im Sommer nahm er uns Kinder im „Bötchen" mit zum Wilhelmstein. Er besaß einen Binnenseeschein und konnte ausgezeichnet manövrieren; zumindest kam es uns so vor. „Schau dir das Boot dort drüben mit einem Auge an", sagte er einmal. „Wenn ich jetzt Kurs halte und die Position des Bootes verändert sich in deinem Auge nicht, dann kommt es zur Kollision. Das heißt, ich muss abdrehen." Beim Anlegen lernten wir, die Klampe mit Kopfschlag zu belegen. Webleinstek, Kreuzknoten, Palstek, alles kein Problem, aye, aye Käpt'n. Im Inselkiosk gab es Sinalco und Eis und Lakritzschnecken.

Seitdem hat sich vieles geändert. Das Schloss Hagenburg mit dem Kanal, der zum Meer führt, ist in andere Hände übergegangen. Das Meer ist – zum Glück! – nicht mehr im Privatbesitz der Familie, aber der Wilhelmstein ist es nach wie vor. Jetzt wird er professionell von der Tourismus GmbH bewirtschaftet, die beliebten Übernachtungsmöglichkeiten habe ich genutzt. Den 18. Geburtstag meines Sohnes feierten wir 2012 nachmittags neben der Festung mit Livemusik; seine Gäste waren mit Auswanderern auf die Insel gekommen. Trotz Nieselregens war das Fest ein Riesenerfolg.

Das alte Gästebuch des Ururgroßvaters haben wir vor Kurzem wieder benutzt. Vielleicht sollten wir jetzt wieder ein paar Jahrzehnte warten, damit es nicht vor der Zeit zu Ende geht mit ihm.

In a shed at the edge of the canal lay the "Graf Wilhelm", later "Graf Wilhelm II", a small motorboat with a canopy; my father called it the "Bötchen" (little boat). In summer, he took us children to Wilhelmstein in the "Bötchen". He had an inland waterway licence and was excellent at manoeuvring; at least that's how it seemed to us. "Look at that boat over there with one eye," he once said. "If I keep my course now and the position of the boat doesn't change in your eye, there will be a collision. That means I have to turn." When we moored, we learnt how to secure the cleat with a cleat hitch. Bowline, reef knot, clove hitch, all no problem, ay ay captain. The island kiosk served Sinalco, ice cream and liquorice snails.

Much has changed since then. Hagenburg Castle and the canal leading to the sea have passed into other hands. The sea is – fortunately! – no longer privately owned by the family, but the Wilhelmstein still is. It is now professionally managed by Tourismus GmbH, and I took advantage of the popular accommodation options. In 2012, we celebrated my son's 18th birthday in the afternoon next to the fortress with live music; his guests had come to the island with emigrants. Despite the drizzle, the party was a huge success.

We recently used our great-great-grandfather's old guest book again. Maybe we should wait a few decades before using it again so that it doesn't wear out and end prematurely.

← Die von Graf Wilhelm vor rund 300 Jahren in Elvas in Portugal erbaute Festung diente der Verteidigung der Portugiesen gegen die Spanier.

← The fortress built by Count Wilhelm around 300 years ago in Elvas in Portugal served to defend the Portuguese against the Spanish.

← Der illuminierte Eingang zur Festung, die inzwischen zum Weltkulturerbe der UNESCO zählt.

← The illuminated entrance to the fortress, which is now a UNESCO World Heritage Site.

Fort de Lippe

York Prinz zu Schaumburg-Lippe
York, Prince of Schaumburg-Lippe

Das 18. Jahrhundert geht langsam zu Ende und auf der Welt herrscht an vielen Orten Krieg. Graf Wilhelm zu Schaumburg-Lippe lebte zeitweilig in England, war als guter und vor allem defensiver Militärstratege bekannt und schlug manche Schlacht für die Briten – und das recht erfolgreich. Der portugiesische König bat ihn daraufhin, Portugal im Kampf gegen die Spanier zu unterstützen. Graf Wilhelm wehrte 1762 als Oberbefehlshaber der verbündeten britischen und portugiesischen Truppen im sogenannten Fantastischen Krieg (Guerra Fantástica) einen spanischen Invasionsversuch ab und bewahrte damit die portugiesische Unabhängigkeit. Er gründete eine Kriegs- und Artillerieschule und reformierte das portugiesische Heer. Nach Vorbild der Festung Wilhelmstein auf dem Steinhuder Meer ließ er im Stile des französischen Baumeisters Vauban das Fort de Nossa Senhora da Graça bei Elvas anlegen, das der König ihm zu Ehren „Fort de Lippe" nannte.

Das Fort wurde noch bis 1979 als Militärgefängnis geführt. Durch die Ernennung zum UNESCO-Weltkulturerbe 2012 bekam die Stadt Elvas die Festung zur Betreuung. Von 2014 bis 2015 wurde das Fort restauriert und als Museum im November 2015 eröffnet.

Es war mir stets ein Bedürfnis, eines der prägendsten und international historischen Ereignisse in Verbindung mit meinen Vorfahren zu erkunden und dieses der Öffentlichkeit zu vermitteln. Die daraus entstehende kulturelle Förderung sehe ich als meine persönliche Verpflichtung an, diese stets zu begleiten. Immer wieder zieht es mich nach Portugal, um den historischen Spirit wahrzunehmen und weitere Spuren des Grafen Wilhelm in Portugal zu entdecken.

The 18th century is slowly coming to an end and war is raging in many places around the world. Count Wilhelm of Schaumburg-Lippe lived in England for a time, was known as a good and above all defensive military strategist and fought many a battle for the British – and quite successfully too. The Portuguese king then asked him to support Portugal in its fight against the Spanish. In 1762, as commander-in-chief of the allied British and Portuguese troops, Count Wilhelm repelled a Spanish invasion attempt in the so-called "Fantastic War" (Guerra Fantástica), thereby preserving Portuguese independence. He founded a military college and artillery school and reformed the Portuguese army. Modelled on the Wilhelmstein fortress on Lake Steinhuder Meer, he had the Fort de Nossa Senhora da Graça near Elvas built in the style of the French master builder Vauban, which the king named "Fort de Lippe" in his honour.

The fort was used as a military prison until 1979. When it was declared a UNESCO World Heritage Site in 2012, the city of Elvas was given the fort to look after. The fort was restored from 2014–2015 and opened as a museum in November 2015.

I have always felt the need to explore one of the most formative and internationally significant events in connection with my ancestors and to communicate this to the public.

I consider the resulting cultural promotion as my personal obligation, one that I am committed to continuously supporting. I am repeatedly drawn to Portugal to experience the historical spirit and discover further traces of of Count Wilhelm's presence in the country.

↑ Blick über ein Feld auf die Abraumhalde von Mesmerode aus.   ↑ The view from a field of the Mesmerode spoil heap.

Kalimandscharo

Kalimanjaro

Heinrich K.-M. Hecht

Egal aus welcher Richtung man über das Steinhuder Meer oder die Landschaft am Meer schaut, der weißgraue Gigant ist nicht zu übersehen. Unter den Seglerinnen und Seglern und Ortsansässigen heißt er nur Kalimandscharo, in Anlehnung an seinen großen Bruder in Afrika.

Obwohl nur rund 120 m hoch, überthront er doch die Landschaft und ist Wahrzeichen und Landmarke zugleich. Entstanden in 120 Jahren als Abraumhalde des Kaliwerks Sigmundshall der Firma K+S Minerals, erinnert der Berg heute an die große Zeit des Kaliabbaus in Deutschland. Im Inneren und vor allem darunter verbirgt sich ein Labyrinth an Gängen, Hallen, fast so groß wie das Innere einer Kathedrale, und ganzen Straßensystemen, die die unterirdischen Arbeitsstätten verbanden und den Abtransport an Abraum ermöglichten, um an die Mineralien zu gelangen.

Nachdem im Jahr 2018 das Werk stillgelegt wurde, wird das Tunnelsystem nach und nach mit großen Mengen Salzwasser geflutet und der Berg langsam begrünt.

No matter from which direction you look across the Lake Steinhuder Meer or the landscape by the sea, you can't miss the white-grey giant. Sailors and locals call it Kalimanjaro, in reference to its big brother, Mount Kilimanjaro in Africa and the German word for potash (Kali).

Although only around 120 metres high, it dominates the landscape and is both a symbol and landmark at the same time. Formed over a period of 120 years as a spoil heap from the Sigmundshall potash plant of the K+S Minerals company, the mountain is now a reminder of the heyday of potash mining in Germany. Inside, and especially underneath, there is a labyrinth of corridors, halls, almost as large as the inside of a cathedral, and entire road systems that connected the underground workplaces and enabled the removal of overburden to get to the minerals.

After the plant was shut down in 2018, the tunnel system is gradually being flooded with large quantities of salt water and the mountain is slowly being greened.

← Bis zum Ende der Förderung im Kaliwerk im Jahr 2018 erleichterten in den letzten Jahrzehnten moderne Maschinen den Abbau von Rohsalz.

← Until the end of mining at the potash plant in 2018, modern machines had made the extraction of crude salt easier in recent decades.

↖↑ Untertageaufnahmen, wahrscheinlich zu Beginn des 20. Jahrhunderts entstanden, die von den früher noch schwierigeren Bedingungen des Salzabbaus zeugen.

↖↑ Underground photographs, probably taken at the beginning of the 20th century, which bear witness to the even more difficult conditions of salt mining in the past.

↑ Von hier aus kann man weit blicken: Der Blick geht vom Kalimandscharo aus in Richtung Steinhuder Meer und wirkt durch leichten Dunst fast wie ein Gemälde von Gerhard Richter, wohlgemerkt – fast.

↑ The view from the Kalimanjaro stretches far and wide, towards Lake Steinhuder Meer. The light haze lends it an almost painterly quality, reminiscent of a Gerhard Richter work – almost.

S. 150–151 Landmarke und Zeugnis vergangener Industrie – die Abraumhalde des Kaliwerks Sigmundshall, im Volksmund und bei Seglerinnen und Seglern gerne Kalimandscharo genannt.

P. 150–151 Landmark and testimony to past industry – the spoil heap of the Sigmundshall potash works, popularly known as Kalimanjaro by locals and sailors.

↑ Der Yachthafen von Idensen. Ein weiteres kleines Idyll in diesem Ort.   ↑   The marina in Idensen. Another little idyll in this village.

Idensen

Heinrich K.-M. Hecht

Eigentlich gehört der kleine Ort Idensen in dieses Buch gar nicht hinein, denn er liegt außerhalb der Grenzen des Naturparks Steinhuder Meer. Wäre da nicht die kleine und mit Fresken versehene Kirche, die mich seit meiner Ankunft im Schaumburger Land fasziniert, wäre es dabei auch geblieben. Aber George Kochbeck hat in diesem Ort auch noch etwas anderes entdeckt ... Aber das ist eine andere Geschichte. Eine weitere Besonderheit ist der Yachthafen von Idensen, der so manche Freizeitkaptäninnen und Freizeitkapitäne anlockt, die den Mittellandkanal nutzen.

Idensen ist uralt und älter als so manche große Stadt in der Nähe, denn es stammt aus dem 12. Jahrhundert. Der Bischof Sigward von Minden gab dem Ort eine Urkunde, in der „Ydanhausen" als Name steht. Im 16. Jahrhundert gab es wohl um die 300 Einwohnerinnen und Einwohner. Inzwischen hat Idensen knapp 1.000 Ortsansässige. Etwas ist recht kurios für einen so kleinen Ort: zwei verschiedene Vorwahlnummern, die aus den 1970er Jahren aufgrund einer Gebietsreform hervorgingen. Aber wer will dort schon anrufen – hinfahren ist wesentlich besser!

The small village of Idensen doesn't really belong in this book, as it lies outside the boundaries of the Lake Steinhude Nature Park. If it weren't for the small, frescoed church, which has fascinated me since my arrival in the Schaumburg region, it would have stayed that way. But George Kochbeck also discovered something else in this place ... But that's another story. Another special feature is Idensen's marina, which attracts many hobby skippers and recreational boaters who use the Mittelland Canal.

Idensen is ancient and older than many large towns in the neighbourhood, dating back to the 12th century. Bishop Sigward of Minden gave the village a document in which the name "Ydanhausen" appears. In the 16th century, there were probably around 300 inhabitants. Idensen now has just under a thousand inhabitants. One curious thing about the village is that it has two different area codes, which are a result of a local government reform in the 1970s. But who wants to call there – it's so much better to visit in person!

↑ Der Weg von Idensen nach Wiedenbrügge führt unter Bäumen hindurch über diese Brücke.

↑ The road from Idensen to Wiedenbrügge leads under trees across this bridge.

↑ Blick von Idensen aus auf den Kaliberg. ↑ View of the Kaliberg, another local name for the slagheap, from Idensen.

↑ Im 12. Jahrhundert von Bischof Sigward von Minden erbaut, gehört die Kirche heute zu den wichtigsten Sakralbauten in der Region.

↑ Built in the 12th century by Bishop Sigward of Minden, the church is now one of the most important religious buildings in the region.

Sigwardskirche
Sigward's Church

Peter Zenker

Im Jahr 1129 ließ Bischof Sigward von Minden den Kirchenbau als Eigen- und Grabkirche errichten, da er im benachbarten Wohnhaus seine Sommerresidenz hatte.

Diese Kirche gilt als eine der bedeutendsten sakralen Kleinbauten der Romanik, ein architektonisches Juwel, das in Niedersachsen seinesgleichen sucht.

Zudem ist sie ein frühes Beispiel engagierter Denkmalpflege im heutigen Niedersachsen, da sie aufgrund des Einsatzes des renommierten Architekten der Hannoverschen Schule, Conrad Wilhelm Hase, vor einem Umbau und Teilabbruch bewahrt und stattdessen nach seinen Plänen ein neugotischer Neubau gegenüber errichtet wurde.

Die Sigwardskirche ist aus behauenen Sandsteinquadern gebaut. Ihr Grundriss besteht aus einem einschiffigen, dreijöchigen Langhaus und einer außen polygonalen, innen halbrunden Apsis mit einem halben Chorjoch. Dem östlichen Langhausjoch sind beidseitig Kapellen angefügt, die den Eindruck eines kurzen Querhauses mit rechteckigem Zentrum (Vierung) erzeugen. Westlich schließt sich an das Langhaus der massive,

In 1129, Bishop Sigward of Minden had the church built as his own church and burial place, as he had his summer residence in the neighbouring house.

This church is considered one of the most important small sacred buildings of the Romanesque period, an architectural jewel that is unrivalled in Lower Saxony.

It is also an early example of committed monument preservation in today's Lower Saxony, as it was saved from being rebuilt and partially demolished thanks to the efforts of the renowned architect of the Hanoverian school, Conrad Wilhelm Hase, and instead a new neo-Gothic building was erected opposite according to his plans.

Sigward's church is built from hewn sandstone blocks. Its floor plan consists of a single-aisle, three-bay nave and an externally polygonal, internally semi-circular apse with a half-choir bay. Chapels are attached to both sides of the eastern nave bay, creating the impression of a short transept with a rectangular centre (crossing). The massive, almost square tower adjoins the nave to the west. It contains a vaulted portal

↑ Wunderschöne romanische Wand- und Deckenmalereien, die verschiedene biblische Szenen und Heilige darstellen.
Im 15. oder 17. Jahrhundert wurden die Malereien mit weißem Kalk übertüncht und erst im 20. Jahrhundert wieder freigelegt.

↑ Beautiful Romanesque wall and ceiling paintings depicting various biblical scenes and saints.
In the 15th or 17th century, the paintings were whitewashed over with white lime and only uncovered again in the 20th century.

↑ Der Innenraum, der nach Osten zeigt. Auch hier wird der romanische Baustil deutlich.

↑ The interior, which faces east. The Romanesque architectural style is also evident here.

↑ Stufen, die durch den jahrhundertelangen Gebrauch ihr Alter nicht verschweigen, führen in den oberen Bereich der Kirche.

↑ Steps, which do not conceal their age due to centuries of use, lead to the upper part of the church.

annähernd quadratische Turm an. Er enthält eine überwölbte Portalhalle, eine ehemals als Bethaus (Oratorium) der Herrschenden genutzte Kapelle mit seitlichem Vierpassfenster sowie Doppelbogenöffnungen zum Kirchenschiff und einem Glockengeschoss.

Im Inneren zeigen romanische Wandmalereien, die einst fast alle Wände und die Decke bedeckten, biblische Szenen und Heiligendarstellungen nach byzantinischen Vorbildern, die von bedeutenden Freskenmalern ihrer Zeit stammen.

hall, a chapel formerly used as a prayer house (oratory) by the ruling class, with a lateral quatrefoil window and double-arch openings to the church nave, as well as a bell storey.

Inside, Romanesque murals, which once covered almost all the walls and the ceiling, depict biblical scenes and depictions of saints based on Byzantine models by important fresco painters of their time.

↑ Auhagen ist bestens bekannt für seine große Störchepopulation.
↑ Auhagen is well known for its large population of storks.

↑ Von diesem Dachfirst in Auhagen lässt sich das Umfeld gut beobachten.
↑ This roof ridge in Auhagen offers a great view of the surrounding area.

Auhagen

Heinrich K.-M. Hecht

Wenn mich jemand fragt, was mir zuerst zu Auhagen einfällt, würde ich ziemlich sicher antworten: Der Blitzerkasten und die Störche und ein Blumenladen. Dabei ist das so ungerecht, denn der Ort hat wesentlich mehr zu bieten, aber man nimmt es meist nicht wahr, wenn man nur durchfährt, um nach Steinhude oder Großenheidorn zu gelangen – und an jener Straße sind nun einmal die zahlreichen Störche, der Blitzer und der Blumenladen. Letzterer ist auch Heimat für die Störche auf dem Dach des Hauses, was seit einigen Jahren mit einer Kamera in das World Wide Web übertragen wird.

Eingebettet in eine Landschaft zwischen dem Steinhuder Meer nach Norden und dem Mittellandkanal im Süden, durch die zahlreiche Bäche mäandern und die Sachsenhäger Aue fließt, fehlt es Auhagen wahrlich nicht an Wasser und sumpfartigen Stellen, um den Störchen den Tisch zu decken, mit Fröschen und was Adebar sonst so mag. Es steckt ja auch schon im Namen, denn Au hieß mal „Land am Wasser".

Auch das könnte man erwähnen: Einen Reiterhof, sogar recht groß gibt es noch, und einen Friedhof, der, wenn ich an ihm im Sommer des Abends spät vorbeifahre, oftmals einen der schönsten Sonnenuntergänge im Hintergrund bietet. Schöner kann man nicht liegen ...

Geschichtlich gibt Auhagen nicht wirklich viel her, keine Könige, die zum Baden oder Jagen kamen wie in Bad Rehburg oder Linsburg, ist ja auch verständlich, denn Frösche, die in Auhagen vorkommen, ließen sich sicherlich als Froschschenkel – wer sie denn mag – gut essen, aber nicht so gut jagen.

Zumindest einen Herzog gab es, in Sachsenhagen. Die ehemals in der Nähe befindliche Burg Sachsenhagen war die Schutzmacht, die anfänglich zu Auhagens Entwicklung beitrug und der Bevölkerung den nötigen Schutz gewährte, das war wohl im 13. Jahrhundert. Und wenn man ehrlich ist, passierte in Auhagen nicht wirklich viel, außer vielleicht der Verlust einer Kapelle während des Dreißigjährigen Kriegs und die Gründung des Männergesangsvereins 1894. Aber stimmt das alles, oder gibt es doch noch viel mehr? Ich bin sicher, wer sich in Auhagen auf die Spurensuche begibt, mit den wunderbaren Menschen dort spricht, wird so manches Geheimnis erfahren, über das ich hier nicht schreiben darf. Und das stimmt ... oder doch nicht?

If someone were to ask me what comes to mind first when I think of Auhagen, I would almost certainly answer: the speed camera box, the storks and a flower shop. But this is so unfair, because the place has much more to offer, but you usually don't notice it if you are only driving through to get to Steinhude or Großenheidorn – and on that road through Auhagen are the numerous storks, the speed camera and the flower shop. The latter is also home to the storks on the roof of the building, which has been transmitted into the World Wide Web with a camera for several years.

Nestled in a landscape between the Lake Steinhuder Meer to the north and the Mittelland Canal to the south, through which numerous streams meander and the river Sachsenhäger Aue flows, Auhagen is certainly not lacking in water and swamp-like areas to provide the storks with a feast of frogs and other delicacies they enjoy. It is evident even in the name, as "Au" once meant "land by the water."

There are a few other things one could also mention about Auhagen: there is still a riding centre, even quite a large one, and a cemetery, which, when I drive past it late in the evening in summer, often provides a stunning backdrop for one of the most beautiful sunsets. You just could not be in a lovelier location ...

Historically, Auhagen doesn't really have much to offer, no kings who came to bathe or hunt as in Bad Rehburg or Linsburg, which is understandable, because frogs, which are common in Auhagen, were certainly good to eat as frogs' legs – if you like them – but not so good to hunt.

At least there was a duke, in Sachsenhagen. Formerly located nearby, Sachsenhagen Castle was the protective power that contributed to Auhagen's early development and provided its inhabitants with the necessary protection, probably in the 13th century. And to be honest, not much really happened in Auhagen, except perhaps the loss of a chapel during the Thirty Years' War and until the men's choral society was founded in 1894. But is that all true: is that all there is, or is there much more? I am sure that if you go in search of clues in Auhagen and talk to the wonderful people there, you will learn many a secret that I am not allowed to write about here. And that's true ... or is it?

S. 160–161   Wer an der richtigen Stelle in Auhagen wohnt, kann einen wunderbaren Sonnenuntergang genießen.

P. 160–162   If you live in the right place in Auhagen, you can enjoy a wonderful sunset.

↖↑ Das Gasthaus „Zur Erholung" – nomen est omen – von Ulrike Fiedler-Meyer. Schon ihr Urgroßvater war Eigentümer der Gaststätte.

↖↑ The inn "Zur Erholung" ("For Recuperation") – nomen est omen – by Ulrike Fiedler-Meyer. The establishment was already owned by her great-grandfather.

↑ „De Düwel" im Kreise der Düdinghäuser Gesellschaft samt Wachhund – natürlich stilvoll mit Bier in der Hand.

↑ "De Düwel" (The Devil) in the company of the Düdinghausen society including guard dog – stylish, of course, with beer in hand.

„De Düwel" von Düdinghausen

Wer lange recherchiert, wird entweder gar nicht fündig oder findet nur sehr wenig Aufschlussreiches, weswegen schon alleine daher ein Besuch in Düdinghausen im Gasthof „Zur Erholung" sinnstiftend sein kann – zumindest für diejenigen, die sich für den dortigen „Düwel" interessieren.

Dass Ulrike Fiedler-Meyer als Inhaberin vom Gasthof einiges dazu beitragen kann, liegt an der Tatsache, dass das Haus sich bereits seit über 300 Jahren in Familienhand befindet. Und da ist verständlich, das so manche Geschichte von Generation zu Generation weitergegeben wird.

Düdinghausen liegt am östlichen Punkt der Rehburger Berge und lag somit auch an der Strecke des Kurfürsten Georg Ludwig vor über 300 Jahren, der unterwegs nach London war, um sich zum König Georg I. krönen zu lassen. Das war 1714 und der Halt am Gasthof in Düdinghausen ist zumindest überliefert.

Nun wäre es grundsätzlich falsch, von König Georg I. auf den obigen Titel und einen „Düwel" zu schließen, aber es ist doch ein netter Nebenschauplatz, der sich da auftat und dem Ort königlichen Glanz verleiht.

Der Sage nach soll es im Mittelalter einen Ritter namens *Dudo* gegeben haben, der seine Burg in Düdinghausen und keine Erben hatte, und dem Ort seinen Namen gab. Als er starb, teilte er seinen Landbesitz in sechs gleiche Teile und vererbte sie seinen Knechten. Noch heute gibt es sechs Höfe, die fast sämtlich die gleich Größe haben und so für diese These sprechen.

In einer der Scheunen, so sprach man vor Jahrhunderten in Düdinghausen, wohne der „Düwel", weshalb sich die Menschen dort fernhielten. Erst viel später, im Jahre 1910, als auf dem Widdelshof in einer Scheune eine Säule gefunden wurde, stellte sich heraus, dass mit „Düwel" eine Pansäule gemeint war, die zu einem Gebäudefries gehörte und nach oben hin einen Teufelskopf aufwies. Woher die Säule tatsächlich stammte, weiß heute keiner mehr. Vermutungen gehen davon aus, dass sie einem alten Kamin aus einem Schloss entstammen könnte, vielleicht aus Sachsenhagen, wo ein Schloss im Dreißigjährigen Krieg zerstört wurde.

Bis in die 1920er Jahre des letzten Jahrhunderts war der „Düwel" ein touristischer Anziehungspunkt, der Ausflüglerinnen und Ausflügler nach Düdinghausen zog. Bis 1925 war die Säule im Gasthof von Wilhelm Meyer, Urgroßvater von Ulrike Fiedler-Meyer, aufgestellt, bis der Pastor Brunstermann aus Steinhude den Ausflüglerinnen und Ausflüglern den Spaß verdarb und den „Düwel" zerstörte.

"De Düwel" of Düdinghausen

Anyone who spends a long time researching will either not find anything or will find very little that is informative, which is why a visit to the inn *Zur Erholung* in Düdinghausen can be worthwhile – at least for those who are interested in the local *Düwel* (Devil).

The fact that Ulrike Fiedler-Meyer, as the owner of the inn, can contribute a lot to this is due to the fact that the house has been in family hands for over 300 years. And so it is understandable that many a story has been passed down from generation to generation.

Düdinghausen is located at the eastern point of the Rehburger hills and was therefore also on the route taken by Elector Georg Ludwig over 300 years ago, who was travelling to London to be crowned King George I That was in 1714 and the stop at the inn in Düdinghausen is at least recorded.

Now, it would be fundamentally wrong to relate the above title and a *Düwel* to King George I, but it does open up a charming side story that lends the place some royal glamour.

According to legend, there was a knight called *Dudo* in the Middle Ages who had his castle in Düdinghausen and no heirs, and he gave the village its name. When he died, he divided his land into six equal parts and bequeathed them to his servants. There are still six farms today, almost all of which are the same size, which supports this theory.

It was said centuries ago in Düdinghausen that the *Düwel* lived in one of the barns, which is why people kept away from there. It was only much later, in 1910, when a pillar was found in a barn on the Widdels farm, that it turned out that *Düwel* meant a pillar that was part of a building frieze and had a devil's head at the top. Today, nobody knows where the pillar actually came from. It is assumed that it could have come from an old fireplace in a castle, perhaps from Sachsenhagen, where a castle was destroyed during the Thirty Years' War.

Until the 1920s, the Düwel was a tourist attraction that drew day trippers to Düdinghausen. Until 1925, the pillar was installed in the inn of Wilhelm Meyer, great-grandfather of Ulrike Fiedler-Meyer, until Pastor Brunstermann from Steinhude spoilt the fun for the day-trippers and destroyed the *Düwel*.

↑ Der Schlossturm und das Amtshaus sind Überbleibsel einer großen Zeit von Sachsenhagen, als die Orte drum herum erst größtenteils entstanden sind.

↑ The castle tower and the Amtshaus (administrative building) are remnants of a grand era in Sachsenhagen, when the villages around it were largely built.

← Dieser aufmerksame Storch hat es sich mit seiner Familie auf dem Schornstein der alten Stadtbücherei mitten im Ort wohnlich eingerichtet.

← This attentive stork and his family have made themselves at home on the chimney of the old library in the centre of the village.

Sachsenhagen

Heinrich K.-M. Hecht

Der Schlossturm und das Amtshaus geben heute noch Auskunft darüber, was für eine imposante Burganlage es einmal gewesen ist – waren die beiden Gebäude doch nur ein kleiner Teil des Areals. Ehemals als Wasserburg im 13. Jahrhundert errichtet, sind die beiden Gebäude heute leider nur noch ein recht bescheidenes Überbleibsel einer ehemals stolzen Siedlung, die auch über seinerzeit neu gegründete Orte wie Auhagen wachte.

Eigentlich nur entstanden, um Gebietsansprüche von Herzog Albrecht I. von Sachsen zu untermauern, gab es über die Jahrhunderte unterschiedlichste Eigentümer der Burg, die nach Entstehung weiter aus- und umgebaut wurde und sich bis hin zur Stadt Sachsenhagen entwickelte. Einzelne Gebäude wurden allerdings bereits im 17. Jahrhundert wieder abgerissen und spätestens zur Mitte des 19. Jahrhundert standen nur noch der Schlossturm und das Amtshaus.

Die heutige Umgebung des Schlossturmes und des Amtshauses ist eher sachlich nüchtern und nicht wie zu Zeiten der Entstehung der Burg ein Urwald namens Dülwald, von dem noch die gleichnamige Straße in Sachsenhagen eine Erinnerung darstellt. Man stelle sich einmal vor, wie es zu diesen Zeiten zuging: Ritter, die zur Burg wollten, Raubritter, die des Weges zogen und ehrliche Bürgerinnen und Bürger, die über den Schutz der Burg froh waren und sich in deren Umfeld niederließen. Heute wacht der Schlossturm eher über den benachbarten Park und naheliegenden Supermarkt.

Was heute am ehesten in Sachsenhagen auffällt, ist die kleine Armee an Störchen, die auf in der Stadt liegenden Gebäuden und Bäumen der Umgebung verteilt ihre Nester hat und regelmäßig Ausflüge zur Sicherung der Nahrung für den Nachwuchs unternimmt. Ein Schauspiel, das beeindruckend ist, wenn es um die Flugkünste der großen, schwarz-weißen Vögel geht, die erst kreisend über dem Nest ihre Runden drehen, um dann zielsicher auf kleinstem Raum zu landen und die Jungtiere zu füttern. Mit rund 100 Störchen zählt Sachsenhagen sicher zu den Orten rund um das Steinhuder Meer mit den meisten Störchen. Storchenhagen anstatt Sachsenhagen wäre da vielleicht auch passend …

Zusammenfassend lässt sich sagen, dass Sachsenhagen eine Stadt ist, die heute im Stadtkern noch das eine oder andere historische Gebäude vorweisen kann und mit rund 2.000 Einwohnerinnen und Einwohnern und 130 Gemeldeten pro Quadratkilometer über eine vergleichbar überschaubare Bevölkerungsdichte verfügt. Den zur Verfügung stehenden Raum teilt sich die Bevölkerung sicher gerne mit den Störchen.

The castle tower and the administrative building still give an idea of what an imposing castle complex it once was – the two buildings were only a small part of the site. Formerly built as a moated castle in the 13th century, today the two buildings are unfortunately only a rather modest remnant of a once proud settlement, which also watched over newly founded villages such as Auhagen.

Originally built to support the territorial claims of Duke Albrecht I of Saxony, the castle has had various owners over the centuries and has been extended and remodelled since its foundation, developing into the town of Sachsenhagen. However, some of the buildings were demolished as early as the 17th century and by the middle of the 19th century at the latest, only the castle tower and the administrative building remained.

The present-day surroundings of the castle tower and the administrative building are rather plain and sober, unlike during the castle's inception when it was surrounded by a primeval forest known as Dülwald, of which the street with the same name in Sachsenhagen serves as a reminder. Imagine what it was like in those days: knights who wanted to get to the castle, robber barons who travelled along the road and honest citizens who were glad of the castle's protection and settled in its vicinity. Today, the castle tower merely watches over the neighbouring park and nearby supermarket.

What is most noticeable in Sachsenhagen today is the small army of storks that have their nests on buildings and trees scattered around the town and make regular trips to secure food for their offspring. It is an impressive spectacle to watch the flying skills of the large, black and white birds, which first circle around the nest and then land unerringly in the smallest of spaces to feed the young. With around one hundred storks, Sachsenhagen is certainly one of the places around Lake Steinhuder Meer with the most storks. Storchenhagen instead of Sachsenhagen might also be fitting …

In summary, it can be said that Sachsenhagen is a town that can still boast one or two historic buildings in the town centre and, with around 2000 inhabitants and 130 inhabitants per square kilometre, it has a comparatively manageable population density. The inhabitants are certainly happy to share the available space with the storks.

↑ Das Rathaus von Sachsenhagen. Zu Beginn des 17. Jahrhunderts erbaut und später durch den Turm ergänzt.

↑ The Sachsenhagen town hall was built in the early 1600s and the tower was added later.

↑ Einer der rund 100 Störche der Stadt auf Nahrungssuche für seine Jungstörche, ganz in der Nähe des Ortes auf einer Wiese.

↑ One of the town's hundred or so storks in search of food for its young in a meadow near the town.

↑ Eine Kirche, die zuerst nur aus dem Saal ohne Turm bestand – der kam erst 1976 hinzu.

↑ A church that initially only consisted of the hall without a tower – that was only added in 1976.

Elisabethkirche
Elisabeth Church

Peter Zenker

Von außen schlicht und schmucklos präsentiert sich die Kirche von Sachsenhagen. Der einfache Saalbau wurde in den Jahren 1663 bis 1676 ohne Turm errichtet, bemerkenswerterweise noch in gotischer Form, nachdem der Flecken 1619 einer Feuersbrunst zum Opfer gefallen war.

Die Kirche ist eine Hallenkirche mit breitem, dreischiffigem Langhaus und fünfseitig geschlossenem Chor unter einem Satteldach. Der Bruchsteinbau wird durch regelmäßig gestufte Strebepfeiler im Wechsel mit schlanken zweibahnigen Maßwerkfenstern und einem umlaufenden Gesims gegliedert. An der Nordfassade gibt es zwei leicht spitzbogige Sandsteinportale mit profilierter Laibungskante und betonten Kämpfergesimsen.

Der Turm wurde erst 1976 mithilfe einer großzügigen Privatspende dem Saalbau hinzugefügt. Er besitzt eine Tordurchfahrt, welche den vorderen mit dem hinteren Friedhofsteil verbindet.

Der überwiegend barock ausgestattete Innenraum der Kirche hat eine flache, von drei Paaren schlanker, achteckiger Holzpfeiler getragenen Holzbalkendecke.

From the outside, the church in Sachsenhagen is simple and unadorned. The simple hall building was erected between 1663 and 1676 without a tower, remarkably still in the Gothic style, after the village fell victim to a fire in 1619.

The church is a hall church with a wide, three-aisled nave and a choir closed on five sides under a gabled roof. The quarry stone building is divided by regularly stepped buttresses alternating with slender two-lane tracery windows and a surrounding cornice. On the north façade there are two slightly pointed arched sandstone portals with a profiled reveals and emphasised impost mouldings.

The tower was only added to the hall building in 1976 with the help of a generous private donation. It has a gateway that connects the front with the rear part of the cemetery.

The predominantly Baroque interior of the church has a flat wooden beam ceiling supported by three pairs of slender, octagonal wooden pillars.

The U-shaped galleries stand on pillars with curved capitals. The choir is separated from the nave by three passages staggered in height, of which the two outer ones have deco-

↑ Die Fenster der Kirche kommen bei fast jedem Licht zur Geltung und müssen sich nicht hinter dem Altar verstecken.

↑ The windows of the church come into their own in almost any light and certainly bear comparison with the altar.

↑ Das beeindruckende Innenleben der Kirche mit seiner wunderschönen und seltenen Holzdecke.

↑ The impressive interior of the church with its beautiful and rare wooden ceiling

← Diese beiden alten Grabplatten haben einen wunderbaren Platz im Durchgang des 1976 eingeweihten Turmes bekommen und schmücken den ehemaligen Eingang der Kirche.

← These two old gravestones have been given a wonderful place in the passageway of the tower, which was consecrated in 1976, and adorn the former entrance to the church.

Die u-förmig angelegten Emporen stehen auf Stützen mit geschwungenen Kopfbändern. Der Chor ist mit drei in der Höhe gestaffelten Durchgängen vom Langhaus abgesondert, von denen die beiden äußeren geschmückte, torartige Einfassungen besitzen. Im Zentrum des zweigeschossigen Altarretabels von 1679 befindet sich ein großes Tafelbild mit der Darstellung des Abendmahls. Darüber ist giebelartig eingerahmt eine Ölberggruppe gemalt. Ein Kruzifix und Putti bekrönen den geteilten Giebel. Vor der polygonalen Brüstung der Kanzel stehen Statuetten der vier Evangelisten.

rated, gate-like surrounds. In the centre of the two-story altarpiece from 1679 is a large panel painting depicting the Last Supper. Above it, framed in a gable-like structure, is an oil painting of the Mount of Olives. A crucifix and putti crown the divided gable. Statuettes of the four Evangelists stand in front of the polygonal parapet of the pulpit.

↑ Ein wunderschöner Rhododendronweg führt in Hagenburg zum Schloss. Die Blütezeit ist gegen Ende Mai, Anfang Juni. Angelegt wurde die Allee zu Beginn des 20. Jahrhunderts.

↑ A beautiful rhododendron path leads to the castle in Hagenburg. The flowering period is around end of May, beginning of June. The avenue was planted at the beginning of the 20th century.

Hagenburg

York Prinz zu Schaumburg-Lippe
York, Prince of Schaumburg-Lippe

Als Kinder sind wir oft und gerne zu unserer Großmutter zu Besuch in das Hagenburger Schloss – vornehmlich im Sommer– gefahren.

Für meine Schwester und mich war es stets ein ehrfürchtiges Wochenende, an diesem wunderschönen Platz am Steinhuder Meer wohnen zu dürfen.

Der für uns große Park mit Teichanlage, gepaart mit Seerosen, Fröschen und Salamandern lud in die einzigartige vorhandene Tierwelt ein, die aus einer weiteren Vielfalt von Vögeln bestand. Der Fischreiher und die Storchfamilie mit Nest auf dem Schloss waren für uns immer eine Sehenswürdigkeit.

Der Baumbestand, die Gartenanlage und die seltene Rhododendronallee ließen uns Kinder endlos spielen, gerne irgendwo versteckt bis in die Abendstunden – zum Leidwesen meiner Eltern.

Unvergessen ist das Motorbootfahren als Zehnjähriger. Alleine mit dem hölzernen Boot mit Badeplattform und aufgesetztem Wellenmotor (wie im Bond-Film in Asien) oder das kleine Kielschlauchboot mit 6,5 PS, was mich durch den Stichkanal aufs offene (Steinhuder) Meer hinaus brachte, in damals für mich atemberaubender Geschwindigkeit. Dies war nicht ohne Tücken zu bewerkstelligen, da der Tiefgang manchmal nur wenige Zentimeter betrug.

Es war etwas unheimlich, wenn man im Kanal badete und die kalte Mudde berührte und das Wasser um einen herum sich schwarz färbte.

Das Knarren im Schloss ließ uns als Kinder in Habachtstellung schlafen und ein Toilettengang war stets ein Himmel-

As children, we often enjoyed visiting our grandmother at Hagenburg Castle – especially in summer.

For my sister and me, it was always an awe-inspiring weekend to be able to stay in this beautiful place on the Lake Steinhuder Meer.

The large park with its pond system, water lilies, frogs and salamanders invited us to enjoy a unique wildlife experience that included a diverse array of birds. The heron and the stork family with their nest on the castle were always a sight to behold for us.

The trees, the gardens and the rare rhododendron plantation allowed us children to play endlessly, often hiding somewhere until the evening hours – much to the chagrin of my parents.

Motor boating as a 10-year-old is unforgettable. Navigating the waters alone was a thrilling experience, whether in the wooden boat with a bathing platform and a mounted outboard motor reminiscent of a scene from a Bond film in Asia, or in the small keel inflatable boat with a 6.5 hp engine that took me through the canal and out onto the open waters of Lake Steinhuder Meer at a speed that was breathtaking for me at the time. This was not without its pitfalls, as the draught was sometimes only a few centimetres.

It was a bit eerie to swim in the canal and feel the cold mud on my skin and see the water around me turn black.

The creaking of the castle made us children sleep on high alert, and a trip to the bathroom always felt like a suicide mission since it wasn't "en-suite" to our bedrooms.

However, we cherished this tradition because the charm of

← Prinzessin Bathildis und Prinz Wolrad zu Schaumburg-Lippe und das Schloss in Hagenburg gegen Ende der 1930er Jahre.

← Princess Bathildis and Prince Wolrad of Schaumburg-Lippe and the castle in Hagenburg, towards the end of the 1930s.

↑ Im Winter ist es möglich, mehr vom Schloss zu sehen, da sonst dichter Baum- und Pflanzenbestand den Blick versperren.

↑ You can see more of the castle in winter, since the trees and plants are bare and don't block the view.

↑ Prinzessin Tatjana und Prinz York zu Schaumburg-Lippe genießen im Sommer 1965 ihre Zeit am Hagenburger Kanal.

↑ Princess Tatjana and Prince York of Schaumburg-Lippe enjoy their time on the Hagenburg Canal in the summer of 1965.

fahrtskommando, da die Toilette nicht „en suite" am Kinderzimmer lag.

Schließlich haben wir dieses Traditionsvermögen geliebt, weil der Charme unserer Großmutter nebst der Bediensteten und Chauffeur Schneidewind, mit seinem schwarzen Mercedes, eine stilvolle und respektvolle Verhaltensweise von uns einforderte.

Schloss Hagenburg war und ist ein ganz besonderer Platz der Erholung gewesen. Ein Schloss, was in Lage und Anmutung seinesgleichen sucht und – zumindest am Steinhuder Meer – nicht finden wird. Ein Schloss, was eine sehr interessante Geschichte beinhaltet und zu den Nachkriegszeiten vom englischen Militär genutzt wurde.

Manchmal vermisse ich diese Ruhe am Meer, im Besitz der Familie Schaumburg-Lippe.

our grandmother, together with the household staff and chauffeur Schneidewind with his black Mercedes, demanded a respectful and dignified behaviour from us.

Hagenburg Castle was and still is a very special place to relax. It is a castle that is unrivalled in terms of its location and elegant appearance and – at least on Lake Steinhuder Meer – will not be found anywhere else. It holds an intriguing history, including its use by the English military in the post-war period.

Sometimes I miss this peace and quiet by the lake and when the castle was a summer residence owned of the Schaumburg-Lippe family.

↑ Der Hagenburger Kanal, der direkt am Schloss endet, ist ein Kleinod und wird gerne für Ausflüge mit dem Boot genommen.

↑ The Hagenburg Canal, which ends directly at the castle, is a gem and is often used for boat trips.

↑ Heinrich „Briller" Schweer, mit Zigarre und seinem Sohn Hein auf dem Eis, irgendwann in den 1940er Jahren. Auch Hein wurde mit Spitznamen später „Briller" gerufen, da die Sehhilfe in der Familie wohl eine gewisse Tradition hatte.

↑ Heinrich "Briller" Schweer, with a cigar and his son Hein on the ice, sometime in the 1940s. Hein was also nicknamed "Briller" later on, as glasses (German: Brille) seem to have been a bit of a tradition in the family.

↑ Auf einem Bauernhof in Hagenburg entdeckt und heute eine Seltenheit: ein Eisschlitten, wie er früher gerne auf dem Steinhuder Meer zum Vergnügen und auch Transport von Menschen benutzt wurde.

↑ Discovered on a farm in Hagenburg and a rarity today: an ice sled, like the ones formerly used on Lake Steinhuder Meer for pleasure and to transport people.

↑ Die St.-Nicolai-Kirche in Hagenburg hat eine Dimension, die sonst rund um das Steinhuder Meer eher ungewöhnlich ist.

↑ The St Nicholas' Church in Hagenburg has a dimension that is otherwise rather unusual around Lake Steinhuder Meer.

St. Nicolai Kirche
St Nicholas' Church

Peter Zenker

Die St.-Nicolai-Kirche in Hagenburg-Altenhagen ist ein repräsentativer Sakralbau, direkt an der Ortsdurchfahrt gelegen. Die Initiative für ihren Bau ging von der schaumburg-lippischen Fürstenfamilie aus, welche im Hagenburger Schloss ihre Sommerresidenz hielt.

Sie wurde im zeitgemäßen Gewand der populären Neugotik der Hannoverschen Schule Mitte des 19. Jahrhunderts von Conrad Wilhelm Hase entworfen und gilt ob ihrer material- und formalästhetisch wohl durchkomponierten Proportionen und Details als eine der bedeutendsten Kirchen aus seiner Zeichenfeder.

St Nicholas' Church in Hagenburg-Altenhagen is a prestigious religious building located directly on the main road through the village. The initiative for its construction came from the Schaumburg-Lippe princely family, who had their summer residence in Hagenburg Castle.

It was designed by Conrad Wilhelm Hase in the contemporary style of the popular neo-Gothic movement of the Hannover School in the mid-19th century and is considered one of the most important churches among his works in terms of material and formal aesthetics due to its carefully composed proportions and details.

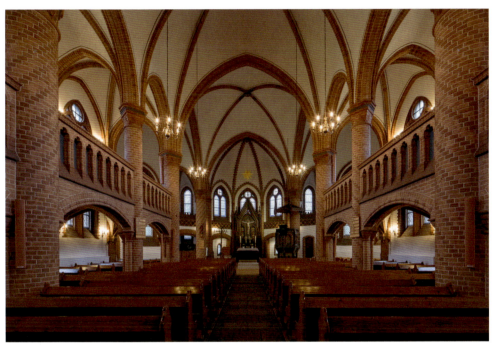

↑ Der imposante neugotische Baustil setzt sich auch im Inneren der Kirche fort.

↑ The neo-Gothic architectural style is just as impressive inside the church as it is outside.

↑ Die gelungene Lichtinszenierung ist schon von weit her zu sehen und bildet zusammen mit der Kirche einen markanten Punkt im Ort.

↑ The church is beautifully lit at night, and it can be seen from far away. The church and the effective light display make a striking landmark in the village.

Ihr mit farbigen Glanz- und Formziegeln gestaltetes Backsteinmauerwerk ist in höchster künstlerischer Qualität ausgeführt.

Die St.-Nicolai-Kirche ist vom Typus her eine dreischiffige Hallenkirche über einem kreuzförmigen Grundriss mit angedeutetem Querhaus, einem fünfseitigen polygonalen Chorschluss und einem quadratischen Westturm.

Diesen prägt ein stattliches, gestuftes Portal sowie der schlanke, polychrome Steinhelm mit seinen flankierenden Zwickelbauten und filigranen Ecktürmchen.

Im Inneren wird das vierjöchige Langhaus mit massiven Seitenschiffemporen unter dem Kreuzrippengewölbe von Rundpfeilern getragen.

Bemerkenswert ist der Altar aus mehrfarbig glasierten Ziegeln in Form eines gotischen Tabernakels mit seiner giebelartigen Bekrönung, ebenso wie die Kanzel.

Its brickwork, designed with coloured glossy and shaped bricks, is of the highest artistic quality.

Nicholas' Church is a three-nave hall church on a cruciform ground plan with an implied transept, a five-sided polygonal chancel and a square west tower.

This is characterised by a stately, stepped portal and the slender, polychrome stone spire with its flanking spandrels and filigree corner turrets.

Inside, the four-bay nave with massive side-aisle galleries is supported by round pillars under the ribbed vault.

The altar made of multi-coloured glazed bricks in the form of a Gothic tabernacle with its gable-like crowning is remarkable, as is the pulpit.

↑ George Kochbeck auf einem seiner Lieblingswege, die es rund um Wiedenbrügge gibt. Dieser wird von ihm gerne mit „Pättchen" tituliert – ein Dialektandenken an seine Herkunft.

↑ George Kochbeck on one of his favourite trails around Wiedenbrügge. He likes to call the path "Pättchen" – a dialect reminder of his origins.

Wiedenbrügge

George Kochbeck

Wiedenbrügge und drum herum – Unsere Schaumburger Toscana

Ich bin George Kochbeck, gebürtiger Ostwestfale, zwanzig Jahre Wahl-Hamburger und seit bald einem Vierteljahrhundert überzeugter Schaumburger. Sabine zog 1996 nach Wiedenbrügge – der Arbeit wegen. Ich folgte ihr 1999 – der Liebe wegen. Seit 2003 sind wir verheiratet und leben mit unseren Kindern nach wie vor hier – wo auch sonst?

Bis Winter 2010 lebten wir in Wiedenbrügge in einem alten Bauernhof. Im April 2011 zogen wir um in unser jetziges Haus. Neben dem Wohnhaus habe ich mir in einer alten Doppelgarage, in der einst Molkereifahrzeuge standen, mein Studio eingerichtet. Hier arbeite ich täglich an meinen Filmprojekten, für die ich Musik komponiere und habe endlich den Platz, um viele meiner Instrumente spielbereit aufzustellen. Ab und zu finden hier auch Proben und Bandaufnahmen statt.

Der 400 qm große Schwimmteich hinten im Garten ist seit 2012 mein geliebtes Hobby und Entspannungsort geworden. Nachdem der Teich zunächst ein trüber Tümpel war und in der Anfangszeit mehrmals Kinder hineingefallen waren, musste eine Entscheidung getroffen werden: Zuschütten oder Pool oder Schwimmteich mit gefahrenloser Ausstiegszone?

Letzteres ist es dann geworden und wir haben diese Entscheidung nie bereut. Die Schwimmsaison beginnt im Mai und geht gern bis Ende September. Ein Pumpensystem nebst Filtern sorgt durch permanente Umwälzung für klares Wasser. Für biologische Reinigung sorgen zudem 600 Pflanzen. Eine Freude ist es zu beobachten, wie jedes Jahr die an die 30 Seerosen abends „schlafen gehen" und morgens sich wieder entfalten. Eine der Rosen pflanzte ich gerade, als mein Freund und Liedermacher Frizz Feick zu Besuch war. Sie heißt seitdem *Frizz* und kommt jedes Jahr als letzte erst gegen Ende August.

Ein Schaumburger versteht es vielleicht, wenn ich von unseren Lieblingsplätzen und unserem täglichen Leben hier berichte: Da wäre zunächst und vor allem unser Haus und unser Garten, von einigen aus dem Freundeskreis auch „Kurpark zu Bultbeckhausen" genannt. An jenem werkelten wir jahrelang, um uns ein Kleinod für unsere Familie und auch unsere Gäste zu schaffen. Seit einiger Zeit haben wir dort in der äußersten Ecke einen Hochsitz mit Blick über die Felder auf das kleine Schloss in Wölpinghausen, perfekt für den Sundowner bis zum letzten Sonnenstrahl.

Wiedenbrügge and all around – our Schaumburg Toscana

I am George Kochbeck, a native of East Westphalia, twenty years a Hamburg resident by choice and a comitted Schaumburger for almost a quarter of a century. Sabine moved to Wiedenbrügge in 1996 – for work. I followed her in 1999 – for love. We have been married since 2003 and still live here with our children – where else?

Until winter 2010, we lived in Wiedenbrügge in an old farmhouse. In April 2011, we moved into our current house. Next to the house, I set up my studio in an old double garage that used to house dairy vehicles. Here I work daily on my film projects for which I compose music and finally have the space to set up many of my instruments ready to play. Rehearsals and band recordings also take place here from time to time.

The 400 square metre swimming pond at the back of the garden has become my favourite hobby and place to relax since 2012. After the pond was initially a large murky puddle and children fell in several times in the early days, a decision had to be made: fill it in or create a pool or swimming pond with a safe exit zone.

We ended up with the latter and have never regretted our decision. The swimming season starts in May and runs until the end of September. A pump system and filters ensure clear water through constant circulation. In addition, 600 plants ensure biological purification. It's a watch every year as the 30 or so water lilies go to sleep in the evening and unfurl again in the morning. I planted one of the lilies when my friend and singer-songwriter Frizz Feick was visiting. It has been called FRIZZ ever since and is the last to bloom every year towards the end of August.

A Schaumburg resident may understand when I talk about our favourite places and our daily life here: first and foremost, there is our house and our garden, which some friends affectionately call the "Kurpark zu Bultbeckhausen" ("Spa gardens of Bultbeckhausen"). We have been working on it for years to create a natural gem and haven for our family and our guests. For some time now, we have had a high seat in the far corner with a view across the fields to the small castle in Wölpinghausen, perfect for sundowners until the last ray of sunshine. On my daily walks with our dog, I often prefer the little path from the Wiedenbrügge village square to Schmalenbruch as a starting point. The atmosphere between the marvellous trees

↑ Von dem versteckten Hochsitz aus wird nicht auf Wild geschossen, sondern abends die Sonne und ein Drink genossen.

↑ The hidden high seat is not there to take shots at wildlife, but to enjoy the sun and a drink in the evening.

Auf meinen täglichen Spaziergängen mit unserem Hund bc vorzuge ich öfter als Ausgangspunkt das kleine „Pättchen" vom Dorfplatz Wiedenbrügge nach Schmalenbruch. Die Stimmung zwischen den wunderbaren Bäumen und Feldern ist jedes Mal anders. Das Steinhuder Meer ist von uns aus mit dem Rad in knapp 30 Minuten erreicht. Wenn nicht gerade Vatertag ist, ein wunderbarer Weg durch die Felder: am Hagenburger Schloss vorbei, mit Blick auf Wasserbüffel und später mit der Insel Wilhelmstein im Rücken entlang des Steinhuder Meeres bis nach Steinhude. Zu den nachfolgenden Orten in der Umgebung haben wir eine bestimmte Beziehung: Hagenburg ist für uns die nächste Möglichkeit zum Einkaufen, Tanken, Post und Sparkasse. Auch dorthin kann man herrlich mit dem Rad durch den Wald entlang der alten Bahnstrecke fahren. Ein weiterer Lieblingsplatz von uns ist der Gasthof „Zur Erholung" unserer Freundin Ulrike Fiedler-Meyer in Düdinghausen. Man kann dort sehr gut speisen und es gibt auch einen Saal, mit dem wir viele schöne Erinnerungen verbinden, wie zum Beispiel die Geburtstagsparty unserer Freunde Walter und Christl, auf der wir unsere Coverband *The Beatgarden* gründeten.

and fields is different every time. Lake Steinhuder Meer can be reached from our home by bike in just under 30 minutes. If it's not the loud and raucous Father's Day, it's a wonderful route through the fields: past Hagenburg Castle, with a view of the water buffalo and later, with the island of Wilhelmstein behind you, along Lake Steinhuder Meer to Steinhude.
We also have a special relationship with the following places in the neighbourhood: Hagenburg is the closest place for us to shop, get gas, go to the post office and the savings bank. It's also a great place to cycle through the forest along the old railway line. Another of our favourite places is the "Zur Erholung" inn run by our friend Ulrike Meyer in Düdinghausen. It's a great place to eat and there's also a hall that holds many cherished memories for us, such as the birthday party of our friends Walter and Christl, where we formed our cover band The Beatgarden.
A truly unique feature is the narrow bridge that you have to cross if you want to go from us to Idensen to eat a delicious piece of cake in the café there.
Bergkirchen is home to the ancient St Catherine's Church, where we were married and our children were baptised. Not

↑ Weite und am Ende der Weite ein kleines Schlösschen. Ein geradezu märchenhafter Ausblick vom Bultbeckhausenschen Hochsitz aus.

↑ An expanse and a small castle at the end of the expanse. An almost fairytale view from the Bultbeckhausenschen high seat.

↑ Im „Kurpark zu Bultbeckhausen", mit viel Zeit und Liebe errichteter Schwimmteich – zum Ausgleich der geistigen Arbeit entstanden.

↑ In the "Kurpark zu Bultbeckhausen", a swimming pond built with a lot of time and love – compensate the mental exertion.

Ein wahrhaftes Unikum ist die schmale Brücke, die es zu überqueren gilt, wenn man von uns aus nach Idensen will, um dort in dem Café ein leckeres Stück Kuchen zu essen.

In Bergkirchen steht die uralte St.-Katharinen-Kirche, in der wir getraut und unsere Kinder getauft wurden. Nicht zuletzt weil ich auch den örtlichen Gemeindechor leite und ab und zu die 400 Jahre alte Orgel bediene, kann man mich dort gelegentlich antreffen. Der Ausblick vom Platz hinter der Kirche auf das Steinhuder Meer ist bestimmt einer der schönsten Ausblicke in ganz Schaumburg.

In Wölpinghausen gibt es unseren Musikclub „Die Kleine Freiheit" im Gebäude des ehemaligen Kindergartens. Dort veranstalten wir regelmäßig Konzerte und andere Events.

Und last, but not least: Wenn wir unsere in- und ausländischen Gäste, die mit der Bahn anreisen, abholen, ist der Bahnhof in Lindhorst das Ziel. Auf dem Weg dorthin kommt man durch Sachsenhagen. Dort gingen unsere Kinder auf die Gerda-Philippson-Grundschule.

Zum Einschulungsgottesdienst 2011 suchte man einen Organisten und ich sprang ein. Mittlerweile habe ich diesen Job nun schon seit zwölf Jahren.

least because I also direct the local parish choir and occasionally play the 400-year-old organ, you can occasionally find me there. The view of Lake Steinhuder Meer from the square behind the church is certainly one of the most beautiful views in the whole of Schaumburg.

In Wölpinghausen there is our music club "Die Kleine Freiheit" in the building of the former children's garden. We regularly organise concerts and other events there.

And last but not least: when we pick up our guests from Germany and abroad travelling by train, the train station in Lindhorst is the destination. On the way there, you pass through Sachsenhagen. Our children go to Gerda Philippson Primary School there.

They were looking for an organist for the school enrolment service in 2011 and I stepped in. I've now had this job for twelve years.

↑ Sicherlich eine der Kirchen im Landkreis, die den schönsten Ausblick hat.

↑ It is certainly one of the churches in the district with the most beautiful view.

St. Katharinen Kirche
St Catherine's Church

Peter Zenker

Die kleine, weithin sichtbare Kirche auf dem Bergrücken der Rehburger Berge ist das älteste bauliche Zeugnis im Ort und ein Kleinod der Kirchenbaukultur des Hochmittelalters. Im Kern findet sich ein romanischer Sakralbau des 12. Jahrhunderts, der im Verlauf der Geschichte dem Zeitgeschmack und funktionalen Anforderungen folgend, ergänzt und umgebaut wurde.

Sie ist vom Gebäudetypus eine Saalkirche mit Querhaus, geradem Chorschluss und leicht querrechteckigem Westturm. Die Fassaden sind aus großen Quadern gemauert und das Satteldach ist mit Sollingplatten gedeckt.

Das rundbogige Portal im Westturm sowie die rechteckigen Schallöffnungen und das Gesims datieren aus dem späten 18. Jahrhundert.

Das Langhaus wird durch kleine, teilweise zugemauerte Rundbogenfenster aus dem 12. Jahrhundert und Strebepfeilern gegliedert.

Den Chor schmücken Maßwerkfenster mit Motiven, die in filigraner Arbeit von Steinmetzen vorgenommen wurden.

The small and prominently visible church on the ridge of the Rehburg Hills is the oldest architectural evidence in the village and a gem of the church building culture in the High Middle Ages. At its core is a Romanesque sacred building from the 12th century, which was added to and remodelled over the course of history in line with contemporary tastes and functional requirements.

In terms of building type, it is a hall church with a transept, straight choir end and a slightly transverse rectangular west tower. The façades are made of large ashlars and the gabled roof is covered with Solling slabs.

The round-arched portal in the west tower as well as the rectangular sound openings and the cornice date from the late 18th century.

The nave is divided by small, partially bricked-up arched windows from the 12th century and buttresses.

The choir is adorned with tracery windows with motifs that were delicately crafted by stonemasons. The south transept façade has an ogival columned portal with floral capitals and

↑ Ein wunderschöner Ausblick in Richtung Steinhuder Meer, ganz in der Nähe der Kirche.
↑ A wonderful view towards Lake Steinhuder Meer very close to the church.

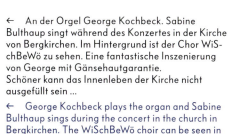

← An der Orgel George Kochbeck. Sabine Bulthaup singt während des Konzertes in der Kirche von Bergkirchen. Im Hintergrund ist der Chor WiSchBeWö zu sehen. Eine fantastische Inszenierung von George mit Gänsehautgarantie.
Schöner kann das Innenleben der Kirche nicht ausgefüllt sein …

← George Kochbeck plays the organ and Sabine Bulthaup sings during the concert in the church in Bergkirchen. The WiSchBeWö choir can be seen in the background. A fantastic production by George with goose bumps guaranteed.
The interior of the church could not be more beautifully filled …

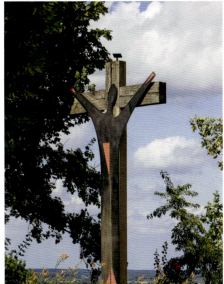

↑ Das Jahrtausendkreuz in Bergkirchen – entstanden zur Weltausstellung EXPO 2000 und entworfen von der Künstlerin Regina Piesbergen.
↑ The Millennium Cross in Bergkirchen – created for the EXPO 2000 world exhibition and designed by the artist Regina Piesbergen.

↑ Was für eine Stimme: Theo DaVinci klingt, als hätten ihn die Götter geküsst.
↑ What a voice: Theo DaVinci sounds like he was kissed by the gods.

Die südliche Querhausfassade hat ein spitzbogiges Säulenportal mit floralen Kapitellen und einem Kreuzrelief. In ihrem Inneren findet sich eine mit Figuren verzierte Kanzel aus dem 17. Jahrhundert, die von einer Mosesstatue getragen wird. Hinter einem schlicht gemauerten Altar mit barockem Kruzifix erhebt sich die vom Orgelbauer Heinrich Clausing gebaute Orgel, die mit einem Pferdefuhrwerk aus Herford angeliefert werden musste.
Links der Orgel steht eine kleine Holzplastik der Heiligen Katharina von Alexandrien, die der Kirche ihren Namen gibt.

a cross relief. Inside there is a 17th century pulpit decorated with figures and supported by a statue of Moses. Behind a simple brick altar with a Baroque crucifix stands the organ built by organ builder Heinrich Clausing, which had to be delivered by horse and cart from Herford.
To the left of the organ is a small wooden sculpture of St Catherine of Alexandria, who gives the church its name.

S. 182–183 Blick von Wölpinghausen aus, vorbei an Edelrindern zum Steinhuder Meer. Der zufällig vorbeifliegende Schwarm von Staren gibt dem Foto das gewisse Extra.

P. 182–183 View from Wölpinghausen, past fine cattle to Lake Steinhuder Meer. The flock of starlings flying past by chance gives the photo that little bit extra.

↑ Ein absolutes Highlight eines Konzerts in Schaumburg: Die Funk-Band „Angels of Libra" mit ihrem charismatischen Sänger Nathan Johnston aus Irland. Die übrigen Bandmitglieder setzen sich aus mehreren Nationen zusammen und haben einen Sound, der direkt ins Herz und die Beine geht.

↑ An absolute highlight of a concert in Schaumburg: the funk band "Angels of Libra" with their charismatic singer Nathan Johnston from Ireland. The other band members come from several nations and have a sound that goes straight to the heart and legs.

↑ Eine Randerscheinung des Kriegs in der Ukraine: Stanislav Kotovski, Bassklarinettenspieler, der sonst in der Ukraine bis 2014 in Symphonieorchestern spielte, zu Besuch in Schaumburg. Er spielt sich für das anstehende Konzert schon mal draußen warm.

↑ A peripheral phenomenon of the war in Ukraine: Stanislav Kotovski, bass clarinet player, who otherwise played in symphony orchestras in Ukraine until 2014, visits Schaumburg. He is warming up outside for the upcoming concert.

↑ Viel Platz gibt es in der Veranstaltungsräumlichkeit „Kleine Freiheit Nr. 4" nicht. Es ist ja auch eine kleine Freiheit ... Das macht aber gerade den Charme dieser Clublocation aus.

↑ There is not much space in the venue "Kleine Freiheit Nr. 4". It is, after all, a "small freedom" ... But that's what makes this club location so charming.

Die kleine Freiheit Nr. 4

Die kleine Freiheit Nr. 4 an der Meeresblickstraße 4 in Wölpinghausen ist seit vielen Jahren ein gemütlicher Veranstaltungsort. Ein Team von ehrenamtlichen Mitarbeitenden kümmert sich um alles. Seit 2021 sind auch Sabine und ich mit im Team.
Einmal im Jahr machen wir um den 6. Dezember herum die sogenannte Nikolaus-Session, zu der wir unseren musikalischen Freundeskreis sowie Kolleginnen und Kollegen aus ganz Schaumburg-Lippe einladen. Ziemlich regelmäßig veranstalten wir aber mittlerweile weitere Konzerte, Kinonachmittage, Theateraufführungen und Performances. Dank einer Förderung durch die Schaumburger Landschaft konnten wir 2022 aufwendig renovieren und neues Equipment anschaffen. Darüber hinaus nutzen einige örtliche Vereine den Saal für Sitzungen und auch die Proben des Posaunenchors und des Kirchenchors finden dort statt.

Kleine Freiheit Nr. 4

Kleine Freiheit Nr. 4 at Meeresblickstrasse 4 in Wölpinghausen has been a cosy venue for many years. A team of volunteers takes care of everything. Sabine and I have also been part of the team since 2021. Once a year, around December 6th, we organise the so-called Nikolaus Session, to which we invite our musical friends and colleagues from all over Schaumburg-Lippe. However, we now organise other concerts, cinema afternoons, theatre shows and performance events on a fairly regular basis. Thanks to funding from the Schaumburger Landschaft, we were able to renovate and purchase new equipment in 2022. In addition, some local clubs use the hall for meetings and the trombone choir and church choir also hold their rehearsals there.

Wölpinghausen

↑ Das Erntefest in Wölpinghausen ist für Groß und Klein immer ein Grund zum Feiern und nebenbei den blankgeputzten Trecker auszuführen – besonders wenn das Wetter mitspielt.
↑ The harvest festival in Wölpinghausen is always a good reason for young and old to celebrate and, by the way, to show off their polished tractors – especially when the weather plays along.

↑ Kunstvoll geschmückte Wagen dürfen nicht fehlen, genauso wenig wie ein Storch, der rund um das Steinhuder Meer inzwischen wieder besonders häufig vorkommt.
↑ Artfully decorated floats are a must, as is the presence of a stork, which has become particularly common again around Lake Steinhuder Meer.

↑ Am Naturfreundehaus in Wölpinghausen wird Tradition des 18. Jahrhunderts gelebt: ein Regiment in historischen Kostümen zu Ehren von Graf Wilhelm Friedrich Ernst zu Schaumburg-Lippe, der vor rund 300 Jahren lebte und der Region unter anderem den Wilhelmstein hinterließ.
↑ At the Naturfreundehaus in Wölpinghausen, 18th century tradition is brought to life: here, through a regiment dressed in historical costumes, honouring Wilhelm Friedrich Ernst, Count of Schaumburg-Lippe, who lived around 300 years ago and left behind landmarks in the region such as the Wilhelmstein.

↑ Diese fünf Sandsteinstelen aus einem Steinbruch in Münchehagen stehen symbolisch für die ehemaligen Einnahmequellen des Ortes: Landwirtschaft, Bergbau, Seefahrt, Steinbrüche und Handwerk.

↑ These five sandstone steles from a quarry in Münchehagen are symbolic of the town's former sources of income: agriculture, mining, seafaring, quarrying and crafts.

Münchehagen

Renate Braselmann

Fährt man von Hannover auf der A2 Richtung Steinhuder Meer, so entdeckt man schon auf der Autobahn ein Hinweisschild des Dinoparks Münchehagen. Dieses kleine beschauliche Dorf, als Ortsteil der Stadt Rehburg-Loccum, hat eine vielfältige Wandlung vollzogen mit unterschiedlichen Schwerpunkten. Aber sicherlich ist der Dinosaurier-Park das absolute touristische Highlight des Dorfes und der gesamten Stadt Rehburg-Loccum.

Entstehung des Dorfes Münchehagen

Dem 1163 gegründeten Kloster Loccum verdankt Münchehagen seine Entstehung und seinen Namen. Die Mönche rodeten östlich des Klosters das Land frei, das in einer Urkunde von 1183 „Hagen" genannt wurde. Damit war die gesamte bewaldete und gerodete Grenzgemarkung gemeint. Auf dieser Hagensiedlung der Mönche – auch Mönichehagen genannt – wurden zunächst Leibeigene und dann Zehnthörige angesiedelt. Grenzgebiete hatten immer unter Herrschaftsstreitigkeiten zu leiden. Die Neuansiedlungen auf dem Gebiet des heutigen Münchehagens geschahen zuerst, um in Kriegen und Fehden durch das Kloster Loccum als dessen Hörige oder Leibeigene geschützt zu sein. Aber auch die klösterlichen Steinbrüche und Kohlengruben zogen Menschen an, die hofften, dort als Steinhauer oder Bergleute arbeiten und leben zu können. In der Schulchronik wird angenommen, dass im 14. Jahrhundert ein Teil der Bergleute aus dem Harz oder dem Erzgebirge angeworben wurde, um deren Wissen und Erfahrungen im Bergbau nutzbar zu machen. Münchehagens ist also schon seit seiner Gründung kein reines Bauerndorf gewesen, sondern sowohl Bauern- als auch Arbeiterdorf.

Landwirtschaft

Die landwirtschaftlichen Betriebe in Münchehagen, von denen es nur ein paar größere gab, die meisten waren eher bescheiden, mussten aufgrund der Gründung des Ortes auf der Fläche des klösterlichen Gebietes den zehnten Teil ihres erwirtschafteten Gutes an das Kloster abgeben, der sogenannte Zehnt. So gab es zum Beispiel einen Hühnerzins, einen Gänsezins, einen Kornzins und die Hand- und Spanndienste. Erst im Jahr 1838 wurde durch die königliche Ablösekommission des Distrikts Stolzenau die Ablösesumme von 14.000 Reichstalern festgelegt, die für jede Haus- und Hofstelle de-

If you drive from Hannover on the A2 towards Lake Steinhuder Meer, you will see a sign for Dinopark Münchehagen on the highway. This small, tranquil village, a district of the town of Rehburg-Loccum, has undergone a variety of transformations with different focuses. But the dinosaur park is certainly the absolute tourist highlight of the village and the entire town of Rehburg-Loccum.

Origin of the village Münchehagen

Münchehagen owes its origins and its name to Loccum Monastery, which was founded in 1163. The monks cleared the land to the east of the monastery, which was called "Hagen" in a document from 1183. This referred to the entire wooded and cleared border area. On this Hagen settlement of the monks – also known as Mönichehagen – serfs and then tithe payers were first settled. Border areas have always suffered from disputes between lords. The new settlements in the area of today's Münchehagen were initially made in order to be protected in wars and feuds by Loccum Monastery as its serfs or villeins. But the monastery's quarries and coal mines also attracted people who hoped to work and live there as stonemasons or miners. The school chronicle assumes that in the 14th century, some of the miners were recruited from the Harz Mountains or the Ore Mountains in order to make use of their knowledge and experience in mining. Münchehagen has therefore not been a purely farming village since its foundation, but both a farming and working village.

Agriculture

The farms in Münchehagen, of which there were only a few larger ones, most of which were rather modest, had to give the monastery a tenth of their produce, the so-called "tithe", due to the founding of the village on the area of the monastic territory. For example, there was a chicken tithe, a goose tithe, a corn tithe and the manual labor. It was not until 1838 that the royal redemption commission of the Stolzenau district set the redemption sum of 14,000 Reichstalers, which was listed in detail for each house and farmstead. However, neither this high sum nor the interest charge of 3.5% could be raised by the inhabitants. This led to unrest among the inhabitants and ultimately to the storming of Loccum Monastery on March 20, 1848. Even later, the income from agriculture

↑ An dieser Stelle wurde im Maximillian-Schacht bis 1921 Kohle gefördert.

↑ Coal was mined at this location in the Maximilian shaft until 1921.

tailliert aufgeführt wurde. Aber weder diese hohe Summe noch die Zinslast von 3,5 Prozent konnte die Bevölkerung aufbringen. Deshalb kam es zu Unruhen unter der Bevölkerung und führte schließlich am 20. März 1848 zur Stürmung des Klosters Loccum. Auch später führten die Einnahmen aus der Landwirtschaft nur bedingt zu einem auskömmlichen Leben. Die Münchehägerinnen und Münchehäger mussten andere Erwerbsquellen suchen, um ihre Familien zu ernähren.

Bergbau und Steinbruch

Seit der Gründung des Ortes Münchehagen arbeiteten die Menschen nicht nur auf ihren kleinen Höfen, sondern ebenfalls im Bergbau und im klösterlichen Steinbruch. Der Bergbau verhalf der Bevölkerung Münchehagens zwar nicht unbedingt zu Wohlstand, so doch zu einem Auskommen. Wann der Kohleabbau in der Gegend um Münchehagen begann, ist bis heute nicht feststellbar. Der älteste Stollen soll aber jener sein, der den Namen Georg-Stollen trägt und mit dessen Bau 1751 in den Rehburger Bergen begonnen wurde. Ein weiterer Stollen wurde 1791 als Kloster-Stollen gegraben und endete

only provided a limited livelihood. The people of Münchehagen had to look for other sources of income to feed their families.

Mining and quarrying

From the time Münchehagen was founded, people not only worked on their small farms, but also in mining and in the monastery quarry. Mining did not necessarily bring prosperity to the people of Münchehagen, but it did provide them with a livelihood. It is still not possible to determine when coal mining began in the area around Münchehagen. However, the oldest adit is said to be the one named Georg-Stollen, the construction of which began in 1751 in the Rehburg mountains. Another tunnel was dug in 1791 as the Kloster-Stollen and ended in 1883 at the Emilien-Schacht on the current site of the Dinopark. It took almost 100 years to get hold of the coal in the five km long tunnel. The tunnels were usually very low, so the miners often had to work lying down. With a depth of 160 meters, the Erlengrund was the deepest shaft. The most famous shaft in Münchehagen is probably the Maximilian

1883 beim Emilien-Schacht auf dem jetzigen Gelände des Dinoparks. Es brauchte fast 100 Jahre, um sich der Steinkohle in dem fünf Kilometer langen Gang zu bemächtigen. Die Stollen waren meist sehr niedrig, so dass die Bergmänner oft im Liegen arbeiten mussten. Am Erlengrund war der tiefste Schacht. Dort ging es rund 160 m hinab. Wohl der bekannteste Schacht in Münchehagen ist der Maximilian-Schacht, dessen Abraum noch heute als Hügel vorhanden ist. Rund 60 m tief mussten die Bergleute dort einsteigen.

Große Kohlevorkommen wurden aber nie gefunden. Da sich bei den jüngsten Grabungen die Flöze als wesentlich weniger mächtig als erwartet herausstellten, wurde der gewerbsmäßige Bergbau in den 1920er Jahren eingestellt. Der immer noch existierende Bergmannsverein stellte als Zeichen dieser Epoche eine Lore in Münchehagen auf. Auch der bekannte Schriftsteller Ernst Jünger, der seine Kindheit in Rehburg verbrachte, schildert in einem seiner Werke die Faszination dieser Welt unter Tage, die er als Junge um 1910 in einem stillgelegten Stollen erlebte.

Die Folgen der Schließung traf die Bevölkerung Münchehagens hart, es haben immerhin ungefähr 120 Männer im Bergbau gearbeitet. Es mussten folglich neue Erwerbsquellen gesucht werden.

Seefahrt

Eine Besonderheit Münchehagens fällt auf, wenn man durch das Dorf fährt und an einer Straßengabelung einen großen Anker sieht. Münchehagen liegt nicht an der Küste, doch sind etliche Münchehäger zur See gefahren. Wie ist es zu dieser Entwicklung gekommen? Der Niedergang des Bergbaus kann es jedenfalls nicht gewesen sein, denn schon vorher gab es verhältnismäßig viele Seeleute.

Die Schulchronik bietet folgende Erklärung an:

Im letzten Viertel des 18. Jahrhunderts fanden sich junge Leute im Alter zwischen 14 und 24 Jahren bereit, von Pfingsten bis Martini nach Holland zu gehen, um durch Gras- und Getreidemähen sowie durch Torfstechen einiges Geld zu verdienen. Man nannte diese Burschen „Hollandgänger". Auch aus anderen Teilen Niedersachsens suchten junge Männer in Holland nach Erwerbsmöglichkeiten. Sie trafen dort ebenfalls auf holländische Fischer und ließen sich anheuern. Beim Heringsfangen konnte man besser Geld verdienen und so fuhren immer mehr Münchehäger im Sommer und im Herbst zur See. Im Winter wohnten sie in Münchehagen. Aber nicht nur junge Menschen zogen hinaus. Den Steinbruch- und Grubenarbeitern wurde ärztlich empfohlen, ihre nach langen Jahren durch Stein und Kohlenstaub schwer geschädigten Lungen in der gesunden Seeluft wieder zu heilen. Viele befolgten den Rat und wechselten im späten Alter noch ihren Beruf. Aus Bergleuten und Steinhauern wurden Seeleute. Auch eine Anzahl junger Mädchen aus dem Dorf folgten den Fischern in Richtung Nordseeküste. Sie arbeiteten während der Sommerzeit in der Gastronomie auf den Nordseeinseln, besonders auf Norderney.

Zwischen den Jahren 1925 bis 1930 verzeichnet das Einwohnerbuch etwa ein Dutzend Kapitäne und Steuerleute sowie 200 weitere Seeleute. Man könnte deshalb auch von einem Fischerdorf im Binnenland sprechen. Als sichtbares Zeichen dieser Epoche hat der Münchehäger Seemannsverein diesen großen Anker im Dorf aufgestellt.

← Die Lore erinnert daran, dass der Bergbau bis in die frühen Jahre des 20. Jahrhunderts viele Familien in Münchehagen ernährte.

← The mining wagon is a reminder that mining fed many families in Münchehagen until the early years of the 20th century.

shaft, the overburden of which still exists today as a mound. The miners had to go down around 60 meters.

However, large coal deposits were never found. As the latest excavations revealed the coal seams to be much less thick than expected, commercial mining was discontinued in the 1920s. The miners' association, which still exists, erected a mining wagon in Münchehagen as a symbol of this era. The well-known writer Ernst Jünger, who spent his childhood in Rehburg, also describes the fascination of this underground world in one of his works, which he experienced as a boy in a disused mine around 1910.

The consequences of the closure hit the people of Münchehagen hard; after all, around 120 men worked in mining. Consequently, new sources of income had to be sought.

Seafaring

A special feature of Münchehagen is noticeable when you drive through the village and see a large anchor at a fork in the road. Münchehagen is not on the coast, but many Münchehageners went to sea. How did this development come about? It certainly cannot have been the decline of mining, as there were already a relatively large number of seafarers before that.

The school chronicle offers the following explanation:

In the last quarter of the 18th century, young people between the ages of 14 and 24 were willing to go to Holland from Whitsun to Martinmas to earn some money by mowing grass and grain and cutting peat. These boys were called "Hollandgangers". Young men from other parts of Lower Saxony also sought employment opportunities in Holland. They also met Dutch fishermen there and were hired out. It was easier to earn money catching herring and so more and more Münchehageners went to sea in the summer and fall. In winter, they lived in Münchchagen. But it wasn't just young people who went out to sea. Quarry and mine workers were advised by doctors to heal their lungs, which had been severely damaged by years of stone and coal dust, in the healthy sea air. Many followed the advice and changed their profession late in life. Miners and stonecutters became sailors. A number of young girls from the village also followed the fishermen to the North Sea coast. During the summer, they worked in the catering trade on the North Sea islands, especially on Norderney.

Between 1925 and 1930, the population register lists around a dozen captains and helmsmen as well as 200 other seamen. One could also refer to it as an inland fishing village. The Münchehäger Seemannsverein has erected this large anchor in the village as a visible symbol of this era.

Porträt von Kapitän Wilhelm Hardich, der zu den ersten Seeleuten gehörte, die um das Jahr 1900 auf Heringsfang gingen, hier allerdings in einer NS-Marineuniform drei Jahrzehnte später. →

Portrait of Captain Wilhelm Hardich, one of the first seamen to go herring fishing around 1900 – here, however, photographed in a Nazi naval uniform around three decades later. →

Hardichhaus
Hardich House

Derek & Marion Meister

Kapitän Hardich

Eines Nachts, wir waren gerade aufs Dorf gezogen und wohnten erst ein paar Wochen in diesem 100 Jahre alten Haus, weckten mich Schritte. Ein wischendes Schlurfen drang durchs dämmrige Mondlicht hinauf bis ins Schlafzimmer. Ich fuhr hoch und lauschte angestrengt in die Dunkelheit. Da war es wieder ... Schritte. Ein Wischen, ein Klickern ... Sofort hatte ich das Bild eines Geisterpiraten vor Augen, der – sein Holzbein hinter sich herziehend, die skelettierten Finger an der Tapete – durch die Zimmer und über die hölzerne Treppe hinauf kam, langsam und bedächtig, um ...
Der Geist eines Piraten im Haus mitten auf dem Land? Zwischen Feldern und Pferdekoppeln? 150 km von der See entfernt und gute 30 Minuten mit dem Rad zum Steinhuder Meer?
Ich bin Autor. Fantasieren und Fabulieren, das ist mein Job und als ich – mit der Nachttischlampe bewaffnet vorsichtig und äußerst mutig aus der Tür und dem Piraten in den Weg trat, war mir klar, wieso ich ausgerechnet auf einen Piraten gekommen war ...
Unser Haus, mitten auf dem flachen Land, ist ein Kapitänshaus. Als wir das zum ersten Mal hörten, sah mich meine Frau Marion mit ihrem unnachahmlichen Die-verkackeiern-uns-doch-Blick an. Mit den Zugezogenen aus Berlin kann man es ja machen. Vom Hackeschen Markt auf die Kuhwiese wollen die, da verschaukeln wir die Neuen mal und erfinden Kapitäne, die inmitten von Mais und Getreide ihre Kähne steuern.
Doch wie sich herausstellte, existierte der Kapitän tatsäch-

Captain Hardich

One night, when we had just moved to the village and had only been living in this hundred-year-old house for a few weeks, I was woken by footsteps. A scurrying shuffle made its way through the dim moonlight up to the bedroom. I jumped up and listened intently into the darkness. There it was again ... footsteps. A wiping, a clicking ... I immediately had the image of a ghost pirate in my mind's eye, dragging his wooden leg behind him, his skeletal fingers on the wallpaper, coming through the rooms and up the wooden stairs, slowly and deliberately to ...
The ghost of a pirate in a house in the middle of the countryside? Between fields and paddocks? One hundred and fifty kilometers from the sea and a good thirty minutes by bike to the Lake Steinhuder Meer?
I am an author. Fantasizing and fabulating, that's my job and when I – armed with a bedside lamp – stepped carefully and extremely bravely out of the door and into the path of the pirate, I realized why I had come across a pirate of all things...
Our house, in the middle of the flat countryside, is a captain's house. When we heard that for the first time, my wife Marion looked at me with her inimitable 'you've got to be kidding me' look. You can do it with the newcomers from Berlin. They want to go from the Hackischer Markt to the Kuhwiese, so we'll take the newcomers for a ride and invent captains to steer their boats amidst the corn and grain.
But as it turned out, the captain actually existed. Captain Hardich had his own cutter and sailed out to sea from Bremerhaven. Catching herrings. He spent the summer months at

← Ein ungewöhnliches Symbol in einem Ort, der weit von der Küste entfernt ist: Der Anker erinnert an eine Blütezeit der Seefahrt in Münchehagen, in der zwanzig Kapitäne und rund 300 Seemänner dem Heringsfang als Broterwerb nachgingen.
← An unusual symbol in a place that is far from the coast: the anchor is a reminder of the heyday of seafaring in Münchehagen, when twenty captains and around 300 sailors fished for herring for a living.

lich. Käpt'n Hardich hatte einen eigenen Kutter und fuhr von Bremerhaven aus zur See. Heringe fangen. Die Sommermonate war er auf See und im Winter in seinem Haus. Und schnitzte und zimmerte und erzählte Geschichten. Käpt'n Hardich muss im Ort sehr beliebt gewesen sein, denn ab und an passiert es, dass jemand in unserem Wohnzimmer steht und meint, er habe exakt hier geheiratet. Vermählt vom Käpt'n, mitten in dessen „Guter Stube".

Wir Meisters waren die ersten Jahre nach unserem Einzug in das Kapitänshaus auch nicht „die Meisters", sondern schlicht „die vom Hardichhaus". Aber so ist das eben auf dem Dorf, wo jeder seinen Spitznamen hat, weil sie – selbstverständlich rein zufällig – allesamt Wesemann heißen.

Das Hardichhaus, unser Kapitänshaus, war das 33. Gemäuer, das wir uns zwischen Stadthagen und Nienburg, zwischen Stolzenau und Mellendorf angesehen hatten. Es hat – kaum waren wir eingetreten – zu Marion und mir sofort gesprochen. Wir waren auf der Suche nach einem neuen Zuhause, weit ab vom hektischen Berlin und absichtlich ein wenig vom Schuss zu Hannover, wo ich geboren wurde.

In Berlin hatten wir uns eine Karte gekauft und Regionen ausgeixt, in die wir nicht ziehen wollten. Dass wir außer einem Schreibtisch, E-Mail und einem Briefkasten nichts zum Arbeiten brauchen, wollten Marion und ich voll ausnutzen. Nachdem wir das Berliner Umland weggestrichen, Bayern dem Rotstift zum Opfer gefallen war und schließlich das Ruhrgebiet ausfiel, schlug ich vor, in meine alte Heimat zu ziehen – jedoch an eine Ecke, dem Steinhuder Meer, die ich nur aus sehr früher Kindheit durch ein paar Ausflüge kannte. Also suchten wir ums Steinhuder Meer herum nach einem Haus für eine Familie, die wir gründen wollten und für die Berlin uns zu stickig und grau vorgekommen war.

Wir betraten das Kapitänshaus der Hardichs und wurden von einer äußerst rüstigen Dame empfangen, die uns durch die Räume führte. Marion und ich sahen uns bereits nach zwei Minuten Hausbesichtigung an, diesmal kein Die-verkackeiern-uns-doch-Blick, und wussten: Das ist es. Dieses Haus oder keins.

Die Gegend um das Steinhuder Meer mit seinen sanft sea and the winter in his house. And he carved and carpentered and told stories. Captain Hardich must have been very popular in the village, because every now and then someone would stand in our living room and say that he got married right here. Married by the captain, in the middle of his "parlor".

For the first few years after we moved into the captain's house, we Meisters weren't called "the Meisters" either, but simply "Die-vom-Hardich-Haus". But that's the way it is in the village, where everyone has their own nickname because they are all called Wesemann – purely by chance, of course.

The Hardichhaus, our captain's house, was the 33rd building we viewed between Stadthagen and Nienburg, between Stolzenau and Mellendorf. As soon as we entered, it immediately spoke to Marion and me. We were looking for a new home, far away from hectic Berlin and deliberately a little out of the way of Hannover, where I was born.

In Berlin, we had bought a map and selected regions that we didn't want to move to. Marion and I wanted to take full advantage of the fact that we didn't need anything to work on apart from a desk, email and a letterbox. After we had eliminated the Berlin area, Bavaria had fallen victim to the red pencil and finally the Ruhr area was ruled out, I suggested moving to my old home – but to a place, the Steinhuder Meer, that I only knew from a few trips in my early childhood. So we looked around the Lake Steinhuder Meer for a house for a family we wanted to start and for which Berlin had seemed too stuffy and gray.

We entered the Hardichs' captain's house and were greeted by an extremely sprightly lady who showed us around the rooms. After just two minutes of viewing the house, Marion and I looked at each other, this time not with a "they're-going-to-crap-us" look, and knew: this is it. This house or no house.

We had already liked the area around the Lake Steinhuder Meer with its gently rolling hills and forests and now we found a house of honest beauty and simple soul. Plenty of space for children to play and for a study full of stories, thrillers, near-future novels, historical crime novels, young adult books and horror stories – everything that Marion and I still create today.

↑ Matrose und Maschinist Fritz Bredemeier an Bord eines Heringsfängers.
↑ Sailor and machinist Fritz Bredemeier on board a herring cutter.

↑ Kapitän Adolf Wesemann (hinter den Matrosen) und seine Seeleute an Bord eines Heringsfängers, auch Logger genannt.
↑ Captain Adolf Wesemann (behind the sailors) and his sailors on board a herring cutter, also known as a lugger.

↑ Das ehemalige Haus von Kapitän Hardich wird nun von dem Schriftsteller Derek Meister mit seiner Familie bewohnt.

↑ Captain Hardich's former house is now occupied by the writer Derek Meister and his family.

geschwungenen Hügeln und den Wäldern hatte uns schon vorher sehr gefallen und nun fanden wir ein Haus von ehrlicher Schönheit und schlichtem Gemüt. Viel Platz für Kinder zum Spielen und für Arbeitszimmer voller Geschichten, voller Thriller, Near-Future-Romane, historischer Krimis, Jugendbücher und Gruselstorys – eben allem, was Marion und ich bis heute erschaffen haben.

Vielleicht sind es auch die exotischen Tiere – der Leopard und Löwe im Flur – oder Hardichs Geschichten, die er in den Wintermonaten hier erzählt hat, die uns sofort das Gefühl gegeben haben, unseren Heimathafen gefunden zu haben.

Man könnte auch sagen: Wir stechen jeden Tag mit dem Kapitänshaus in die kreative See.

Ich umklammerte die Schreibtischlampe fester und trat in den mondkalten Flur, dem Geisterpiraten entgegen. Wieder Schritte, nein, ein Trippeln ... Da! Ein Schatten ... Klein und flink und ... Es war ein Marder. Kein Geisterpirat, auch wenn ich hätte schwören können, dass er eine Augenklappe trug. Der Marder flitzte dreist an mir vorbei und verschwand im Bodenloch, das wir für die neue Heizung erst gestern gesetzt hatten.

Ich schlich mich hin und spähte hinein. Sehen konnte ich unseren Geist nicht mehr, aber ich hörte ihn lachen. Wirklich. Er lachte. Er lachte laut.

Aber das ist eine andere Geschichte und soll ein andermal bei einem Schlückchen Grog im Kapitänshaus nahe dem Steinhuder Meer erzählt werden ...

Perhaps it is also the exotic animals – the leopard and lion in the hallway – or Hardich's stories, which he told here during the winter months, that immediately gave us the feeling of having found our home port.

You could also say that we set sail into the creative sea with the captain's house every day.

I clutched the desk lamp tighter and stepped into the moonlit hallway, towards the ghost pirate. Footsteps again, no, a shuffling ... There! A shadow ... Small and swift and ... It was a marten. Not a ghost pirate, although I could have sworn he was wearing an eye patch. The marten flashed past me brazenly and disappeared into the hole in the floor that we'd just dug yesterday for the new heating system.

I crept over and peeked in. I could no longer see our ghost, but I could hear him laughing. I really did. He was laughing. He laughed out loud.

But that's another story and will be told another time over a sip of grog in the captain's house near Lake Steinhuder Meer ...

↑ Die Musikkneipe Kanbach war eine Institution.
↑ The Kanbach music pub was an institution.

↑ Gastronom und Entertainer Wilhelm „Willi" Kanbach.
↑ Restaurant owner and entertainer Wilhelm "Willi" Kanbach.

Kanbach
Heinrich K.-M. Hecht

Kanbach! Was werden bei diesem Namen für Erinnerungen wach! Es war Anfang der 1970er Jahre. Ich bemühte mich, ein guter Musiker zu sein, mir so viele Livebands anzusehen wie irgendwie möglich. Irgendwann kam jemand aus unserer Clique mit der Information, dass in dem kleinen und beschaulichen Örtchen Münchehagen in Schaumburg live die Post abgeht! Das Kanbach war für uns in Hannover nicht gerade um die Ecke, aber mein Vater war so freundlich, uns seinen Wagen am Wochenende zur Verfügung zu stellen, den mein Freund und Gitarrist Horst – bereits achtzehn und im Besitz eines Führerscheines – fahren durfte. Wie fieberten dem Wochenende entgegen, um loszufahren und mit einem Bier und Currywurst als Nahrung, den Konzerten zu lauschen. Das Kanbach war jedes Mal proppenvoll. Im Gegensatz zum eher rockigen Publikum und der harten Musik, lieferte der Kellner Heinz seine Getränke und Speisen in Sakko und Fliege aus. Um in sein Blickfeld zu geraten, brachte man die Korblampe überm Tisch zum Schwingen ... Legendär auch die Durchsagen von Wilhelm „Onkel Willi" Kanbach:
„Meine sehr verehrten Damen und Herren, es ist 22 Uhr! Sollten sich hier kleine Mädchen bzw. lüttsche Jungs unter sechzehn aufhalten, bitte ich sie sofort das Lokal zu verlassen. Ich erinnere an den Jugendschutz."
Kanbach ist eine Legende! Eröffnet wurde es als „Münchehagener Hof" 1963 und schloss leider endgültig nach einem tragischen Tod in der Familie im Jahr 2014.

Kanbach
Heinrich K.-M. Hecht

Kanbach! What memories does this name bring back! It was the early 70s. I was trying to be a good musician and hear as many live bands as possible. At some point, someone from our clique came up with the information that the small and tranquil village of Münchehagen in Schaumburg was a live venue! The Kanbach was not exactly around the corner for us in Hannover, but my father was kind enough to let us use his car for the weekend, which my friend and guitarist Horst – already eighteen and in possession of a driver's license – was allowed to drive. We eagerly awaited the weekend so that we could drive off and listen to the concerts with a beer and currywurst for sustenance. The Kanbach was packed every time. In contrast to the rather rocky audience and the hard music, the waiter Heinz delivered his drinks and food in a jacket and bow tie. To get into his field of vision, the wicker lamp above the table was made to swing ... Wilhelm "Uncle Willi" Kanbach's announcements were also legendary:
"Ladies and gentlemen, it's 10 pm! If there are any little girls or boys under sixteen here, please leave the restaurant immediately. I remind you of the protection of minors."
Kanbach is a legend! It opened as the "Münchehagener Hof" in 1963 and unfortunately closed for good after a tragic death in the family in 2014.

↑ Einst als Kapelle für das Kloster in Loccum gebaut.   ↑ Once built as a chapel for the monastery in Loccum.

Ehemalige Klosterkapelle
Former monastery chapel

Peter Zenker

Die kleine Kirche mitten im Dorf wurde vom Kloster Loccum ursprünglich als Friedhofskapelle für das Dorf Münchehagen gebaut. Mit den Jahren wurden hier immer regelmäßiger Gottesdienste gefeiert, so dass schließlich eine eigene Pfarrstelle eingerichtet wurde. Die Kirche liegt auf dem Pilgerweg von Loccum nach Volkenroda in Thüringen.

Sie wurde 1713 als kleiner, rechteckiger Bruchsteinbau errichtet und ist, in markanter Lage stehend, von prägendem Einfluss auf das Straßen- und Ortsbild Münchehagens.

Der Kirchraum trägt ein Satteldach, das im Osten abgewalmt ist. Über dem Westgiebel mit Rundbogenportal erhebt sich ein sechsseitiger, verschieferter Dachreiter mit einem mit Kugel und Kreuz bekrönten Helm. Darunter finden sich rechteckige Schallöffnungen und eine Turmuhr.

Zwei mächtige Stützpfeiler stehen an den Westecken, zwei weitere an der Südwand. Je drei Rechteckfenster mit Mittelstützen orientieren sich nach Norden und Süden, ein weiteres nach Osten.

Ein Vorgängerbau der Kirche, noch aus Holz gebaut, wurde

The small church in the centre of the village was originally built by Loccum Monastery as a cemetery chapel for the village of Münchehagen. Over the years, church services were held here more and more regularly, so that eventually a separate parish was established. The church is located on the pilgrimage route from Loccum to Volkenroda in Thuringia.

It was built in 1713 as a small, rectangular quarry stone building and, standing in a prominent position, has a formative influence on the streetscape and townscape of Münchehagen.

The church has a gabled roof, which is hipped in the east. A six-sided, slated ridge turret with a helmet crowned with a ball and cross rises above the west gable with a round arch portal. Below this are rectangular sound openings and a tower clock.

Two mighty supporting pillars stand at the west corners, two more on the south wall. Three rectangular windows with central pillars face north and south, with another facing east.

A predecessor building of the church, still made of wood, was first mentioned in 1463, but was largely destroyed during the

← Das Altarbild erinnert an die Zeiten des Heringsfangs, dem einige aus der Bevölkerung Münchehagens nachgingen und zeigt im Mittelteil die Erscheinung des auferstandenen Jesus Christus am See Genezareth.
← The altarpiece is reminiscent of the times of herring fishing, which some citizens of Münchehagen pursued, and shows the appearance of the Risen Christ on the Sea of Galilee in the central section.

← Das Innere der Kirche mit den blauen Bänken, die der Kirche gut stehen und zum maritimen Thema des Altars passen.
← The interior of the church with the blue pews, which look good in the church and match the maritime theme of the altar.

erstmals 1463 erwähnt, doch während des Dreißigjährigen Kriegs weitgehend zerstört.
Im Jahre 1996 wurde im Altarraum ein großes Altarbild von dem zeitgenössischen Maler Werner Petzold aufgestellt, das im Mittelteil den auferstandenen Jesus Christus am See Genezareth darstellt. Dieses Bildmotiv weist auf die Fischer- und Heringsfängertradition der Gemeinde hin, die über viele Jahrzehnte lebendig war.

Thirty Years' War.
In 1996, a large altarpiece by the contemporary painter Werner Petzold was installed in the chancel, which depicts the resurrected Jesus Christ on the Sea of Galilee in the centre. This motif refers to the fishing and herring fishing tradition of the parish, which was alive for many decades.

Dinopark

Renate Braselmann / Benjamin Englich

Dinosaurier-Park

Die vielen Wandlungen des Dorfes Münchehagen führten vor einigen Jahren zu einem außergewöhnlichen Ereignis und brachten dem Dorf eine Berühmtheit weit über Kreis- und Landesgrenzen hinweg. Im Steinbruch der Firma Ferdinand Wesling, in dem bis heute noch abgebaut wird, entdeckten Steinhauer im Jahr 1980 seltsame Spuren. Schnell konnte von wissenschaftlicher Seite bestätigt werden: Es waren Fußabdrücke eines Dinosauriers! Das war eine Sensation! Schließlich gab es nicht viele Stellen weltweit, die einen solchen Fund präsentieren konnten. Damit begann die Geschichte des Dinosaurier-Parks. Die Lokalzeitung *Die Harke* betitelte einen Bericht am 15. September 1990 mit der Überschrift „In Münchehagen wimmelt es von Sauriern: 150 Urwelttiere werden für Park aufgebaut." Der Betreiber des Steinbruchs, Ferdinand Wesling, nahm nach dem sensationellen Fund im Jahr 1980 Kontakt auf zu örtlichen Behörden, zum Kloster Loccum als Besitzer der Ländereien sowie zum Land Niedersachsen, um diese einmaligen Funde der Öffentlichkeit zugänglich zu machen. Um bei einem späteren Besuch eine Vorstellung davon zu erhalten, wie groß die Urzeittiere waren, die diese Trittspuren im Gestein hinterließen, plante man, diese Urzeitriesen in Originalgröße aufzustellen. Es war die Firma Bernd Wolter Design in Schweden, die in ihrem Atelier lebensgroße prähistorische Tiermodelle für Museen, Freizeitparks und Ausstellungen anfertigte. Die einzelnen Modelle wurden in Handarbeit gefertigt und mussten ihrer Größe wegen in Einzelteile zerlegt werden, um sie dann nach ihrem Transport in Münchehagen wieder zusammenzufügen. Des-

Dinosaur Park

The many transformations of the village of Münchehagen led to an extraordinary event a few years ago and brought the village fame far beyond the district and state borders. In 1980, stonemasons discovered strange traces in the quarry of the Ferdinand Wesling company, which is still being quarried today. It was quickly confirmed by scientists: They were the footprints of a dinosaur! That was a sensation! After all, there were not many places in the world that could present such a find. Thus began the history of the dinosaur park. The local newspaper *Die Harke* ran a report on 15.09.1990 with the headline "Münchehagen is teeming with dinosaurs: 150 prehistoric animals are being set up for the park." After the sensational discovery in 1980, the operator of the quarry, Ferdinand Wesling, contacted the local authorities, Loccum Monastery as the owner of the land and the state of Lower Saxony in order to make these unique finds accessible to the public. In order to give later visitors an idea of the size of the prehistoric animals that had left the footprints in the rock, the plan was to set up these prehistoric giants in their original size. It was the company Bernd Wolter Design in Sweden that produced life-size prehistoric animal models for museums, theme parks and exhibitions in its studio. The individual mo-dels were made by hand and, due to their size, had to be dismantled into individual parts and then reassembled in Münchehagen after transportation. That's why, according to the local newspaper, Münchehagen was "teeming" with dinosaurs. Numerous buildings were erected on the site of the discovery, including a large hall that covered the entire trackway to protect it from

↖ Direkt auf dem nationalen Geotop „Saurierfährten" steht eine von den Funden inspirierte Szene von Langhals- und Raubsauriern.

↖ A scene of long-necked and predatory dinosaurs inspired by the finds stands directly on the national geotope "Saurierfährten".

↑ Über 300 Fußabdrücke riesiger Langhalsdinosaurier wurden bis heute auf dem Naturdenkmal im Zentrum des Dinosaurier-Parks gefunden.

↑ Over 300 footprints of giant long-necked dinosaurs have been found on the natural monument in the centre of the dinosaur park.

↑ Die Raubsaurierspuren heben sich durch drei Zehen an der Spitze des Abdrucks der Krallen deutlich von den anderen Spurenfunden ab.

↑ The predatory dinosaur tracks stand out from the other tracks found due to the three toes, at the tip of which the imprint of the claws is clearly visible.

↑ Im Aktionsbereich des Dinosaurier-Parks wird spielerisch an die Forschungsarbeit herangeführt.

↑ In the activity area of the dinosaur park, visitors are introduced to research work in a playful way.

halb „wimmelte" es, laut Lokalzeitung, in Münchehagen von Dinosauriern. Es fanden zahlreiche Baumaßnahmen auf dem Gelände des Fundortes statt, unter anderem wurde eine große Halle errichtet, die die gesamte Fährtenspur überdachte, um sie gegen Verwitterung zu schützen. Schließlich konnte im Juni 1992 das – mittlerweile – staatlich anerkannte Dinosaurier-Freilichtmuseum Münchehagen mit dem Naturdenkmal „Saurierfährten" eröffnet werden. Ein zweieinhalb Kilometer langer Rundweg führt die Besucherinnen und Besucher durch die verschiedenen Erdzeitalter mit entsprechenden Texttafeln und natürlich zur Begegnung mit den damals lebenden Dinosauriern und anderen Urtieren.

Heute ist der Dinosaurier-Park Münchehagen eine feste Instanz in der nationalen und internationalen Forschung. Der wissenschaftliche Sektor des Dinosaurier-Parks beschränkt sich allerdings längst nicht mehr ausschließlich auf die vor Ort gefundenen Dinosaurierspuren. Diese werden zwar nach wie vor aktiv untersucht und es finden sogar nach wie vor regelmäßige Grabungen unter anderem in Kooperation mit lokalen Schulen statt, dennoch ist dies nur eines der Forschungsfelder, in denen der Park aktiv ist.

Auch eiszeitliche Funde aus der Weserregion werden im Park präpariert und erforscht. Vor einigen Jahren konnte eine große Sammlung aus privater Hand übernommen werden. Diese zählt durch ihre hohe Diversität zu den umfassendsten der Welt und zeigt eine enorme Bandbreite der Tiere, die vor 115.000 Jahren bis 11.000 Jahren hier bei uns lebten.

Unter dem Titel „Jurassic Harz" werden am Nordharzrand seit 2002 aktiv Fossilien durch das Dinopark-Team in Koope-

weathering. Finally, in June 1992, the Münchehagen Dinosaur Open-Air Museum, now recognized by the state, was opened with the "Dinosaur Tracks" natural monument. A 2.5-kilometer circular trail leads visitors through the different geological eras with corresponding text panels and, of course, an encounter with the dinosaurs and other prehistoric animals that lived at that time.

Today, the Münchehagen Dinosaur Park is an established institution in national and international research. However, the scientific sector of the Dinosaur Park is no longer limited to the dinosaur tracks found on site. Although these are still being actively investigated and regular excavations are still taking place, including in cooperation with local schools, this is only one of the fields of research in which the park is active.

Ice Age finds from the Weser region are also prepared and researched in the park. A few years ago, a large collection was acquired from a private collection.

Due to its high diversity, it is one of the most comprehensive in the world and shows an enormous range of animals that lived here between 115,000 and 11,000 years ago.

Under the title "Jurassic Harz", fossils have been actively excavated by the Dinopark team in cooperation with the Hannover State Museum and the University of Bonn on the northern edge of the Harz since 2002. In addition to the oldest mammals in Germany, numerous prehistoric crocodiles and turtles, the project has also unearthed a very special dinosaur. *Europasaurus holgeri*, a dwarfed long-necked dinosaur species that has so far only been found in a single quarry here in Lower Saxony. To date, 22 animals of this species have been found,

↑ Im Präparationslabor des Dinosaurier-Parks werden unter anderem über 240 Millionen Jahre alte Knochen von Dinosauriern wissenschaftlich untersucht und gesäubert.

↑ In the Dinosaur Park's taxidermy laboratory, dinosaur bones over 240 million years old are scientifically examined and cleaned.

↑ Auch die Forschungsgeschichte wird im Park interaktiv dargestellt, wie hier die Zeit des Goldrauschs im Yukon.

↑ The history of exploration is also presented interactively in the park, such as the time of the gold rush in the Yukon.

↑ Bei Sonderveranstaltungen, wie den „Jurassic Days", sind auch „echte" Dinosaurier zu sehen.

↑ At special events, such as the "Jurassic Days", "real" dinosaurs can also be seen.

↑ Edutainment nennt sich das einmalige Konzept des Dinoparks, in dem jüngste Erkenntnisse aus der Forschung spielerisch vermittelt werden.

↑ Edutainment is the name of Dinopark's unique concept, in which the latest findings from research are communicated in a playful way.

↑ In einer großen Sonderausstellung werden eiszeitliche Fossilien gezeigt.

↑ Ice-age fossils are on display in a large special exhibition.

ration mit dem Landesmuseum Hannover und der Universität Bonn ausgegraben. Das Projekt hat neben den ältesten Säugetieren Deutschlands, zahlreichen prähistorischen Krokodilen und Schildkröten auch einen ganz besonderen Dinosaurier zutage gefördert. *Europasaurus holgeri*, eine verzwergte Langhalssaurierart, die bisher ausschließlich in einem einzigen Steinbruch hier in Niedersachsen gefunden wurde. Bis heute wurden 22 Tiere dieser Art gefunden, darunter alle Altersstadien vom Schlüpfling bis zum ausgewachsenen Tier. *Europasaurus* gehört heute zu den am besten untersuchten Dinosauriern der Welt.

Das jüngste Projekt sind „Emil & Emily", zwei 240 Millionen Jahre alte *Plateosaurier*, die in der Schweiz gefunden wurden. Die Fossilien wurden in großen Steinblöcken geborgen und werden aktuell im Präparationslabor des Dinoparks aus dem Gestein herausgearbeitet. Anschließend werden die Knochen

including all age stages from hatchlings to adults. *Europasaurus* is now one of the best-studied dinosaurs in the world.

The most recent project is "Emil & Emily", two 240-million-year-old *plateosaurs* found in Switzerland. The fossils were recovered in large blocks of stone and are currently being worked out of the rock in the Dinopark's preparation laboratory. The bones are then stabilized and digitized using high-resolution, high-tech 3D scanners. This step enables the researchers to share the data directly with cooperation partners all over the world and examine the fossils together. Visitors to the park can observe and experience all these processes live.

The new findings naturally also have an influence on the presentation of the models in the park. Year after year, work is carried out to improve and expand the open-air museum and new figures are constantly being added. One dinosaur, the

↑ *Spinosaurus aegyptiacus* – einer der größten, aber auch kontroversesten Raubsaurier der Welt lauert am Waldrand.

↑ *Spinosaurus aegyptiacus* – one of the largest but also most controversial predatory dinosaurs in the world lurks at the edge of the forest

stabilisiert und mit hochauflösenden Hightech-3-D-Scannern digitalisiert. Dieser Schritt ermöglicht es den Forschenden, die Daten direkt mit Kooperationspartnern auf der ganzen Welt zu teilen und gemeinsam die Fossilien zu untersuchen. All diese Prozesse können die Besucherinnen und Besucher des Parks live beobachten und miterleben. Die neuen Erkenntnisse haben natürlich auch Einfluss auf die Darstellung der Modelle im Park. Jahr für Jahr wird an der Verbesserung und Erweiterung des Freilichtmuseums gearbeitet und fortwährend werden ebenfalls neue Figuren aufgestellt. Ein Dinosaurier, der 45 m lange *Seismosaurus*, musste per Hubschrauber eingeflogen werden. Die gesamte Anlage mit über 300 versteinerten Dinosaurierspuren und inzwischen ebenso vielen lebensechten Dinosaurier-Rekonstruktionen und anderen Urzeittieren in Originalgröße hat sich zu Europas größtem Dinosaurier-Freilichtmuseum entwickelt. Jüngst wurde das Forschercamp eröffnet, in dem die Museumspädagoginnen und Museumspädagogen des Parks interessierten Besuchenden in Talkrunden die Forschungsarbeiten der Dinopark-Teams

45-metre-long *Seismosaurus*, had to be flown in by helicopter. The entire complex with over 300 fossilized dinosaur tracks and just as many lifelike dinosaur reconstructions and other prehistoric animals in original size has developed into Europe's largest open-air dinosaur museum. The research camp was recently opened, where the park's museum educators present and discuss the research work of the Dinopark teams to interested visitors in talks. A visit to the Dinopark is part of the standard program for school classes from the surrounding schools. But the constantly growing number of visitors also shows that interest in dinosaurs and their history is not waning. The fame that Münchehagen has gained with this park is reflected in the many road signs in the surrounding area. Apparently, the Dinopark is so popular that our former German Chancellor Angela Merkel also paid a visit to the park, along with other high-ranking ministers. So the history of Münchehagen did not begin with the settlement of the Loccum monks, but much, much earlier. It was not humans, but the dinosaur *Iguanodon*, for example, which left its mark here in Münche-

↑ Auch vom großen *Iguanodon* wurden Spuren in der Region gefunden. ↑ Traces of the large *Iguanodon* have also been found in the region.

präsentieren und diese diskutieren. Für die Schulklassen der umliegenden Schulen gehört ein Besuch des Dinoparks zum Standardprogramm. Aber auch die stetig wachsenden Besucherinnen- und Besucherzahlen zeigen, dass das Interesse an Dinosauriern und deren Geschichte nicht nachlässt. Die Berühmtheit, die Münchehagen mit diesem Park erlangt hat, zeigt sich an den vielfältigen Hinweisschildern in der näheren und weiteren Umgebung. Offensichtlich ist der Dinopark so populär, dass, neben anderen hochrangigen Ministerinnen und Ministern, auch unsere ehemalige Bundeskanzlerin Angela Merkel dem Park einen Besuch abstattete. Die Geschichte Münchehagens begann also nicht erst mit der Siedlung der Loccumer Mönche, sondern schon viel, viel früher. Es waren keine Menschen, sondern zum Beispiel der Dinosaurier *Iguanodon*, der vor 139 Millionen Jahren hier in Münchehagen seine Spuren hinterließ. Möge die Strahlkraft dieses touristischen Highlights dem Ort und der gesamten Region erhalten bleiben!

hagen 139 million years ago. May the charisma of this tourist highlight be preserved for the town and the entire region!

S. 206–207 Im Nebel des frühen Morgens lauert ein *Deinonychus* dem deutlich größeren *Centrosaurus* auf.

P. 206–207 In the early morning mist, a *Deinonychus* lies in wait for the much larger *Centrosaurus*.

 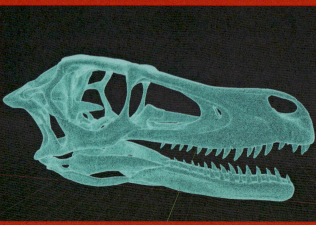

← Mit Hightech-Scannern werden die unbezahlbaren Fossilien schonend erfasst und digitalisiert.

← The priceless fossils are carefully recorded and digitized using high-tech scanners.

▶ **Der Dinopark** ist international stark vernetzt. Der Schwesterpark in Lourinha, Portugal befindet sich ebenfalls auf einer Originalfundstelle.
▶ **Mittels Volontariats- und Praktikumsangeboten** für Auszubildende und Studierende fördert der Dinosaurier-Park Münchehagen aktiv den Forschungsnachwuchs.
▶ **Zu den festen Kooperationspartnern** aus dem Forschungsbereich gehören heute die Universitäten Bonn, Greifswald, Hannover sowie die Museen Braunschweig, Münster, Hannover und weitere in Deutschland sowie einige internationale Museumspartner.
▶ **Der Dinopark** gründete zu Beginn der 2000er Jahre einen eigenen Förderverein für die regionale Paläontologie. Hochleistungsrechner und moderne 3-D-Scanner ermöglichen es, die Fossilien in sehr kurzer Zeit vollständig zu digitalisieren und sie so Wissenschaftlerinnen und Wissenschaftlern auf der ganzen Welt zugänglich zu machen.

▶ The Dinopark has a strong international network. The sister park in Lourinha, Portugal is also located on an original site.
▶ Dinosaur Park Münchehagen actively promotes the next generation of researchers by offering traineeships and internships for apprentices and students.
▶ Permanent cooperation partners in the field of research today include the universities of Bonn, Greifswald and Hannover, as well as the museums of Braunschweig, Münster, Hannover and others in Germany, and a number of international museum partners.
▶ At the beginning of the 2000s, Dinopark founded its own support association for regional palaeontology.
High-performance computers and modern 3D scanners make it possible to completely digitize the fossils in a very short time and thus make them accessible to scientists all over the world.

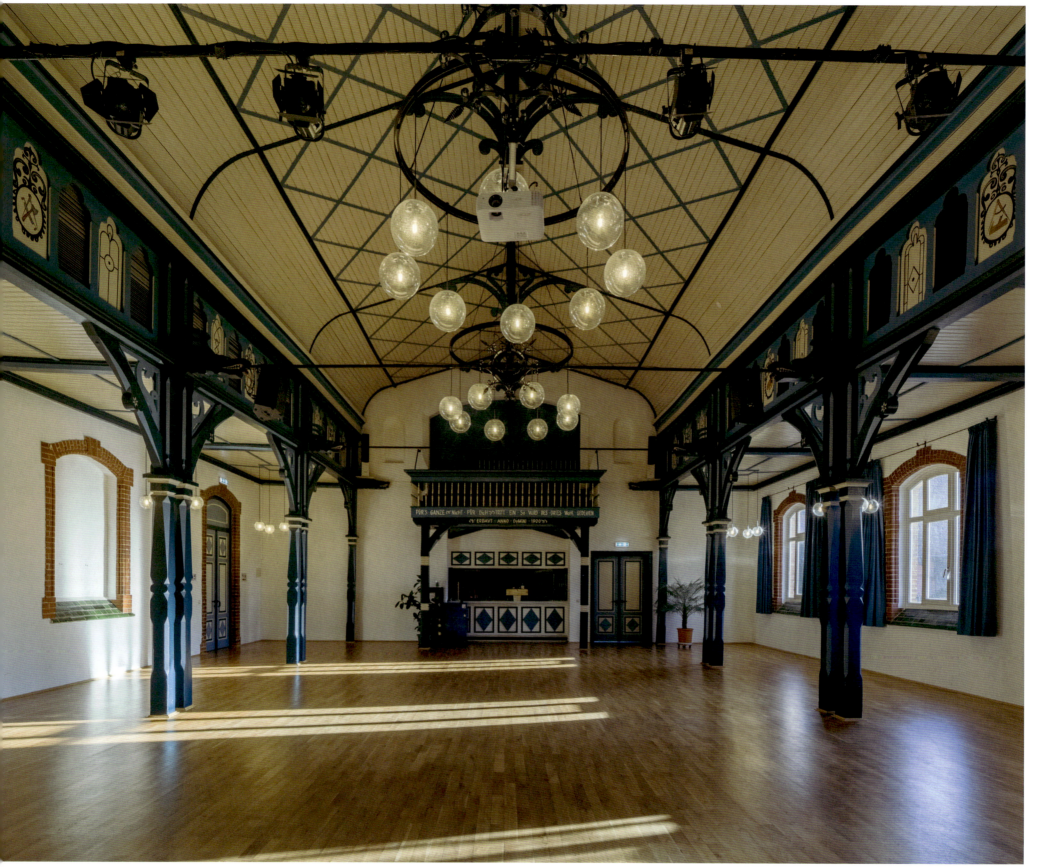

↑ Die wunderbaren Schnitzereien links und rechts oben im „Rathskellersaal", die verschiedene Handwerksberufe darstellen, zeugen von der Vergangenheit des Gebäudes als Bauschule.

↑ The wonderful carvings at the top left and right of the "Rathskeller hall", which depict various trades, bear witness to the building's past as a construction school.

Rehburg-Loccum

Heinrich K.-M. Hecht

Rehe und eine Burg habe ich während meiner Besuche in Rehburg vergeblich gesucht. „Reheburgk" hieß tatsächlich eine alte Burg, die bereits vorhanden war, als dem Ort 1648 die Stadtrechte verliehen wurden. Lange nannte man den Ort „Rehborgh". Die Stadt gibt es noch, die Burg schon lange nicht mehr – bis auf einen kleinen alten Gewölbekeller, der sich im 1754 erbauten Rathaus der Stadt befindet. Immerhin gab es nahe Rehburg in frühen Zeiten zumindest eine weitere Burg und eine Siedlung, aus der eine recht bekannte Adelsfamilie hervorging.

Im Frühmittelalter gab es im Westen die Ringwallanlage Düsselburg – Reste davon sind noch heute zu sehen, und im Süden lag im Mittelalter auf einem Hügel namens Haarberg die Siedlung Munichehausen, der Stammsitz des Geschlechts der Münchhausens, bis die bekannte Familie nach Brokeloh umzog, weil ihre Siedlung wahrscheinlich während der Hildesheimer Stiftsfehde zu Anfang des 16. Jahrhunderts zerstört wurde.

Die meisten Aufenthalte führten mich – offen gesagt – nicht nach Rehburg, sondern durch Rehburg. Egal ob ich zum Kloster Loccum, nach Mardorf oder Schneeren fuhr, jedes Mal ging es durch Rehburg hindurch. Was mir am ehesten auffiel, waren der kürzlich neugestaltete Kreisverkehr mit seinen teils wunderbaren Gebäuden drum herum, die zahlreichen Störche, die sogar auf der Polizeistation ihr Nest hatten, das Werk einer Milchfabrik und natürlich die Villa des Schriftstellers Ernst Jünger, die 1901 von dem Architekten und ehemaligen

I searched in vain for deer and a castle during my visits to Rehburg. "Reheburgk" was indeed the name of an old castle that already existed when the town was granted its town charter in 1648. For a long time the place was called "Rehborgh". The town still exists, but the castle has long since disappeared – apart from a small old vaulted cellar in the town hall, which was built in 1754. Nevertheless, there was at least one other castle and a settlement near Rehburg in early times, from which a fairly well-known noble family emerged.

In the early Middle Ages, there was the Düsselburg, a hill fort with circular rampart, in the west – remains of which can still be seen today – and in the south, on a hill called Haarberg, there was the settlement of Munichehausen, the ancestral seat of the Münchhausen family, until the famous family moved to Brokeloh because their settlement was probably destroyed during the Hildesheim Diocesan Feud at the beginning of the 16th century.

To be honest, most of my journeys did not take me to Rehburg, but through Rehburg. Whether I was travelling to Loccum Monastery, Mardorf or Schneeren, I passed through Rehburg every time. The things that most caught my eye were the recently redesigned roundabout with some wonderful buildings around it, the numerous storks that even had their nest on the police station, the factory of a dairy company and, of course, the villa of the writer Ernst Jünger, which was designed in 1901 by the architect and former mayor of Rehburg, Ernst Meßwarb. The enterprising Ernst and his father Wil-

↑ Schöner als mit dieser Baumallee kann man kaum empfangen werden, zumindest wenn man von Loccum aus kommt.
↑ Few places can welcome someone as beautifully as with this avenue of trees, at least if you come from Loccum.

↑ Der Steinhuder Meerbach kann theoretisch mit einem kleinen Paddelboot oder ähnlichem Gefährt vom Steinhuder Meer aus bis zur Weser befahren werden.
↑ In theory, the Steinhuder Meerbach can be navigated from Lake Steinhuder Meer to the Weser River using a small paddleboat or similar watercraft.

Bürgermeister von Rehburg, Ernst Meßwarb entworfen wurde. Von dem umtriebigen Sohn Ernst und seinem Vater Wilhelm, die übrigens beide Bürgermeister und Architekten waren, stammen unter anderem auch der Uhr- und Feuerwehrturm und die Städtische Bauschule mit „Rathskeller" in Rehburg. Im „Rathskeller" zeugen noch die hervorragend in Holz geschnitzten Zunftzeichen an der Galerie des 1900 entstandenen Raumes von der Vergangenheit der Bauschule.

Wer vom Kloster in Loccum in Richtung Rehburg fährt, dem fällt zuerst die sehr schöne Baumallee auf, die ihn direkt bis in den Ort begleitet. Auf dem Weg nach Mardorf liegt gleich links das Benelli-Museum. Nichts für Naturbegeisterte, es sei denn, sie wären auf einem Motorrad unterwegs, aber ich erinnere mich bei dem Namen Benelli sofort an das erste serienmäßige Sechszylinder-Motorrad – Benelli 750 Sei, das mich in meiner Jugend begeisterte.

Wer sich für das Steinhuder Meer und den Naturpark im Detail interessiert, stellt ferner fest, dass der Steinhuder Meerbach direkt durch Rehburg fließt. Theoretisch könnte man mit einem Kanu oder Paddelboot vom Steinhuder Meer aus bis in die Weser gelangen und würde durch malerische Landschaften kommen. Aber dann wäre man nicht mehr in Rehburg – was ja schade wäre.

helm, who were both mayors and architects, also designed the clock and fire station tower and the municipal building school with "Raths-Keller" in Rehburg. In the "Raths-Keller", the excellently carved wooden guild signs on the gallery of the room built in 1900 still bear witness to the building school's past.

If you drive from the monastery in Loccum towards Rehburg, the first thing you will notice is the beautiful avenue of trees that accompanies you right into the village. On the way to Mardorf, the Benelli Museum is immediately on the left. Not a venue for nature lovers, unless they are nature lovers travelling on a motorbike, but the name Benelli immediately reminds me of the first standard six-cylinder motorbike, the Benelli 750 Sei, which inspired me in my youth.

Anyone interested in Lake Steinhuder Meer and the nature park in detail will also notice that the Steinhuder Meerbach flows directly through Rehburg. Theoretically, you could take a canoe or paddle boat from Lake Steinhuder Meer to the Weser River and would pass through picturesque landscapes. But then you would no longer be in Rehburg – and that would be a shame.

↖←↓ Der „Rathskeller" war einmal eine Bauschule, die Polizeistation eine Gemeindeschule – nur die Villa von Schriftsteller Ernst Jünger war und ist eine Villa. Eines aber haben alle drei Gebäude gemeinsam: den Architekten Ernst Meßwarb.

↖←↓ The "Raths-Keller" was once a construction school, the police station a community school – only the villa of writer Ernst Jünger was and is a villa. But all three buildings have one thing in common: the architect Ernst Meßwarb.

↑ Die St.-Martini-Kirche, mit einem Taufstein, der älter als die Kirche selbst ist.

↑ St Martin's Church, with a baptismal font that is older than the church itself.

St. Martini Kirche
St Martin's Church

Peter Zenker

An der Stelle, wo heute die Kirche St. Martini am Stadtplatz Rehburgs steht, gab es zuvor einen Kirchenbau aus Holz aus der Mitte des 16. Jahrhunderts, der an der Ostseite eines ehemaligen Wachturmes errichtet worden war.

Dieser Wehrturm auf quadratischem Grundriss bekam 1585 seine elegante schlanke Spitze aufgesetzt und ist bis heute noch als Kirchturm erhalten. 1748, 100 Jahre nach dem Dreißigjährigen Krieg, entstand wahrscheinlich unter Verwendung der alten Fundamente das heute erhaltene Kirchenschiff aus Bruchsteinmauerwerk mit dem geräumigen Rechtecksaal unter dem leicht abgewalmten Dach. Flachbogige Sprossenfenster bestimmen das ruhige Erscheinungsbild aller Fassaden. Die Decke des Innenraumes ist als verputztes Spiegelgewölbe (Gewölbe mit flacher Decke in der Mitte) ausgeführt, unter dem auf leicht geschwungenem Grundriss ein säulenflankierter Rokokoaltar steht. Über dem Altar, auf einer fast ringsum verlaufenden Holzempore mit Sängerbühne, befindet sich die Orgel mit ihrem rankengeschmückten, kastenförmigen Prospekt.

On the site where St Martin's Church now stands on Rehburg's town square, there was previously a wooden church building from the mid-16th century, which was erected on the east side of a former watchtower.

This square-based defence tower was given its elegantly slender spire in 1585 and is still preserved as a church tower today. In 1748, one hundred years after the Thirty Years' War, the nave, which has survived to this day, was probably built using the old foundations in quarrystone masonry with its spacious rectangular hall under a slightly hipped roof. Flat-arched lattice windows characterise the calm appearance of all the facades. The ceiling of the interior is designed as a plastered mirror vault (vault with a flat ceiling in the centre), under which stands a rococo altar flanked by columns on a slightly curved floor plan. Above the altar, on a wooden gallery with a choir loft that runs almost all the way around, is the organ with its box-shaped façade adorned with ornamental vines.

Next to the altar on one side is the Gothic baptismal font with tracery decoration from the 12th century, which was redisco-

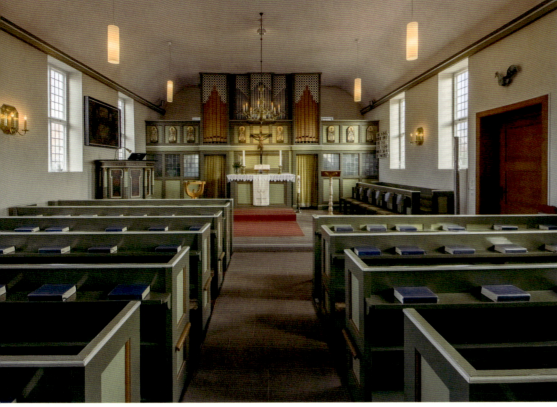

↑ Blick vom Eingang in Richtung Altar.
↑ View from the entrance towards the altar.

↑ Dieses Altarbild war lange Zeit verschwunden und durch ein anderes ersetzt worden, was nun entgegengesetzt über der Empore hängt. Erst vor Kurzem wurde das ursprüngliche Bild aufgefunden und wieder an seinen richtigen Platz gebracht.
↑ This altarpiece had been missing for a long time and was replaced by another one, which now hangs in the opposite direction above the gallery. Recently, the original painting was rediscovered and restored to its rightful place.

← Der Taufstein, um den sich Legenden ranken.
← The baptismal font, which is the subject of several legends.

Neben dem Altar steht auf der einen Seite der 1960 wiederentdeckte gotische Taufstein mit Maßwerkdekorverzierung aus dem 12. Jahrhundert. Dieser, so sagt die Legende, ist wohl vom Geschlecht der von Münchhausens gestiftet worden, nachdem sie ihre Siedlung auf dem Haarberg, zwischen Rehburg und Winzlar gelegen, nach einer Wüstung des Ortes verlassen hatten. Auf der anderen Seite vom Altar befindet sich die Kanzel, deren Brüstungen mit Evangelistenbildern geschmückt sind, laut Inschrift 1674/75 datierend. Ein expressives, barockes Kruzifix bestimmt die Südwand. Mit der Friederikenkapelle im herrlichen Buchenwald auf dem Brunnenberg von Bad Rehburg und der St.-Martini-Kirche ist die Gemeinde mit zwei Gotteshäusern gesegnet, in denen ein aktives Gemeindeleben stattfindet.

vered in 1960. According to legend, this was probably donated by the von Münchhausen family after they abandoned their settlement on the Haarberg, located between Rehburg and Winzlar, following the desolation of the village. On the other side of the altar is the pulpit, the parapets of which are decorated with images of the Evangelists, dated 1674/75 according to the inscription. An expressive, baroque crucifix dominates the south wall. With the Friederike Chapel in the beautiful beech forest on the Brunnenberg in Bad Rehburg and the St Martin's Church, the parish is blessed with two places of worship in which an active parish life takes place.

↑ Die historische Wandelhalle, die heute ein gern besuchter Veranstaltungsort ist und die Tourist-Information der Stadt Rehburg-Loccum beherbergt.

↑ The historic Wandelhalle, the former spa town's promenade hall, which is now a popular venue for events and houses the tourist information centre of the town of Rehburg-Loccum.

Bad Rehburg

Heinrich K.-M. Hecht

Promenieren in der Epoche der Romantik

Der Bruder vom König, Adolphos Friedrich, Herzog von Cambridge, war der am häufigsten in Bad Rehburg weilende prominente Gast aus dem hannoverschen Welfenhaus. Das verwundert nicht, denn einst als Rehburger Brunnen gegründet, wurde Bad Rehburg rasch zu einem staatlichen Kurort. Es war 1752 mit der Proclama des hannoverschen Königs Georg II. der Beginn einer großartigen Entwicklung, die mit dem Bau eines Bade- und Gästehauses einherging. Schon ein Jahr später konnte das Badehaus mit seinen vier Bädern und Kabinetten genutzt werden. Leider existiert das Gebäude heute nicht mehr. Ein neues Badehaus wurde von 1779 bis 1786 errichtet und besteht heute noch. Einer der Räume, die sogenannte Königinnenzelle, enthält an Italien erinnernde Fliesen mit spätbarocken und frühklassizistischen Motiven und Ornamenten, und wirkt in seinem Gesamtbild sehr romantisch. Erst 1978 hat man die Fliesen wiederentdeckt, nachdem darüberliegende Tapeten entfernt wurden. Im 19. Jahrhundert entstand die Säulenhalle, die – wenn auch architektonisch verändert – den Ort heute noch, samt kleiner davorstehender Fontäne, verschönert.

Die Friederikenkapelle, etwas außerhalb des Ortskerns als Waldkapelle gelegen, wurde vom König Ernst August II. von Hannover gestiftet und deren Errichtung 1842 mit einer festlichen Einweihung gefeiert. Leider konnte die Königin Friederike, die zumindest ab und an in Bad Rehburg weilte, diesen

Promenading in the era of Romanticism

The king's brother, Adolphus Frederick, Duke of Cambridge, was the most frequent prominent guest from the Hanoverian Guelph dynasty in Bad Rehburg. This is not surprising, as Bad Rehburg was once founded as the Rehburg Fountain and quickly became a state health resort. In 1752, the proclamation of the Hanoverian King George II marked the beginning of a great development, which was accompanied by the construction of a bathhouse and guest house. Just one year later, the bathhouse with its four baths and cabinets was ready for use. Unfortunately, the building no longer exists today. A new bathhouse was built between 1779 and 1786 and still exists. One of the rooms, the so-called Queen's Cell, contains tiles reminiscent of Italy with late baroque and early classicist motifs and ornamentation, and its overall appearance is very romantic. The tiles were only rediscovered in 1978 after the wallpaper above them was removed. In the 19th century, the portico was built, which – although architecturally altered – still embellishes the place today, along with the small fountain in front of it.

The Friederike Chapel, located just outside the town centre as a forest chapel, was donated by King Ernst August II of Hannover and its construction was celebrated with a festive inauguration in 1842. Unfortunately, Queen Friederike, who at least occasionally stayed in Bad Rehburg, did not live to see this moment, as she had died a year earlier.

← Das ursprüngliche Badehaus beinhaltet historische Baderäume und im Obergeschoss Platz für wechselnde Ausstellungen, wo früher die herrschaftlichen Aufenthaltsräume waren.
← The original bathhouse contains historic bathing rooms and space for temporary exhibitions on the upper floor, where the stately lounges used to be.

↑ Porträt der Königin Friederike von Hannover, die ab und an in Bad Rehburg weilte.
↑ Portrait of Queen Friederike of Hannover, who stayed in Bad Rehburg from time to time.

↑ So gingen zu früheren Zeiten die Menschen aus dem Adel baden.
↑ This is how people from the nobility used to go bathing.

↑ Königinnenzelle nennt man diesen Raum, der mit Fliesen ausgestattet wurde, die man erst in den 1970er Jahren wiederentdeckte und freilegte.
↑ This room is called the Queen's Cell and was furnished with tiles that were only rediscovered and uncovered in the 1970s.

Moment nicht mehr erleben, denn sie verstarb bereits ein Jahr zuvor.

Der Ort Bad Rehburg, gerne auch Madeira des Nordens genannt, liegt reizvoll auf der Höhe der Rehburger Berge und bietet auch außerhalb seiner Historie so allerlei zu entdecken. Wanderungen, zum Beispiel zum Wilhelmsturm, der 1848 vom Fürsten Georg Wilhelm zu Schaumburg-Lippe als Turm für die Landvermessung errichtet wurde und an seinen Vater, Graf Wilhelm, erinnern sollte, bieten bei entsprechendem Wetter einen hervorragenden Rundumblick in das Schaumburger Land.

Seit fast 50 Jahren gibt es die Deutsche Märchenstraße und seit 2019 gehört Bad Rehburg mit seinem Brüder-Grimm-Märchenweg dazu. Auf neunzehn Stationen, entlang der historischen Promenaden, lässt sich sowohl das Deutsche Märchen als auch die wunderbare Landschaft in und um Rehburg erkunden.

The town of Bad Rehburg, also known as the Madeira of the North, is charmingly situated on the heights of the Rehburg Hills and offers all sorts of things to discover beyond its history. Hikes, for example to the Wilhelmsturm, which was built in 1848 by Georg Wilhelm, Prince of Schaumburg-Lippe as a tower for land surveying and was intended to commemorate his father, Count Wilhelm, offer an excellent panoramic view of the Schaumburg countryside in good weather.

The German Fairy Tale Route has been in existence for almost 50 years and Bad Rehburg has been part of it since 2019 with its Brothers Grimm Fairy Tale Trail. There are nineteen stations along the historic promenades where you can explore both German fairy tales and the wonderful landscape in and around Rehburg.

← Ein sehr schönes Ziel für eine kleine Wanderung von Bad Rehburg aus – der Wilhelmsturm.
← A very nice destination for a short hike from Bad Rehburg – the Wilhelmsturm.

← Die historische Wandelhalle noch im ursprünglichen Zustand mit den vor dem Gebäude liegenden Säulen.
← The historic Wandelhalle still in its original state with the columns in front of the building.

↑ So sieht der Bereich der kleinen Fontäne heute aus.
↑ This is what the small fountain area looks like today.

↑ Lange Zeit, vor allem im 18. und 19. Jahrhundert, ein Treffpunkt der höheren Gesellschaft aus Hannover.
↑ For a long time, especially in the 18th and 19th centuries, it was a meeting place for Hannover's high society.

↑ Eine Aufnahme zu Beginn des 20. Jahrhunderts: Die ehemalige Villa der königlichen Klosterheilanstalt existiert leider nicht mehr.
↑ A photo taken at the beginning of the 20th century: the former villa of the royal monastery sanatorium unfortunately no longer exists.

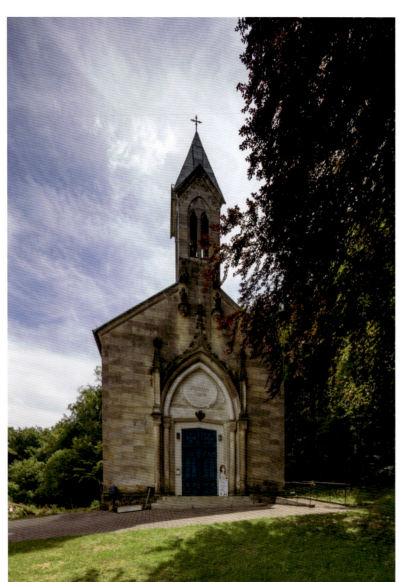

← Die Friederikenkapelle, ein Geschenk des Königshauses aus Hannover im 19. Jahrhundert.

← The Friederike Chapel, a gift from the Royal House of Hannover in the 19th century.

Friederikenkapelle
Friederike Chapel

Peter Zenker

Idyllisch am Waldrand in südlicher Lage der historischen Kuranlage Bad Rehburgs gelegen und im Jahre 1842 fertiggestellt. Mit steigender Bedeutung Bad Rehburgs und zunehmender Beliebtheit des Ortes durch den Kurbetrieb im 18. Jahrhundert wurde der Wunsch nach einem angemessenen Gotteshaus laut. Bis dato hatte es auch in Rehburg kein Gotteshaus gegeben.

Königin Friederike Karoline Sophie Alexandrine von Mecklenburg-Strelitz, die gemeinsam mit ihrem Mann Ernst August I. von Hannover in den Sommern regelmäßig in Bad Rehburg weilte, gab den Anstoß für den Bau der Kapelle. Die finanzielle Unterstützung war somit durch das Königshaus gesichert.

Idyllically situated on the edge of the forest to the south of Bad Rehburg's historic spa complex, the chapel was completed in 1842. With the growing importance of Bad Rehburg and the increasing popularity of the town as a spa resort in the 18th century, the need for a suitable place of worship became more and more apparent. Until then, there had been no place of worship in Rehburg either.

Queen Friederike Karoline Sophie Alexandrine of Mecklenburg-Strelitz, who regularly spent summers in Bad Rehburg with her husband Ernst August I von Hannover, provided the impetus for the construction of the chapel. Financial support was thus secured from the royal family.

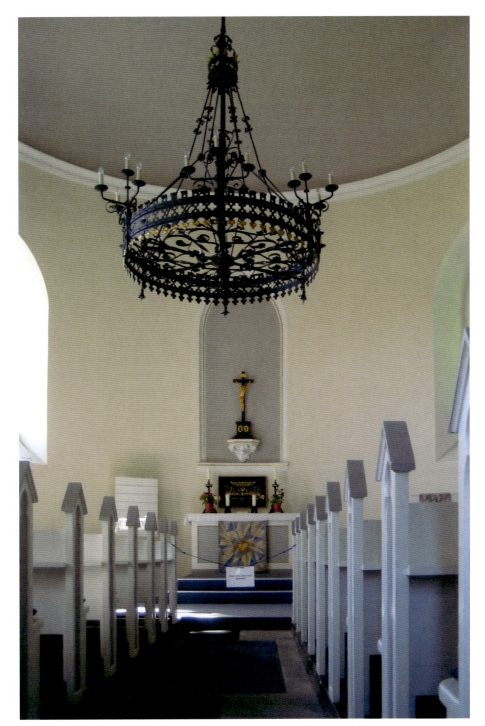

↑ Das Innere der Kapelle wird zurzeit saniert und ist nicht öffentlich zugänglich.
↑ The interior of the chapel is currently being renovated and is not open to the public.

Die ihr zu Ehren benannte Friederikenkapelle wurde nach einem Entwurf des in Rinteln geborenen Malers Georg Osterwald gebaut.

Die Architektur im neugotischen Stil mit dem tonnengewölbten Saalbau auf rechteckigem Grundriss und dem runden Chorschluss ist eher schlicht gehalten.

Nur die dem Ort zugewandte Eingangsfassade ist mit einem aufwendiger dekorierten, von Säulen flankierten und mit kleinen Kreuzblumen und einem Wimperg (giebelartige Bekrönung) geschmückten Portal versehen.

The Friederike Chapel, named in her honour, was built according to a design by the Rinteln-born painter Georg Osterwald.

The architecture in the neo-Gothic style with the barrel-vaulted hall building on a rectangular floor plan and the round choir end is rather simple.

Only the entrance façade facing the town has an elaborately decorated portal flanked by columns and adorned with small finials and a wimperg (gable-like crowning).

↑ Das Konventshaus der Klosteranlage präsentiert sich den Besuchenden schier endlos und bietet einen wunderbaren Kontrast zwischen dem aus Obernkirchener Sandstein bestehenden Sockel und dem darüberliegenden Fachwerk.

↑ The convent house of the monastery complex presents itself to the visitor as almost endless and offers a wonderful contrast between the Obernkirchen sandstone base and the half-timbering above.

Kloster Loccum

Loccum Monastery

Ralf Meister, Abt zu Kloster Loccum
Ralf Meister, abbot of the Loccum monastery

QUAM TERRIBILIS EST LOCUS ISTE

NON EST HIC ALIUD NISI DOMUS DEI EST ET PORTA COELI

VERE DOMINUS EST IN LOCO ISTO

GENES XXVIII

Wie heilig ist diese Stätte
Hier gibt es nichts außer dem Haus
Gottes und dem Tor des Himmels
Der Herr ist wirklich an diesem Ort

Genesis 28

How holy is this place
There is nothing here but the house of
God and the gate of heaven
The Lord really is in this place

Genesis 28

Ein Ort für die Ewigkeit

Auf halber Strecke zwischen dem Steinhuder Meer und der Weser liegt ein Ort der Ewigkeit, das Kloster Loccum, eine der am besten erhaltenen mittelalterlichen Klosteranlagen Deutschlands. „Porta patet, cor magis" – Die Tür steht offen, das Herz noch mehr. Das ist das zisterziensische Motto des Klosters. Zwölf Zisterziensermönche und ein Abt aus dem thüringischen Volkenroda machten sich auf den Weg Richtung Nordwesten, um im Jahr 1163 das Kloster Loccum zu gründen. Graf Wulbrand von Hallermund hatte im Dom zu Minden dem Zisterzienserorden die Stiftungsurkunde über ein Stück Land rund um die Burg Lucca ausgestellt. Von dieser Burg kann man noch heute eine Fluchtanhöhe im ausgedehnten Wald südlich von Loccum betreten. Dieser historische Marsch der Mönche ist heute zu einem Pilgerweg geworden. Er verbindet das Kloster Loccum mit Volkenroda und wird von vielen Menschen zur geistlichen Einkehr begangen.

Das Kloster Loccum, umringt von einer kilometerlangen, drei Meter hohen Steinmauer, war nicht eine abgeschlossene Welt, sondern durch alle Jahrhunderte eng verbunden mit den Menschen, die vor den Toren lebten und arbeiteten. Der große Forst musste genauso bewirtschaftet werden wie die Ländereien, eine Bibliothek aufgebaut und gepflegt und die vielen Gebäude unterhalten werden. Auch als das Kloster Ende des 16. Jahrhunderts evangelisch wurde, blieben die Mönche, feierten ihre Gebetszeiten und bewirtschafteten das Land.

A place for eternity

Halfway between the Lake Steinhuder Meer and the Weser River lies a place of eternity, the Loccum Monastery, one of the best-preserved medieval monasteries in Germany. "Porta patet, cor magis" – The door is open, the heart even more so. This is the Cistercian motto of the monastery. Twelve Cistercian monks and an abbot from Volkenroda in Thuringia made their way north-west to found Loccum Monastery in 1163. Count Wulbrand von Hallermund had issued a deed of foundation to the Cistercian order in Minden Cathedral for a piece of land around Lucca Castle. Today, you can still walk an escape route from this castle to a refuge hill in the extensive forest south of Loccum. This historic march of the monks has now become a pilgrimage route. It connects Loccum Monastery with Volkenroda and is walked by many people for spiritual contemplation.

Loccum Monastery, surrounded by a kilometre-long, three-metre-high stone wall, was not a closed-off world, but was closely connected to the people who lived and worked outside its gates throughout the centuries. The large forest had to be managed just like the agricultural estates, a library had to be established and maintained, and the many buildings had to be looked after. Even when the monastery became Protestant at the end of the 16th century, the monks remained, continuing to celebrate their prayer times and farm the land.

The piety that has characterised this place for centuries has

↑ Der Innenhof des Klosters mit Blick auf den Kreuzgang und Dachreiter wird gerne als Paradies bezeichnet.

↑ The inner courtyard of the monastery with a view of the cloister and ridge turret is often referred to as paradise.

Die Frömmigkeit, die diesen Ort jahrhundertelang geprägt hat, wurde von den evangelischen Erben weiter gepflegt. Wer einmal das Abendgebet mitfeiert, die Hora, die werktags von Montag bis Samstag um 18 Uhr in dieser Kirche gehalten wird, spürt etwas von der geistlichen Schönheit der klösterlichen Tradition. Das alte Stundengebet der Zisterziensermönche, der Gesang, das Gebet und die Stille klingen lange nach, wenn man den weiten Kirchenraum wieder verlässt. Seit fast neun Jahrhunderten, eine halbe Ewigkeit, klingen die biblischen Sätze, die Abendlieder und das „Verleih uns Frieden". Das Gehen im Kreuzgang des Klosters führt Besucherinnen und Besucher in einen Rhythmus, den vor uns schon viele erfahren haben. Im Refektorium, dem historischen Speisesaal, findet auf Einladung der Landeskirche Hannovers immer am 6. Januar der erste Neujahrsempfang in Niedersachsen statt; die politischen und gesellschaftlichen Vertretenden treffen sich an diesem spirituellen Ort, denn in aller menschlichen Kunst und unserer Fertigkeit, diese Gesellschaft zu gestalten, die Schöpfung zu bewahren und dem Frieden zu dienen, bleiben wir angewiesen auf den Segen Gottes. Das Kloster Loccum fügt uns ein in eine Zeit menschlicher Demut und tiefen Gottesglaubens.

been cultivated by the Protestant heirs. Anyone who attends the evening prayer, the Hora, which is held in this church on weekdays from Monday to Saturday at 6.00 pm, will feel something of the spiritual beauty of the monastic tradition. The old Liturgy of the Hours of the Cistercian monks, the singing, the prayer and the silence linger long after you leave the spacious church. For nearly nine centuries, a span of time that feels like an eternity, the biblical verses, evening hymns, and the prayer "Grant us peace" have resonated within these walls. Walking through the cloisters of the monastery leads visitors into a rhythm that many have experienced before us. The historic refectory, or dining hall, of the monastery is the setting for the first New Year's reception in Lower Saxony, held annually on January 6th at the invitation of the Evangelical Lutheran Church of Hannover; Political and social leaders gather in this spiritual space, acknowledging that in all our human endeavours – in shaping society, preserving creation, and serving peace – we remain dependent on God's blessing. Loccum Monastery connects us to a time of human humility and deep faith in God.

All visitors enter the monastery grounds in Loccum through an old heavy wooden gate, which is open day and night, and

↑ „Priors Garten" und die neue Bibliothek. Letztere passt trotz ihres modernen Erscheinungsbildes sehr gut zur gesamten Klosteranlage. Der Garten wurde ebenfalls neu angelegt und zählt zu den Lieblingsorten des Abts im Kloster.

↑ "Prior's Garden" and the new library. Despite its modern appearance, the latter fits in very well with the entire monastery complex. The garden was also redesigned and is one of the abbot's favourite places in the monastery.

Alle Besuchenden betreten das Klostergelände in Loccum durch eine alte schwere Holzpforte, die Tag und Nacht geöffnet ist, und schreiten durch einen lang gestreckten Torbogen am Torhaus vorüber. Auf diesem Weg senkt sich für einige Momente der Blick unter dem Gemäuer, das man durchschreitet. Und dann öffnet er sich wieder und nimmt die Weite des Klosterbezirks und die Größe der Stiftskirche wahr. Ein Domherr aus Hamburg schrieb vor mehr als 200 Jahren über seinen Besuch im Kloster Loccum: „Es ist Segen des Reisens, dich einer Gegend zu nähern, wo du die früh Verlornen wiederfindest, oder den Umarmungen derer entgegeneilst, die du bis dahin nur ungesehen liebtest. Diesen Segen gab uns das stille freundliche, gastfreie Kloster Loccum. Wiedersehen, geknüpfte neue Bande dauernder Freundschaft und der Vollgenuß der herrlichen Natur, bereiteten uns dort Tage, denen nur wenige im Leben gleichen."

Doch nicht nur die Tradition, sondern auch die Moderne prägt das Leben im Kloster. Das Kloster Loccum ist eine „selbstständige geistliche Körperschaft" in der Evangelisch-lutherischen Landeskirche Hannovers. Es unterhält Kontakte zum katholischen Orden der Zisterzienser. Als Abt leite ich zusammen mit dem Prior sowie einem Konvent von Männern walk through an elongated archway past the gatehouse. For a few moments along the way, your gaze lowers beneath the structure you are walking through. Then, emerging from the passageway, you are greeted by the vastness of the monastery grounds and the majesty of the collegiate church. More than 200 years ago, a canon from Hamburg wrote about his visit to Loccum Monastery: "It is the blessing of travelling to approach a place where you can find those you lost early, or rush towards the embrace of those you have only loved unseen until then. The quiet, friendly, hospitable Loccum Monastery gave us this blessing. Reunions, new bonds of lasting friendship and the full enjoyment of the marvellous nature provided us with days there that few in life can match."

But not only tradition, but also modernity characterises life in the monastery. Loccum Monastery is an "independent spiritual body" within the Evangelical Lutheran Church of Hannover. It maintains contact with the Catholic order of Cistercians. As abbot, I manage the fortunes of the monastery together with the prior and a convent of men and women. At the same time, the collegiate church is the church of the Loccum parish and has been home to the "Predigerseminar", the training centre for future pastors, for over 200 years. Young people spend

↑ Dieser wunderbare Gebetsleuchter steht im linken Seitenschiff der Stiftskirche.

↑ This marvellous prayer candelabra stands in the left aisle of the collegiate church.

und Frauen die Geschicke des Klosters. Zugleich ist die Stiftskirche die Kirche der Kirchengemeinde Loccum und beherbergt seit über 200 Jahren das „Predigerseminar", die Ausbildungsstätte für künftige Pastorinnen und Pastoren. Junge Menschen verbringen viele Wochen in dieser historischen Umgebung und dieses Kloster wird eine Heimat auf Zeit. Wer das Klostergelände besucht, begegnet ihnen und vielen anderen Gästen, die das Tagungshaus für Seminare nutzen. Pilgerinnen und Pilger finden Übernachtungsmöglichkeiten im Pilgerhaus, Gäste der angrenzenden Evangelischen Akademie flanieren in ihren Seminarpausen über das Gelände und Loccumerinnen und Loccumer spazieren durch den Klosterforst. Während der Sommermonate werden für Besuchende Führungen durch das Kloster Loccum angeboten. Der Mittelpunkt dieser Führungen ist die schlichte Kirche mit Triumpfkreuz, Marien- und Laienaltar, Reliquienschrein und der Seifert-Orgel. Auch die neue Bibliothek mit einem Bestand von 120.000 Exemplaren, darunter viele aus dem 15. und 16. Jahrhundert, ist ein Kulturschatz. „Portas patet, cor magis": Das Kloster Loccum ist ein offener, geistlicher Raum für alle Suchenden. Und in seinen Mauern wächst die Dankbarkeit für die Bewahrung, die über unserem Leben liegt. So wie der Theologe Jörg Zink schrieb:

> „Millionen Jahre waren, ehe es mich gab, Gott.
> Jahrmillionen werden vielleicht nach mir sein.
> Irgendwo in ihrer Mitte sind ein paar Sommer,
> in denen für mich Tag ist auf dieser Erde.
> Für diese Spanne Zeit danke ich dir.
> Kloster Loccum, ein Ort der Ewigkeit."

many weeks in these historic surroundings and this monastery becomes a temporary home. Anyone visiting the monastery grounds will meet them and many other guests who use the conference house for seminars. Pilgrims find overnight accommodation in the pilgrims' house, guests from the neighbouring Protestant Academy stroll through the grounds during their seminar breaks and Loccum residents stroll through the monastery forest. During the summer months, guided tours of Loccum Monastery are organised for visitors. The centrepiece of these tours is the simple church with its triumphal cross, Marian and lay altar, reliquary and Seifert organ. The new library with a collection of 120,000 books, including many from the 15th and 16th centuries, is also a cultural treasure. "Portas patet, cor magis": Loccum Monastery is an open, spiritual space for all seekers. And within its walls, gratitude grows for the protection that lies over our lives. As the theologian Jörg Zink wrote:

> "Millions of years were before I existed, God.
> Millions of years will perhaps be after me.
> Somewhere in their midst are a few summers
> in which it is daytime for me on this earth.
> I thank you for this span of time.
> Loccum Monastery, a place of eternity."

↑ Der Blick geht vom westlichen Teil der Stiftskirche aus auf das Taufbecken und das sehr detailreiche Tauffenster, das wohl Johannes den Täufer zeigt.

↑ The view from the western part of the collegiate church is of the baptismal font and the very detailed baptismal window, which probably shows St John the Baptist.

↑ Auf dem Foto ist nur ein Bereich des Kreuzgangs zu sehen, auf diesem Foto der östliche Teil.

↑ Only one part of the cloister, the eastern part, can be seen in this photo.

↑ Abt Ralf Meister im Kapitelsaal, dessen Decke von wunderschön verzierten Säulen abgestützt wird.

↑ Abbot Ralf Meister in the chapter house, the ceiling of which is supported by beautifully decorated columns.

↑ Im linken Teil des Fotos befindet sich die Stiftskirche mit gut zu erkennendem Dachreiter, rechts daneben die sehr schönen Bäume der Klosteranlage, die im Sommer unverzichtbar sind und Schatten spenden.

↑ On the left of the photo is the collegiate church with its clearly recognisable ridge turret, and to the right are the beautiful trees of the monastery grounds, which are indispensable during the summer, providing much-needed shade.

↑ Im Jahr 1913, vor Ausbruch des Ersten Weltkriegs, beehrte Kaiser Wilhelm mit einem Besuch das Kloster Loccum.

↑ In 1913, before the outbreak of the First World War, Kaiser Wilhelm honoured Loccum Monastery with a visit.

↑ Eine Ansicht aus dem Jahre 1892 vom Kloster Loccum mit dem davorliegenden Teich.

↑ A view from 1892 of Loccum Monastery with the pond in front of it.

S. 230–231 Das großzügige Innere der Stiftskirche mit der Seifert-Orgel auf der hinteren linken Seite und Blick auf den Altar. Im Vordergrund angeschnitten der Taufstein.

P. 230–231 The spacious interior of the collegiate church with the Seifert organ at the rear left and a view of the altar. The baptismal font is partially visible in the foreground.

← Die Ansicht auf die Klosteranlage von Osten aus, mit der Stiftskirche links. Im Vordergrund der ehemalige Kammerteich mit grasenden Rindern vor der Klostermauer.

← View of the monastery complex from the east with the collegiate church on the left. In the foreground is the former Kammerteich pond with grazing cattle in front of the monastery wall.

↑ Auf dem Weg nach Winzlar bietet sich einer der schönen Blicke in Richtung des Steinhuder Meeres.

↑ On the way to Winzlar, you can enjoy one of the lovely views looking out towards Lake Steinhuder Meer.

Winzlar

Thomas Brandt

Winzlar – Ein Kleinod aus dem 12. Jahrhundert

Die kleine beschauliche Ortschaft Winzlar liegt dort, wo vor etwa 10.000 Jahren noch das westliche Ufer des Steinhuder Meeres verlief. Heute liegt das Ufer des Sees etwa eineinhalb Kilometer weiter östlich – bedingt durch jahrtausendelange Verlandungsprozesse. Doch tatsächlich gehört auch heute noch ein gar nicht mal so kleines Stück des Seeufers, immerhin 375 m, zur Gemarkung Winzlar. Dieses liegt mitten im 2021 neu ausgewiesenen Naturschutzgebiet „Westufer Steinhuder Meer", welches das ehemalige Naturschutzgebiet Meerbruch ablöste, und zwar direkt nördlich des beliebten Beobachtungsturmes am Westufer.

Bereits 1196 wurde der hübsche Ort Winzlar urkundlich erwähnt. Zweifellos besiedelten aber auch schon lange zuvor Menschen die Gegend, wie Funde aus der vorchristlichen Zeit belegen. 1974 schloss sich die bis dahin eigenständige Gemeinde Winzlar mit Rehburg, Münchehagen, Bad Rehburg und Loccum zur Stadt Rehburg-Loccum zusammen. 1996, zum 800. Jubiläum Winzlars, schrieb Konrad Droste in seiner umfangreichen und lesenswerten Dorfchronik die lange Geschichte des Ortes auf. Heute leben etwa 1.000 Einwohnerinnen und Einwohner im Ort.

Winzlar – a gem from the 12th century

The small, tranquil village of Winzlar is located where the western shore of Lake Steinhuder Meer used to be around 10,000 years ago. Today, the shore of the lake lies around one and a half kilometres further east – due to thousands of years of sedimentation. But even today, a not-so-small section of the lake shore, 375 metres in length, still belongs to the district of Winzlar. This is located in the centre of the "Westufer Steinhuder Meer" nature reserve, which was newly designated in 2021 and replaced the former Meerbruch nature reserve, directly north of the popular observation tower on the western shore.

The pretty village of Winzlar was mentioned in documents as early as 1196. However, the area was undoubtedly inhabited long before that, as finds from pre-Christian times prove. In 1974, the previously independent municipality of Winzlar merged with Rehburg, Münchehagen, Bad Rehburg and Loccum to form the town of Rehburg-Loccum. In 1996, to mark Winzlar's 800th anniversary, Konrad Droste wrote down the long history of the village in his comprehensive and readable village chronicle. Today, around 1,000 inhabitants live in the village.

↑ Das Zuhause der ÖSSM in Winzlar mit einer detailreichen Ausstellung im Inneren.

↑ The home of the ÖSSM in Winzlar with a detailed exhibition inside.

Die Ökologische Schutzstation Steinhuder Meer (ÖSSM) in Winzlar

Im Jahr 1991 gründeten die örtlichen Naturschutzgruppen den Verein „Ökologische Schutzstation Steinhuder Meer", kurz „ÖSSM", um die Kräfte des außerbehördlichen Naturschutzes zu bündeln. Seit 1992 ist der Verein Eigentümer eines rund 160 Jahre alten Hofgebäudes, das weitgehend nach historischen und ökologischen Gesichtspunkten renoviert wurde. Es liegt an der Hagenburger Straße in Winzlar.

Hier arbeiten heute Forschende und Teilnehmende des Freiwilligen Ökologischen Jahres (FÖJ) und Bundesfreiwilligendienstes (BfD), Praktikantinnen und Praktikanten, Studierende sowie ehrenamtliche Naturschützerinnen und Naturschützer daran, auf wissenschaftlicher Basis den Naturschutz in der Region zu stärken. Der Verein übernimmt darüber hinaus für das Land Niedersachsen die wissenschaftliche Betreuung der Naturschutzgebiete, plant Pflege und Entwicklungsmaßnahmen und setzt diese mit verschiedenen Partnern, zum Beispiel mit den Landkreisen, den Umweltverbänden und dem Naturpark Steinhuder Meer, um. Außerdem bietet der Verein eine thematisch breite Palette naturkundlicher Führungen und Vorträge an, erstellt Informationsblätter und betreut eine Ausstellung im Stationsgebäude. Die ÖSSM ist außerdem als außerschulischer Lernstandort, als ein Regionales Umweltbildungszentrum (RUZ) anerkannt.

The Steinhuder Meer Ecological Conservation Station (ÖSSM) in Winzlar

In 1991, the local nature conservation groups founded the association "Ecological Protection Station Steinhuder Meer", or "ÖSSM" for short, in order to pool the forces of nongovernmental nature conservation. Since 1992, the association has been the owner of a 160-year-old farm building, which has been largely renovated according to historical and ecological criteria. It is located on Hagenburger Straße in Winzlar.

Scientists, participants in the Voluntary Ecological Year (FÖJ) and the Federal Voluntary Service (BfD), interns, students and volunteer conservationists are working here today to enhance nature conservation in the region on a scientific basis. The association also takes over the scientific management of the nature reserves for the state of Lower Saxony, plans maintenance and development measures, and implements these with various partners, e.g. with the district administrations, the environmental associations and the Lake Steinhude Nature Park. The association also offers a wide range of natural history tours and lectures, creates information sheets and maintains an exhibition in the station building. The ÖSSM is also recognised as an extracurricular learning location and as a Regional Environmental Education Centre (RUZ).

↑ Hier können sich die kleinen Tiere wohlfühlen: ein mit viel Liebe errichtetes Insektenhaus.

↑ Here, the small creatures can feel at home: an insect house constructed with great care and love.

↑ Angezüchtete Moose und Glockenheide mit der dahinter liegenden Geflügelvoliere.

↑ Cultivated mosses and bell heather with the poultry aviary behind them.

↑ Geweiht am 24. August im Jahre 1740, am Tag des Apostels Bartholomäus – die Fachwerkkapelle von Winzlar.

↑ Consecrated on 24 August 1740 on the day of St Bartholomew the Apostle – the half-timbered chapel of Winzlar.

Fachwerkkapelle
Half-timbered chapel

Peter Zenker

Die Fachwerkkapelle zu Winzlar ist wegen des Zeugnis- und Schauwertes für die Bau- und Kunstgeschichte – im Hinblick auf die beispielhafte Ausprägung einer dörflichen Fachwerkkapelle des 18. Jahrhunderts – von historischer Bedeutung. Dieser rechteckige Fachwerkbau mit kleinem Vorbau an der westlichen Giebelseite wurde 1740 erbaut und prägt trotz seiner Kleinheit das Straßenbild.

Das Satteldach der Kapelle ist nach Osten abgewalmt. Im Westen überragt das Dach ein vierseitiger, verschieferter Dachreiter mit Pyramidenhelm und kleinen Schallöffnungen, der mit Kugel und Kreuz bekrönt ist.

Die Ziegelausfachungen an der Westseite des Vorbaus aus sechs kreuzförmig angeordneten Gefachen sind verglast und das westliche Giebeldreieck mit Pfannen behängt. Hochrechteckige Fenster bestimmen die Längsseiten.

Der Kirchraum wird von einer flachen Decke mit seitlichen Vouten überspannt. Kleine Emporen befinden sich auf der Ost- und Westseite. In ihm steht ein schlichter, hölzerner Blockaltar sowie leicht erhöht die hölzerne Kanzel, deren

The half-timbered chapel in Winzlar is of historical importance due to its exemplary character as a village half-timbered chapel of the 18th century and its value as a testimony to and showcase for architectural and art history. This rectangular half-timbered building with a small extension on the western gable end was built in 1740 and has a defining impact on the streetscape despite its small size.

The gabled roof of the chapel is hipped to the east. To the west, the roof is surmounted by a four-sided, slated ridge turret with a pyramid helmet and small sound openings, which is crowned with a sphere and cross.

The brick infills on the west side of the extension, consisting of six cross-shaped compartments, are glazed and the western gable triangle is hung with pantiles. High rectangular windows characterise the long sides.

The church is spanned by a flat ceiling with lateral coving. Small galleries are located on the east and west sides. There is a simple, wooden block altar and a slightly raised wooden pulpit with ornamentally painted walls and a wooden baptis-

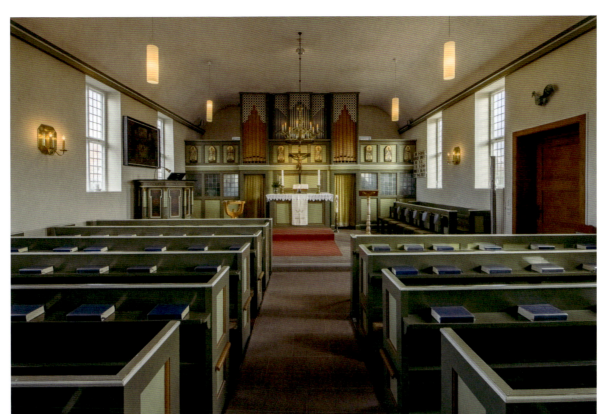

← In den 1960er Jahren erfuhr die Kapelle eine umfassende Sanierung mit neuen Bänken.

← In the 1960s, the chapel underwent extensive renovation with new pews.

← Ehemals hinter dem Altar befindlich, hängt dieses mit Bauernmalerei versehene Abendmahlsbild über der kleinen Kanzel.

← Formerly located behind the altar, this picture of the Last Supper, which features a naive, rustic-style painting style, hangs above the small pulpit.

Wandungen ornamental bemalt sind, und ein hölzerner Taufständer. An der Brüstung der Ostempore sieht man acht Gemälde mit Engelsdarstellungen. Zudem gibt es noch ein Gemälde mit Abendmahlsdarstellung in hübscher, barocker Bauernmalerei.

mal font. Eight paintings depicting angels can be seen on the parapet of the east gallery. There is also a painting depicting the Last Supper in a charming, Baroque folk art style.

↑ Der Aloys-Bunge-Platz mit seinen restaurierten Häusern ist der charmante Kern von Mardorf.

↑ The Aloys-Bunge-Platz with its restored houses is the charming centre of Mardorf.

Stuart Orme

Mardorf ein Ort mit vielen Facetten

Im Jahr 1997 zog unsere Familie, bestehend aus meinen Eltern Ron und Hilary, meinem Bruder David, seiner Frau Bianka und ihrem Sohn Liam sowie meiner Frau Yvonne und mir, nach Mardorf. Anfangs hatte ich große Bedenken, in einen Ort zu ziehen, der als eine regionale touristische Attraktion bekannt ist. Wollte ich wirklich die damit einhergehende Hektik in mein Leben lassen? Meine Heimat sollte doch ein Ort der Ruhe und der Besinnlichkeit sein. Ein Ort, an dem man sich wohlfühlt, am liebsten weit, weit weg vom stressigen Alltag. Könnte das gut gehen in Mardorf?

Die Gründe für den Umzug waren sowohl unsere Selbstständigkeit, da wir uns hier eine neue Existenz aufbauen wollten, als auch die Begeisterung für die traumhafte Gegend am Steinhuder Meer. Mardorf, direkt am See gelegen, bietet eine wunderschöne und ruhige Umgebung, in der wir unsere Kinder sicher aufwachsen lassen können. Mardorf kombiniert aktives Erleben, entspannte Erholung, unberührte Natur und kulinarische Leckerbissen auf eine Art und Weise, dass jeder selbst entscheiden kann, worauf man gerade Lust hat. Noch im Jahr des Umzugs gründeten wir unser Familienunternehmen, den Golf Park Steinhuder Meer. Die Golfanlage eröffnete erfolgreich und gewann im Laufe der Jahre immer mehr Mitglieder. Unser Erfolg beruhte auf unserem Engagement, unserer harten Arbeit, unserem englischen Charme, den wir in den Golfsport integrierten – und der Lage des Golfparks. Mit dem Slogan „Golf für jedermann, Golf für die ganze Familie" lockten wir nicht nur erfahrene Golferinnen und Golfer, sondern auch Neulinge und Familien an.

Mardorf a place with many facets

In 1997, our family, consisting of my parents Ron and Hilary, my brother David, his wife Bianka and their son Liam, as well as my wife Yvonne and myself, moved to Mardorf. Initially, I was very apprehensive about moving to a place that is known as a regional tourist attraction. Did I really want the hustle and bustle that comes with it in my life? After all, my home should be a place of peace and tranquillity. A place where you feel at ease, preferably far away from the stress of everyday life. Could that be possible in Mardorf?

The reasons for the move were both our self-employment, as we wanted to set up a new business here, and our enthusiasm for the beautiful area around Lake Steinhuder Meer. Mardorf, located directly on the lake, offers a beautiful and peaceful environment in which we can let our children grow up safely. Mardorf combines active experiences, relaxed recreation, unspoiled nature and culinary delights in such a way that everyone can decide for themselves what they feel like doing. We founded our family business, Golf Park Lake Steinhuder Meer, in the same year as the move. The golf course opened successfully and gained more and more members over the years. Our success was based on our commitment,
our hard work, our English charm, which we integrated into the sport of golf – and the location of the golf park. With the slogan "Golf for everyone, golf for the whole family", we attracted not only experienced golfers, but also beginners and families.

We found our new home in Mardorf, both professionally and privately. I became involved in local politics, while our wives

↑ Die mehrmalige Schützenkönigin Angelina Orme.
↑ The multiple shooting queen Angelina Orme.

↖ Die seltener zu sehende Rückseite des Hauses des Gastes in Mardorf. Von hier aus sieht man besonders schön und in Ruhe das Storchennest.
↖ The rarely seen rear of the Haus des Gastes in Mardorf. From here you can see the stork's nest.

← Als Schule 1842 erbaut und 1959 überflüssig geworden aufgrund der neuen Schule, beherbergt das schöne Gebäude heute ein gutes Restaurant – „Alte Schule".
← Built as a school in 1842 and made redundant in 1959 due to the new school, the beautiful building now houses a good restaurant – "Alte Schule".

Sowohl beruflich als auch privat fanden wir in Mardorf unsere neue Heimat. Ich engagierte mich in der lokalen Politik, während unsere Frauen alle im örtlichen Schützenverein aktiv wurden. Besonders stolz sind wir darauf, dass unsere Tochter Angelina dreimalige Jugendschützenkönigin wurde. Die Gemeinschaft in Mardorf nahm uns herzlich auf, und wir fühlten uns in dieser kleinen Dorfgemeinschaft glücklich und geborgen. Der Tourismus im Ort, den ich vor unserem Umzug scheute, bietet eben auch Vorteile: Radfahren, Segeln, Surfen, Segway, Angeln, Kiten, Reiten, Golfen, Tennis, Fußball, Klettern und vieles mehr – und das alles fußläufig vom Wohnhaus entfernt. Über die Jahre haben wir uns an die Schönheit der Landschaft und die Ruhe in Mardorf gewöhnt. Nach einem arbeitsreichen Tag lieben wir es, Spaziergänge um den Golf-

all became active in the local shooting club. We are particularly proud of the fact that our daughter Angelina became three-time youth shooting queen. The community in Mardorf welcomed us warmly and we felt happy and secure in this small village community. The tourism in the village, which I shied away from before we moved, also offers advantages: Cycling, sailing, surfing, Segway, fishing, kiting, horse riding, golf, tennis, soccer, climbing and much more – all within walking distance of the house.

Over the years, we have become accustomed to the beauty of the landscape and the tranquillity of Mardorf. After a busy day, we love to go for walks around the golf course or along the lake. We like to explore the surrounding area by bike and enjoy nature.

↑ Das Naturpark-Haus mit seiner gut strukturierten Fassade, die wie ein Vorhang wirkt und aus Cortenstahl besteht. Der Entwurf stammt vom Büro der btp Architekten aus Hannover.

↑ The Nature Park House with its well-structured façade, which looks like a curtain and is made of Corten steel. The design was created by btp Architekten from Hannover.

↖ Die zahlreichen Stege vor Mardorf. Etwa in der Mitte der aus Dünen und Kiefern bestehenden Landschaft steht das Naturpark-Haus an der Küste des Nordufers.

↖ The numerous jetties off Mardorf. The nature park house on the northern shore is located roughly in the middle of the landscape of dunes and pines.

← Der Kiosk, der bereits seit den 50er Jahren des letzten Jahrhunderts besteht und eigentlich als Fördermaßnahme zum Verkauf von Milch entstand, entzückt auch heute noch die Besucherinnen und Besucher von Mardorf.

← The kiosk, which has been in existence since the 1950s and was originally set up as a promotional measure to sell milk, still delights visitors to Mardorf today.

platz oder entlang des Meeres zu unternehmen. Mit dem Fahrrad erkunden wir gerne die Umgebung und genießen die Natur. Nun, rund 25 Jahre später, sind wir fest in Mardorf verwurzelt. Unsere Familie hat es zu keinem Zeitpunkt bereut, nach Mardorf gezogen zu sein, und ein Wegziehen kommt für uns nicht mehr infrage. Wir sind dankbar für die Gemeinschaft und die Möglichkeit, in dieser wundervollen Gegend zu leben.
Aus einer Notlösung vor 25 Jahren wurde der schönste Ort zum Leben und zum Arbeiten, den ich nicht mehr missen möchte.

Now, some 25 years later, we are firmly rooted in Mardorf. Our family has never regretted moving to Mardorf and moving away is no longer an option for us. We are grateful for the community and the opportunity to live in this wonderful area. What started out as an emergency solution 25 years ago has become the most beautiful place to live and work, and I wouldn't want to be without it

↑ Die Christuskapelle ist sehr klein, hat im Inneren eine ebenso kleine Orgel, steht aber bereits seit über 300 Jahren.

↑ The Christ Chapel is very small, has an equally small organ inside, but has been standing for over 300 years.

Christuskapelle
Christ Chapel

Peter Zenker

Mardorf gehörte im späten Mittelalter zu Rehburg, später zu Husum und seit 1522 zu Schneeren. Seitdem war der Pastor von Schneeren auch für Mardorf zuständig. Das bedeutete, dass die Mardorferinnen und Mardorfer regelmäßig den damals beschwerlichen Weg nach Schneeren auf sich nehmen mussten, für die Gottesdienste, aber auch für jede Taufe, jede Eheschließung und jede Beerdigung.

Im Jahr 1722 wurde schließlich die Kapelle in zweifacher Funktion genutzt, nämlich als Kirch- sowie Schulraum. In der Doppelnutzung dokumentiert sie das Nützlichkeitsdenken und die Innovation der einsetzenden Aufklärung.

Von der Straße zurückgesetzt steht der eingeschossige, mit Schrägstreben und Andreaskreuzen geschmückte Bau aus dunklem Fachwerk mit verputzten und weiß gestrichenen Ausfachungen aus Lehm und Weidengeflecht. An den Längs-

In the late Middle Ages, Mardorf belonged to Rehburg, later to Husum and since 1522 to Schneeren. Since then, the pastor of Schneeren was also responsible for Mardorf. This meant that the people of Mardorf regularly had to make the arduous journey to Schneeren for church services, but also for every baptism, every marriage and every funeral.

In 1722, the chapel was finally used for two purposes, namely as a church and as a schoolroom. In its dual use, it documents the utilitarian thinking and innovation of the incipient Enlightenment.

Set back from the street, the single-storey building, decorated with diagonal struts and St Andrew's crosses, is made of dark half-timbering with plastered and white-painted infill panels made of clay and wickerwork. On the long sides there are large, partly offset rectangular windows and a low door. The

↑ Klein, aber trotzdem mit wundervollem Klang.
↑ Small, but still with a wonderful sound.

↑ Die 300 Jahre sind dem Inneren der Kapelle nach einer gelungenen Sanierung nicht anzusehen und sie hat trotzdem ihren Charme behalten.
↑ After a successful renovation, the chapel's 300 years are not visible inside, but it has nevertheless retained its charm.

seiten gibt es große, teils versetzte Rechteckfenster und eine niedrige Tür. Die Kapelle ist über einem gestreckt achteckigen Grundriss mit langem Saalraum und Satteldach traufständig zur Straße gebaut. Das Dach trägt einen kleinen, hölzernen Dachreiter mit Pyramidendach als Glockenstuhl, bekrönt mit Kugel und Wetterfahne.

In ihrem Inneren stammen der Opferstock mit der Inschrift und die hölzerne Taube über der Kanzel aus der Bauzeit.

chapel is built on an elongated octagonal floor plan with a long hall and gabled roof, facing the street. The roof bears a small, wooden ridge turret with a pyramid roof as a belfry crowned with a ball and weather vane.

Inside, the offering box with the inscription and the wooden dove above the pulpit date from the time of construction.

↑ Bis vor wenigen Jahren wurde hier im Mardorfer Feld (zwischen Neustadt und Mardorf) Torf abgebaut. Nach dem Abbau wurde das Hochmoor wieder vernässt und zaghaft bildet sich die Moorvegetation zurück.

↑ Until a few years ago, peat was mined here in the Mardorfer Feld (between Neustadt and Mardorf). After extraction, the raised bog was rewetted and the bog vegetation is tentatively returning.

↑ Dort, wo heute Teichrosen und Schilf wachsen, stand einst eine Sanddüne. Aus deren Sand wurde vor über einem halben Jahrhundert die Moorstraße gebaut.

↑ A sand dune once stood where pond lilies and reeds grow today. Its sand was used to build the moor road over half a century ago.

↑ Ein wichtiger Schritt auf dem Weg zu einem naturnahen Hochmoor: Torfmoose bilden einen grünen Teppich auf den Wasserflächen zwischen den Bulten aus Pfeifengras und fruchtendem Wollgras.

↑ An important step on the way to a near-natural raised bog: peat mosses form a green carpet on the water surfaces between the bulbs of moor grass and flowering cotton grass.

↑↑ Der Holzsteg durch die feuchte Moorheide ermöglicht Einblicke auf die Vegetationszusammensetzung der Moorvegetation. An feuchten Stellen wächst hier sogar der Rundblättrige Sonnentau.

↑↑ The wooden walkway through the damp moorland heath provides an insight into the composition of the moorland vegetation. The round-leaved sundew even grows here in damp places.

↑ Auf dieser Luftaufnahme wird deutlich, wie gut sich der Golf Park Steinhuder Meer in den vorhandenen Waldbereich integriert. Gut zu sehen sind auch die Neuanpflanzungen von Bäumen neben dem Teich, der sich zwischen den Bahnen 7 und 8 befindet.

↑ This aerial view clearly shows how well Golf Park Steinhuder Meer is integrated into the existing woodland area. You can also clearly see the trees planted next to the pond between holes 7 and 8.

↑↑ Die Golferinnen und Golfer nennen einen großen Bereich von Sand im Spielbereich „Waste Area", aus dem hier ein Spieler seinen Ball schlagen muss. In diesem Fall auf Bahn 8 des Golf Parks Steinhuder Meer.

↑↑ Golfers call a large area of sand in the playing area a waste area, from which players have to hit their ball. In this case on hole 8 of the Golf Park Steinhuder Meer.

↑ Das sogenannte Signature Hole am Grün der Bahn 14. Dieses Grün ist unverwechselbar für den Golf Park Steinhuder Meer. Aus dem Bunker schlägt gerade der Gründer des GPSM, Ron Orme.

↑ The so-called signature hole on the green of hole 14, which is unmistakable for the Steinhuder Meer Golf Park. The founder of the GPSM, Ron Orme, is hitting out of the bunker.

↑↑ Falko Schade schlägt seinen Ball aus einem tiefen Bunker auf der Bahn 9, der ein Hindernis auf dem Weg zum Grün darstellt.

↑↑ Falko Schade hits his ball out of a deep bunker on hole 9, which is an obstacle on the way to the green.

↑ Ein typischer lichter Kiefernwald im Naturpark, neben der Straße von Mardorf nach Schneeren gelegen, direkt im Anschluss an den Golfplatz.

↑ A typical sparse pine forest in the nature park next to the road from Mardorf to Schneeren, directly adjacent to the golf course.

Schneeren

Claudia Gondry

Windmühle Schneeren

Woum, woum, woum... Wir Kinder wachten mitten in der Nacht von einem unglaublich lauten, rhythmischen Geräusch auf, das die runden Wände unserer kleinen, wie Kuchenstücke geformten Zimmer im ersten Stock unseres neuen Zuhauses erschütterte. Dann hörte man von oben unsere Eltern zum Telefon laufen und kurz danach stiegen Männer über die Wendeltreppe hinauf unter das Dach der Windmühle, in der wir jetzt lebten, machten sich lange und unter lauten Rufen dort zu schaffen und dann hörte das schreckliche Geräusch endlich auf.

Die Windrose, die früher das gesamte Dach in die günstigste Windrichtung gedreht hatte, jetzt aber fixiert war, hatte sich im Sturm losgerissen und musste unter großen Anstrengungen durch Helfer aus dem Dorf wieder festgestellt werden, damit nicht der gesamte Dachstuhl abhob.

Das war nicht das einzige Mal, dass das passierte.

Unsere Eltern waren beide eigentlich Studierte, die nach dem Krieg in den USA als Medienschaffende gearbeitet hatten. Wegen eines Todesfalls in der Familie kamen sie 1952 nach Hannover zurück, stiegen ins Familienunternehmen ein und gründeten eine Familie. Diese wuchs in den nächsten Jahren schnell auf vier Kinder an und das Haus in der Stadt wurde zu klein.

Um Kosten zu sparen und weil sie – schon damals – daran glaubten, dass Kinder „in der Natur" besser aufgehoben seien als im Großstadtverkehr, suchten unsere Eltern nach einer preiswerten Unterkunft außerhalb von Hannover. Schneeren war, durch Beziehungen unserer Großmutter, schon als Zu-

Schneeren Windmill

Woum, woum, woum ... we children were woken up in the middle of the night by an unbelievably loud, rhythmic noise that shook the round walls of our little rooms, shaped like pieces of cake, on the second floor of our new home. Then from upstairs we heard our parents running to the telephone and shortly after that men climbed up the spiral staircase to the roof of the windmill in which we now lived, made their way there for a long time, shouting loudly, and then the terrible noise finally stopped.

The wind rose, which had previously turned the entire roof in the most favorable wind direction, but was now fixed, had torn loose in the storm and had to be fixed again with great effort by helpers from the village, so that the entire roof structure did not lift off.

This was not the only time this happened.

Both our parents were actually academics who had worked as journalists in the USA after the war. Owing to a death in the family, they returned to Hannover in 1952, joined the family business and started a family. This quickly grew to four children over the next few years and the house in the city became too small.

To save costs and because they believed – even then – that children were better off 'in nature' than in big city traffic, our parents were looking for inexpensive housing outside of Hannover. Schneeren was, through relations of our grandmother, already known as a refuge in the countryside and so they must have come across the ruined mill there and fell in love with it. The condition of the building was ruinous and the location, on

↖ In dieser Windmühle verbrachte die Autorin ihre Kindheit. Im Jahr 1871 als dreigeschossiger Erdholländer erbaut, gehört die Mühle zum Wappen von Schneeren.

↖ The author spent her childhood in this windmill. Built in 1871 as a three-story earthen bollard, the mill is part of the coat of arms of Schneeren.

↑ Der Eingang lädt zum Entdecken der Mühle ein. ↑ The entrance invites you to discover the mill.

fluchtsort auf dem Land bekannt und so sind sie wohl auf die dortige Mühlenruine gestoßen und haben sich in sie verliebt. Der Zustand des Gebäudes war ruinös und die Lage, auf einem kahlen, windigen Hügel, etwa einen Kilometer vom Dorf entfernt, unwirtlich und von allen Seiten weithin einsehbar. Es gehörte schon eine gehörige Portion Mut, die finanzielle Notlage in den frühen 1950er Jahren und der damals noch nicht so weit verbreitete „Glaube an die Natur" dazu, mit vier kleinen Kindern nach Schneeren auf den Schopersberg zu ziehen. Geholfen hat bei dem Vorhaben sicher auch die monetäre Unterstützung durch die Familie und die fachliche Hilfe durch den Bruder unseres Vaters, eines angehenden Architekten aus München.

Das Gebäude, das unsere Eltern auf dem leeren Hügel bei Schneeren als unser zukünftiges Familiendomizil kauften, war die zerlöcherte Ruine einer 1871 erbauten Turmholländer Windmühle, die vor dem Krieg lange als Getreidemühle betrieben, dann durch Blitzschlag zerstört und aufgegeben worden war. Die verrückten Großstädterinnen und Großstädter, die das baufällige Gemäuer als Einfamilienhaus nutzen wollten, müssen damals im Dorf schon genauso viel mitleidiges Kopfschütteln ausgelöst haben wie die erneute Renovierung der Mühle im Jahre 2012: „Lat se man maken ... de Verrückten vom Berg" ...

1956 wurde der Kaufvertrag unterschrieben, die alten Mühlräder und Mühlsteine aus dem Gebäude entfernt, das danebenstehende Maschinenhaus entkernt und der Bau begonnen. Unsere Großmutter legte eine Apfelwiese an und pflanzte einen Mammutbaum. Die heute noch vollständig

a bare, windy hill about 1 km from the village was inhospitable and visible from all sides for miles. It took a fair amount of courage, with the financial hardship in the early fifties and the then not so widespread 'faith in nature' to move with four small children to Schneeren on the Schopersberg. The monetary support from the family and the professional help from our father's brother, a budding architect, from Munich certainly helped with the project.

The building that our parents bought on the empty hill near Schneeren as our future family domicile was the holey ruin of a Turmholländer windmill built in 1871, which had long been operated as a flour mill before the war, then destroyed by lightning and abandoned. The crazy city dwellers who wanted to use the dilapidated masonry as a family home must have caused as much pitying head-shaking in the village back then as the renewed renovation of the mill in 2012: *Let them have their own way, these crazy folks from the mountain.*

In 1956 the purchase contract was signed, the old mill wheels and stones were removed from the building, the adjacent machine house was gutted and construction began. Our grandmother laid out an apple orchard and planted a redwood tree. Our uncle's plans, which are still complete today, show the many ideas, attempts and changes that were required to convert the historic industrial architecture into a modern single-family home, and they also demonstrate the – for financial reasons – very slow progress of the transformation.

In 1960 we – parents, children (seven, 2 times five and one year old) and our Great Dane Leu – moved into the still unfinished building. Life on the construction site was adventurous

↑ Das Mühlwerk ist mit Flügelwelle und Kammrad noch erhalten.
↑ The millwork is still preserved with the wingshaft and comb wheel.

← Ein Blick aus dem Fenster gibt den Blick auf die vor vielen Jahren nachgebildeten Flügel frei.
← A look out the window reveals the wings recreated many years ago.

↑ Auch der Hof wurde liebevoll mit alten Mühlsteinen gestaltet.
↑ The courtyard has also been lovingly decorated with old millstones.

vorhandenen Pläne unseres Onkels zeigen die vielen Ideen, Anläufe und Änderungen, die der Umbau der historischen Industriearchitekur in ein modernes Einfamilienhaus erforderte und sie demonstrieren auch den – aus finanziellen Gründen – sehr langsamen Fortschritt der Umwandlung.

1960 zogen wir – Eltern, Kinder (sieben, zweimal fünf und ein Jahr alt) und unsere Dogge Leu – in das noch unfertige Gebäude ein. Das Leben auf der Baustelle war abenteuerlich und ungewohnt, nicht nur wegen der nächtlichen Überraschungen wie der Geschichte mit der Windrose. Wir untersuchten auf klapprigen Leitern die (auch heute noch vorhandene) Mühlentechnik hoch oben unter dem Dach, folgten eigenartig aussehenden Männern, die mit Wünschelruten auf dem Gelände nach Wasser suchten (bis 2012 hatten wir noch unseren eigenen Brunnen) und schlugen uns mit den Kindern aus dem Dorf herum. Meine Brüder und ich waren immer auf Kriegsfuß mit den Einheimischen. Erst unsere sehr viel jüngere Schwester hat den Anschluss zum Dorf geschafft.

Als sich nach wenigen Jahren herausstellte, dass der Lebensraum in der Mühle für eine sechsköpfige Familie doch ziemlich eingeschränkt war, entwarf unser Onkel auf dem Grundriss des alten Maschinenhauses nebenan einen modernen, unterkellerten Anbau mit Flachdach. Nicht nur das, die Mühle, die aus Backstein gebaut und teilweise mit Teerpappe verkleidet worden war, bekam neue, schwarze Holzflügel und wurde weiß verputzt. Ein moderner 1960er-Jahre-Bau auf dem leeren Hügel: die Dorfbevölkerung fühlte sich zweifellos in ihrem Urteil über die verrückten Zugezogenen bestätigt.

Aber in den folgenden Jahrzehnten wuchsen die Bäume, bei

and unusual, not only because of the nightly surprises like the story with the wind rose. We investigated the mill technology (which still exists today) high up under the roof on rickety ladders, followed strange-looking men searching for water on the site with dowsing rods (until 2012 we still had our own well), and fought with the children from the village. My brothers and I were always at war with the locals. Only our much younger sister made the connection to the village.

When after a few years it became clear that the living space in the mill was rather limited for a family of 6, our uncle designed a modern extension with a basement and a flat roof on the floor plan of the old engine house next door. Not only that, the mill, which had been built of brick and partially covered with tar paper, got new black wooden sashes and was plastered white. A modern 60's building on the empty hill: the villagers undoubtedly felt confirmed in their judgment of the crazy newcomers.

But with the decades that followed, the trees grew, which we were allowed to help plant as children. We learned how to drive, our father went to work in Hannover and we integrated ourselves.

Only when all of us slowly left the nest and our mother finally remained on the Schopersberg as the only one with little financial means, the mill went downhill again. After the death of our parents it was almost a ruin again. The monument conservator from Neustadt told us at that time that one could 'flatten' it!

But we did not do that and from 2012 our family has renovated the mill once again: with a young architect and an imagina-

↑ Ein wunderbarer Ausblick auf einen Mammutbaum, der recht selten in unseren Breiten ist. Davor lädt ein Tisch zum Verweilen ein.

↑ A wonderful view of a redwood tree, which is quite rare in our latitudes. In front of it, a table invites you to stop a while.

↑ Bis 1947 noch als Mühle in Betrieb, wurde sie in den 1950er und 1960er Jahren zum Wohnraum umgebaut.

↑ Still in operation as a mill until 1947, it was converted to residential use in the 1950s and 1960s.

↑ Eine der zahlreichen Ansichten auf Schneeren – hier vom Weg an der Mühle aufgenommen.

↑ One of the numerous views on Schneeren – here taken from the path at the mill.

deren Pflanzung wir als Kinder mithelfen durften, wir machten den Führerschein, unser Vater fuhr zur Arbeit nach Hannover und man integrierte sich.

Erst als wir alle langsam das Nest verließen und unsere Mutter schließlich mit geringen finanziellen Mitteln als Einzige auf dem Schopersberg zurückgeblieben war, ging es mit der Mühle wieder bergab. Nach dem Tod unserer Eltern war sie fast wieder eine Ruine. Der Denkmalpfleger aus Neustadt sagte uns damals, dass man sie ja auch „plattmachen" könne! Das haben wir aber nicht gemacht und von 2012 an hat unsere Familie die Mühle noch einmal renoviert: mit einem jungen Architekten und einem einfallsreichen Bauunternehmer aus Hannover, dessen ausgezeichneten Handwerkern aus der weiteren Umgebung, unter Mithilfe der Deutschen Stiftung Denkmalschutz, der Bingo-Umweltstiftung, des Niedersächsischen Landesamtes für Denkmalpflege und mit viel Nachbarschaftshilfe, Eigenarbeit und Liebe.

Jetzt kann man die Mühle auf dem Schopersberg wieder von

tive builder from Hannover, his excellent craftsmen from the wider area, with the help of the German Foundation for Monument Protection, the Bingo Foundation, the Lower Saxony Monument Preservation Office, and with a lot of neighborly help, personal work, and love.

Now the mill on the Schopersberg can be seen again from afar, with its new Dutch aluminum wings, freshly plastered and with our grandmother's redwood tree as a backdrop behind it. Life in the village, which our parents had hoped for so much, nevertheless did not keep any of us in Schneeren, because the idea that city dwellers have of the idyll of country life rarely coincides with the reality of working farmers and their views of nature.

Schneeren is a beautiful village, with 42 listed houses, a traditional 'Eichenbrink' (small forest) with an idyllic village pond in the middle of the village and forest and moors in the surrounding area. Sometimes you can find here, in the midst of intensively farmed land, even places that seem almost enchanted.

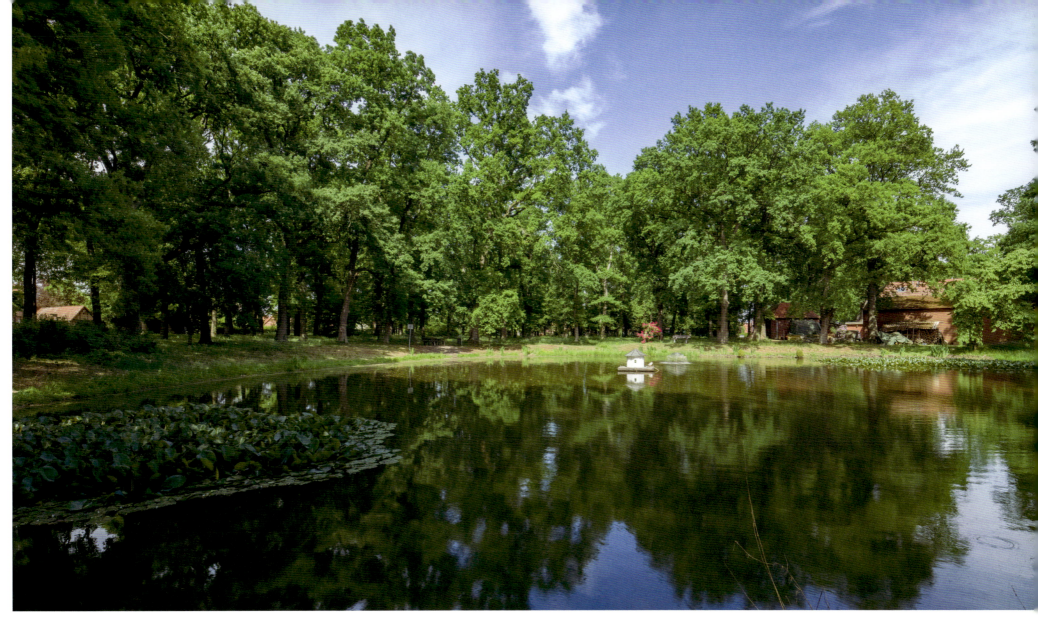

↑ Ein idyllischer Ort – der Dorfteich, auch Queemoor genannt.

↑ An idyllic place – the village pond, also called Queemoor.

Weitem sehen, mit ihren neuen holländischen Aluminiumflügeln, frisch verputzt und mit dem Mammutbaum unserer Großmutter als Kulisse dahinter.

Das Leben auf dem Dorf, von dem sich unsere Eltern so viel erhofft hatten, hat dennoch keinen von uns in Schneeren gehalten, denn die Vorstellung, die Großstädterinnen und Großstädter von der Idylle des Landlebens haben, deckt sich ja in den wenigsten Fällen mit der Realität der arbeitenden Bäuerinnen und Bauern und deren Ansichten von der Natur. Schneeren ist ein schönes Dorf, mit 42 denkmalgeschützten Häusern, einem traditionellen „Eichenbrink" (Wäldchen) mit idyllischem Dorfteich in der Mitte des Ortes und viel Wald und Mooren in der Umgebung. Manchmal findet man hier, inmitten der intensiv von der Landwirtschaft bewirtschafteten Flächen, sogar noch Orte, die verwunschen zu sein scheinen.

Wahlenhorst

Wahlenhorst is such a place. It's a small beech grove that we used to visit on our bikes when we were kids, because it was so beautiful and so eerie. On the map, it appears like an island behind the Häfern, the large forest located to the northeast of the village. We always thought the big beech trees were ancient, and you could find red sandstone slabs there under the fallen trees, which don't exist elsewhere in our terminal moraine area. The 'island' is surrounded by a ditch, along which weathered old boundary stones stand, and the small bridge, which forms the only access to the place, makes the whole seem like a natural fortress. The chronicler of Mardorf, Friedrich Dankenbrink, tells of legends that a treasure was buried there in the Middle Ages. That was of course particularly exciting for us children.

Today Wahlenhorst is far enough away from my mill to give my dachshund enough exercise. When he has run as far as

S. 258–259 Die Wahlenhorst, nahe bei Schneeren und ein geradezu mystischer Ort. Der Sage nach sollen hier Raubritter einen Schatz vergraben haben.

P. 258–259 Wahlenhorst, near Schneeren, is a mystical place. According to legend, robber barons buried a treasure here.

↑ Die Autorin an einem ihrer Lieblingsplätze rund um Schneeren: die Wahlenhorst.

↑ The author at one of her favorite places around Schneeren: the Wahlenhorst.

Wahlenhorst

Die *Wahlenhorst* ist so ein Ort. Ein kleines Buchenwäldchen, das wir schon als Kinder immer wieder auf unseren Fahrrädern besucht haben, weil es so schön und so unheimlich war. Auf der Karte erscheint es wie eine Insel hinter dem Häfern, dem großen, im Nordosten des Ortes gelegenen Wald. Wir dachten immer, die großen Buchen seien uralt, und man konnte dort unter den umgestürzten Bäumen Buntsandsteinplatten finden, die es sonst in unserer Endmoränengegend gar nicht gibt. Die „Insel" ist von einem Graben umzogen, an dem entlang verwitterte alte Grenzsteine stehen, und die kleine Brücke, die den einzigen Zugang zu dem Ort bildet, lässt das Ganze wie eine natürliche Festung erscheinen. Der Mardorfer Chronist Friedrich Dankenbrink berichtet von Legenden, wonach im Mittelalter dort ein Schatz vergraben wurde. Das war natürlich besonders aufregend für uns Kinder.

Heute ist die Wahlenhorst weit genug von meiner Mühle entfernt, um meinem Dackel genügend Auslauf zu verschaffen. Wenn er bis hinter den Häfern am Fahrrad gelaufen ist, kommt er wenigstens nicht auf die Idee, ins Mühlenfeld zu laufen und sich dort bei meinen Nachbarn, deren Schlafzimmer auf ebener Erde liegt und mit einer großen, oft offenen Schiebetür versehen ist, ins Bett zu legen. So geschehen vor einiger Zeit ... Geschichten vom Land halt.

behind the oats on the bicycle, at least he doesn't get the idea of running into the mill field and lying down in bed with my neighbors, whose bedroom is on the ground level and has a large, often open sliding door. That's what happened some time ago ... Stories from the country.

↑ Noch heute wird eine Torfbahn in der Nähe von Schneeren betrieben, um den Torf abzutransportieren.

↑ Even today, a peat railroad is operated near Schneeren to transport the peat away.

Torfbahn

Doch dann kam einer der ersten schönen Frühlingstage dieses Jahr und ich war zufällig in der Nähe und dachte mir: Wir versuchen es noch mal miteinander, das Steinhuder Meer und ich. Schon der Weg dorthin hat mich verzaubert, denn es war nicht dieser typische Überlandweg durch Felder, sondern wir rauschten durch einen lichten Birkenwald, der, total surreal, auf einer Seite komplett im Moor stand. Baumstümpfe ragten aus dem Wasser. Tote Birkenstämme, die wohl in vielen tausend Jahren wieder zu Torf werden. Denn, das ist ja irgendwie bekannt, Torf ist ein Rohstoff, der ganz langsam wächst und tausende von Jahren braucht, um richtig dicke Schichten zu bilden.

Peat railroad

But then one of the first beautiful spring days of the year arrived and I happened to be in the neighbourhood and thought to myself: let's try it again, the Lake Steinhuder Meer and me. Even the way there enchanted me, because it wasn't the typical overland route through fields, but we rushed through a sparse birch forest, which, totally surreal, stood completely in the moor on one side. Tree stumps protruded from the water. Dead birch trunks that will probably turn back into peat in many thousands of years. Because, as we all know, peat is a raw material that grows very slowly and takes thousands of years to form really thick layers.

← Die evangelische „Kirche zum guten Hirten". Wahrscheinlich bereits die dritte Kirche, die an diesem Platz 1724 erbaut wurde.

← The Protestant "Church of the Good Shepherd". Probably the third church built on this site in 1724.

Kirche zum guten Hirten
Church of the Good Shepherd

Peter Zenker

Die Kirche wurde 1724 an der Stelle eines 1588 geweihten Vorgängerbaus auf dem leicht erhöhten Kirchplatz im südöstlichen Teil des 1215 erstmals erwähnten Ortes Schneeren errichtet. Sie bekam 1913 ihren markant pfannenverschalten Turmaufsatz, der das 1792 durch Blitzschlag zerstörte Fachwerkobergeschoss ersetzte.

Mit ihren beiden Bauabschnitten und aufgrund ihrer städtebaulichen Bedeutung als Gesamtgefüge einer Kirchenanlage mit prägendem Einfluss auf das Ortsbild ist sie von Bedeutung für die Bau- und Kunstgeschichte.

Sie ist als Saalkirche auf rechteckigem Grundriss aus Feldsteinmauerwerk gebaut. Ihr schlichtes Satteldach ist über dem Chor zur Hälfte abgewalmt und grenzt an einen Westturm auf quadratischer Basis, der mit einem Satteldach mit Dachreiter unter polygonalem, spitzem Turmhelm gedeckt ist. Das Langhaus wird durch je fünf Segmentbogenfenster mit Sandsteinrahmung gegliedert und durch Strebepfeiler gesichert. Der Innenraum ist von einer hölzernen Segmentbogen-

The church was built in 1724 on the site of a previous building consecrated in 1588 on the slightly elevated church square in the south-eastern part of the village of Schneeren, which was first mentioned in 1215. In 1913, it was given its striking pantiled tower, which replaced the half-timbered upper storey that had been destroyed by lightning in 1792.

With its two construction phases and due to its urban significance as the overall structure of a church complex with a formative influence on the townscape, it is important for the history of architecture and art.

It is built as a hall church on a rectangular ground plan of fieldstone masonry. Its simple gabled roof is half hipped over the choir and adjoins a west tower on a square base, which is covered with a gabled roof with a ridge turret under a polygonal, pointed spire.

The nave is divided by five segmental arched windows with sandstone frames and secured by buttresses. The interior is spanned by a wooden segmental arched barrel vault. The

↑ Recht ungewöhnlich für eine Kirche dieser Art und Größe: der lichtdurchflutete Innenraum.

↑ Quite unusual for a church of this type and size: the light-flooded interior of the church.

tonne überspannt. Der Chorraum wird dominiert von einem um 1780 gefertigten Umgangsaltar, der von der 1830 erbauten Orgel der Gebrüder Meyer aus Hannover mit siebzehn Registern in zwei Manualen und einem Pedal bekrönt wird. Davor steht der Kanzelkorb aus der Zeit um 1600 und ein Taufstein von 1729. Der Holzaufsatz des Altars wurde 1780 gefertigt.
1988 erst erhielt die Kirche den Namen „Kirche zum guten Hirten".

choir is dominated by an altar made around 1780, which is crowned by the organ built in 1830 by the Meyer brothers from Hannover with seventeen stops in two manuals and a pedal. In front of it is the pulpit from around 1600 and a baptismal font from 1729, while the wooden altarpiece was made in 1780.
The church was only given the name "Church of the Good Shepherd" in 1988.

↑ Die den heute ausgestorbenen, wilden Auerochsen ähnelnden Heckrinder sind besonders robust und werden im Rahmen eines Naturschutzprojektes der Region Hannover als Landschaftspfleger eingesetzt.

↑ The Heck cattle, which resemble the now extinct wild aurochs, are particularly robust and are used as landscape conservationists as part of a nature conservation project in the Hannover region.

Heckrinder
Heck cattle

Thomas Brandt

Landschaftspfleger wie aus der Urzeit

Nein, unsere Landschaft war kein einheitlich dunkler Wald, bevor wir Menschen nach Europa einwanderten, denn auch hier gab es ein Mosaik aus verschiedenen offenen Landschaftstypen und Wäldern. Neben den offenen Mooren, Biberwiesen und von Naturkatastrophen heimgesuchten Flächen lagen Flächen, die – selbst noch nach der letzten Eiszeit – von großen, pflanzenfressenden Säugetieren mehr oder weniger gebüsch- und baumfrei gehalten wurden. Doch nur wenige dieser „Großherbivoren", wie Biologinnen und Biologen sie nennen, haben den Druck durch die wachsende Menschheit überlebt. Eines dieser großen Weidetiere kennt man immerhin noch aus Kreuzworträtseln: den Auerochsen *Bos primigenius*, auch kurz *Ur* genannt. Auch er wurde ausgerottet, obwohl sich sein riesiges damaliges Verbreitungsgebiet von Spanien bis Korea und von Südskandinavien bis Nordafrika erstreckte. Das letzte bekannte Individuum dieser bis zu 1.000 kg schweren Tierart starb wohl 1627 in Polen. Fast drei Jahrhunderte später versuchten die Brüder Heinz und Lutz Heck die Rückzüchtung von Auerochsen aus Rindern, die man etwa 9.000 Jahre zuvor aus den wilden Vorfahren domestizierte. Das Ergebnis dieser und vieler anschließender Zuchterfolge, ein durchaus dem Auerochsen ähnelndes Rind, nach den Züchtern „Heckrind" genannt, kann man derzeit im Toten Moor bewundern. Die Heckrinder werden dort im Rahmen eines spannenden und erfolgreichen Naturschutzprojektes der Region Hannover als Landschaftspfleger eingesetzt, um unliebsame Gehölze, wie die Nordamerikanische Traubenkirsche, kurzzuhalten und um Lebensräume für zahlreiche

Landscape conservationists from prehistoric times

No, our landscape was not a uniform dark forest before we humans migrated to Europe, because here too there was a mosaic of different open landscape types and forests. In addition to the open moors, beaver meadows and areas affected by natural disasters, there were areas that – even after the last ice age – were kept more or less free of shrubs and trees by large, herbivorous mammals. However, only a few of these "large herbivores", as biologists call them, have survived the pressure of growing mankind. One of these large grazing animals is still known from crossword puzzles: the aurochs *Bos primigenius*, or *Ur* for short. It too was wiped out, although its huge former range stretched from Spain to Korea and from southern Scandinavia to North Africa. The last known individual of this species, which weighed up to 1,000 kg, probably died in Poland in 1627. Almost three centuries later, the brothers Heinz and Lutz Heck attempted to breed aurochs back from cattle that had been domesticated from their wild ancestors around 9,000 years earlier. The result of this and many subsequent breeding successes, a cattle very similar to the aurochs, called "Heck cattle" after the breeders, can currently be admired in the Dead Moor.

The Heck cattle are used there as part of an exciting and successful nature conservation project by the Hannover region as landscape conservationists to keep unwelcome shrubs short, such as the North American bird cherry, as well as to create habitats for numerous endangered animal and plant species. And they are actually as robust as the "originals". Central European winters do not bother the Heck cattle, they can defend

↑ Auch die Kühe machen einen durchaus wehrhaften Eindruck. Und sie sind es auch – Wölfe aufgepasst!

↑ The cows look as if they can defend themselves. And they can – wolves beware!

heute bedrohte Tier- und Pflanzenarten zu schaffen. Und tatsächlich sind sie so robust wie die „Originale". Mitteleuropäische Winter machen den Heckrindern nichts aus, gegen die heimischen Wolfsrudel können sie sich wehren und bei der Nahrungswahl sind sie wahrlich nicht wählerisch. Beobachtet man die Herde, kann man sich fast in das Mittelalter zurückträumen – wenn da der stabile Zaun um die großen Weideflächen nicht wäre.

themselves against the local wolf packs and they are truly not picky when it comes to their choice of food. Watching the herd, you could almost dream yourself back to the Middle Ages – if it weren't for the sturdy fence around the large grazing areas.

↑ Familienidylle im Toten Moor. Die robusten Rinder schaffen offene Lebensräume für eine Vielzahl von Tier- und Pflanzenarten, die heute selten geworden sind.

↑ Family idyll in the Dead Moor. The robust cattle create open habitats for a variety of animal and plant species that have become rare today.

↑ Rittergut Brokeloh, von Clamor von Münchhausen 1545 im Stile der Weserrenaissance als Wasserburg erbaut, zählt zu den Highlights in der Gegend von Brokeloh und Husum.
Dank eines Vorfahren des heutigen Eigentümers wurde das seinerzeit baufällige Rittergut in der Mitte des 19. Jahrhunderts nicht abgerissen, sondern erfuhr in den Jahren 1871 bis 1875 eine umfangreiche Sanierung.

↑ Brokeloh Manor, built by Clamor von Münchhausen in 1545 in the Weser Renaissance style as a moated castle, is one of the highlights in the Brokeloh and Husum area.
Thanks to an ancestor of the current owner, the then dilapidated manor house was not demolished in the middle of the 19th century, but underwent extensive renovation between 1871 and 1875.

Brokeloh und Husum

Heinrich K.-M. Hecht

Ehemaliger Sitz der Familie von Münchhausen

Im Nordwesten des Naturparks Steinhuder Meer liegen die Ortschaften Husum und Brokeloh am Rande der Meerbachniederung in einer leicht hügeligen Landschaft, gebildet von Endmoränen, die die Saale-Eiszeit mit der Schneerener und Husumer Staffel geformt hat. Die ertragsarmen Sand- und Moorböden bedingten eine vielfältige landwirtschaftliche Nutzung, so dass eine Kulturlandschaft entstand, die durch ihren Wechsel von Acker, Grünland und Wald in Teilen von noch vielen erhaltenen Landschaftselementen geprägt ist. Mit einem großen Humusanteil und damit verbundenen niedrigen pH-Werten bietet die Landschaft bei Brokeloh perfekte Voraussetzungen auch für den Heidelbeeranbau.

Der Name Brokeloh leitet sich in der Bedeutung wohl von den Worten „Loh" und „Brok" ab, was so viel wie erhöhter Waldplatz im Sumpfgebiet bedeutete. Diese Beschreibung passt auch heute noch, denn der Ort Brokeloh ist umgeben von reichlich Sumpf- und Moorgebieten.

Die abgeschiedene Lage bewegte Clamor von Münchhausen, 1545 am Ortsrand von Brokeloh das Herrenhaus des Rittergutes Brokeloh als Wasserburg im Stil der Weserrenaissance zu errichten. Er nutzte dazu Steine der verfallenen Kirche des in der Hildesheimer Stiftsfehde 1519 zerstörten Dorfes nahe des Gutes der Münchhausens am Haarberg. Auf einer Anhöhe zwischen Rehburg und Winzlar gelegen, befand sich ursprünglich der Stammsitz der bedeutenden Familie: „In Brokeloh allzeit sicher wohnen gewesen sei" heißt es 1636 in einem Erbteilungsvertrag der Familie von Helversen, die das Rittergut von den von Münchhausens zuvor erwarb.

Former seat of the von Münchhausen family

In the north-west of the Lake Steinhude Nature Park, the villages of Husum and Brokeloh are located on the edge of the Meerbach lowlands in a slightly hilly landscape formed by terminal moraines shaped by the Saale Ice Age with the Schneeren/Husumer Staffel. The low-yielding sandy and peaty soils require diverse agricultural use, resulting in a cultural landscape characterized by the alternation of arable land, grassland, forest and, in parts, many preserved landscape elements. With a high humus content and the associated low pH values, the landscape near Brokeloh also offers perfect conditions for blueberry cultivation.

The name Brokeloh is probably derived from the words "Loh" and "Brok", which meant something like an elevated wooded area in the marshland. This description still fits today, as the village of Brokeloh is surrounded by abundant swamp and moorland.

The remote location prompted Clamor von Münchhausen to build the manor house of the Brokeloh manor as a moated castle in the Weser Renaissance style on the outskirts of Brokeloh in 1545. He used stones from the ruined church of the village, which had been destroyed in the Hildesheim Collegiate Feud of 1519. This was the ancestral seat of the important von Münchhausen family, located on the Haarberg, a hill between Rehburg and Winzlar: "It was always safe to live in Brokeloh", according to a 1636 inheritance contract of the Von Helversen family, who had previously acquired the manor from the von Münchhausens.

Today, the landscape around Brokeloh can be experienced on

↑ Vor dem Eingang zum Herrenhaus steht rechts das Pächterhaus, gebaut 1843. Eine Besonderheit sind die Öffnungen im Kniestock, die der Getreidelagerung dienten, sowie die recht niedrigen Gauben.

↑ In front of the entrance to the manor house on the right is the tenant's house, built in 1843. A special feature are the openings in the kneeling storey, which were used to store grain, and the rather low dormers.

↑ Ein Blick in den Innenhof des Herrenhauses auf die rechte Seite: Fachwerk vom 16. Jahrhundert, saniert im 19. Jahrhundert, aus dem auch die Fenstergrößen stammen.

↑ A view into the inner courtyard of the manor house on the right-hand side: half-timbering from the 16th century, renovated in the 19th century, from which the window sizes also originate.

Heute lässt sich die Landschaft um Brokeloh eindrucksvoll auf den gut ausgeschilderten Rundwanderwegen „Lönsweg" und dem „Teichweg" rund um Husum erleben. Brokeloh ist ferner bekannt durch den Bickbeernhof Brokeloh. In der Saison von Mai bis September bietet er einer großen Fangemeinde seine Blaubeerspezialitäten zum direktem Verzehr an. Auf Wiesen, Feldern und in den Wäldern rund um das Rittergut Brokeloh findet auf fast 60 Hektar seit 2004 alljährlich das weltgrößte Live-Rollenspiel – „ConQuest of Mythodea" (Eroberung von Mythodea) statt. Fast 10.000 Teilnehmende aus über 25 Nationen spielen eine Woche Anfang August in einer mittelalterlichen Fantasiewelt den immer wieder neuen Kampf Gut gegen Böse. Ein unvergleichliches Schauspiel.

Brokeloh ist seit 1974 Ortsteil der Gemeinde Landesbergen, gehört aber seit alters her zum Kirchspiel Husum.

the well-signposted circular hiking trails "Lönsweg" and the "Teichweg" around Husum. Brokeloh is also known for the Bickbeernhof Brokeloh. In the season from May to September, it offers its blueberry specialties to a large fan base for direct consumption.

Every year since 2004, the world's largest live role-playing game – "ConQuest of Mythodea" – has taken place on almost 60 hectares of meadows, fields and in the woods around the Brokeloh manor. Almost 10,000 participants from over 25 nations spend a week at the beginning of August playing the ever-changing battle of good versus evil in a medieval fantasy world. An incomparable spectacle.

Brokeloh has been part of the municipality of Landesbergen since 1974, but has belonged to the parish of Husum since time immemorial.

S. 272–273   Rötlicher Granitgneis-Findling, der in der Eiszeit wohl von Skandinavien bis in unsere Gefilde vordrang – als Naturdenkmal registriert und geschützt.

P. 272–273   Reddish granite gneiss boulder that probably travelled from Scandinavia to our region during the Ice Age – registered and protected as a natural monument.

↑ Eine von den zwei architektonischen Sehenswürdigkeiten in Husum – die St.-Jacobi-Kirche mit ihrem imposanten Gebäude.

↑ One of the two architectural sights in Husum – the St Jacob's Church with its imposing building.

St. Jacobi Kirche
St Jacob's Church

Peter Zenker

Die Kirche stammt aus dem 18. Jahrhundert und bildet mit dem ebenso alten Pfarrhaus und seinem großen Pfarrgarten ein ausgesprochen hübsches Ensemble mit prägendem Einfluss auf das Straßenbild des Ortes. Zudem erfährt sie ihre Bedeutung im Rahmen der Ortsgeschichte Husums.

1522 wird Husum nachweislich als selbstständige Gemeinde mit eigener Kirche benannt. Diese blieb im Dreißigjährigen Krieg im Wesentlichen verschont, nur die Glocke wurde gestohlen. Sie wurde allerdings aufgrund zunehmender Baufälligkeit 1737 durch eine neue Kirche ersetzt, die aber wenige Jahrzehnte nach der Errichtung durch einen Brand zerstört wurde und 1775 wiederaufgebaut werden musste. Immerhin sind der Taufstein und der Opferstock von der alten Kirche übrig geblieben, die noch heute benutzt werden.

Die Architektur zeigt den Typus einer lang gestreckt rechteck-

The church dates back to the 18th century and, together with the equally old vicarage and its large parish garden, forms an extremely pretty ensemble with a formative influence on the streetscape of the village. It also plays an important role in Husum's local history.

In 1522, Husum is documented as an independent parish with its own church. It was largely spared during the Thirty Years' War, when only the bell was stolen. However, due to increasing dilapidation, it was replaced by a new church in 1737, which was destroyed by fire a few decades after its construction and had to be rebuilt in 1775. Nevertheless, the baptismal font and the offering box from the old church remain and are still in use today.

The architecture is typical of an elongated rectangular hall church. Its walls are probably made of quarry stone and thick-

↑ Die außenliegende Treppe der Kirche führt zu einer Empore, in der sich die Prieche (Sitzplatz der höheren Stände) des Rittergutes Brokeloh befand.

↑ The outside staircase of the church leads to a gallery where the Prieche (seating area for the higher classes) of the Brokeloh manor was located.

↑↑ Das Gemeindehaus stammt ebenfalls wie die Kirche aus dem 18. Jahrhundert.

↑↑ Like the church, the parish hall dates back to the 18th century.

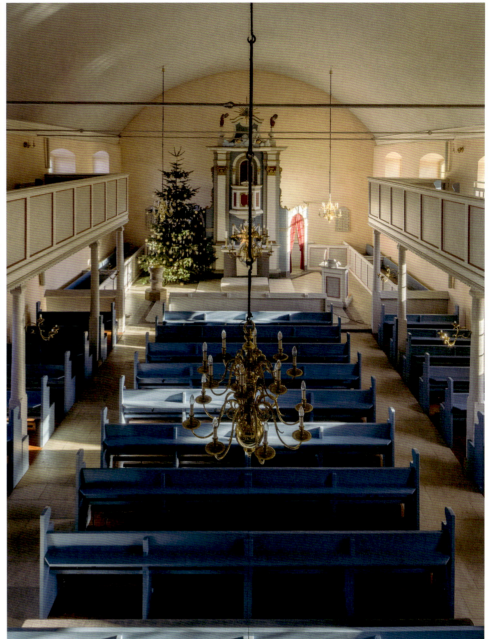

↑ Die erste Innenausstattung der Kirche verbrannte im Oktober 1774. Im Jahr 1777 wurde ein neuer Altar installiert. Auch die Galerie und die restlichen Holzarbeiten wurden neu geschaffen und blieben bis heute erhalten.

↑ The first interior of the church burnt down in October 1774. In 1777, a new altar was installed and the gallery and the remaining woodwork were recreated and have been preserved to this day.

igen Hallenkirche. Ihre Wände sind wohl aus Bruchstein gebaut und dick verputzt. Sie werden durch allseits farblich hell abgesetzte Strebepfeiler gestützt. Jeweils sechs hochrechteckige Fenster mit flachbogigem Sturz dienen der Belichtung des Innenraumes. Das Dach ist als Krüppelwalmdach ausgebildet und wird durch einen achteckigen, verschieferter Dachreiter unter spitzem Helm bekrönt.

Der Kirchraum wird durch eine glatt verputzte, helle Tonnendecke überspannt. 1777 wurde er mit einem barocken Kanzelaltar ausgerüstet, der zusammen mit den hölzernen Emporen an den beiden Längsseiten den Reiz der Kirche ausmacht. Der Altarbau stammt von Johann Christian Lauber aus Hannover, die Schnitzereien stammen vom Hofbildhauer Johann Friedrich Ziesenis.

ly plastered. They are supported by lightly coloured buttresses on all sides. The interior is lit by six high rectangular windows with flat arched lintels. The roof is designed as a half-hipped roof and is crowned by an octagonal, slated ridge turret under a pointed helmet.

The church is spanned by a smoothly plastered, light-coloured barrel ceiling. In 1777, it was equipped with a Baroque pulpit altar, which, together with the wooden galleries on both long sides, makes the church so attractive. The altarpiece was made by Johann Christian Lauber from Hannover, the carvings are by the court sculptor Johann Friedrich Ziesenis.

↑ Die Reste des Schlossteichs, die auf eine ruhmreiche Vergangenheit des Ortes hinweisen: Hier weilten die hannoverschen Könige Georg I. und Georg II., wenn sie zur Jagd im Grinderwald gingen.

↑ The remains of the castle pond, a reminder of the village's glorious past: the Hanoverian kings George I and George II stayed here when they went hunting in the Grinderwald forest.

Linsburg

Ecki Stieg

Linsburg und Umgebung

Manchmal machen ein paar Kilometer schon einen gewaltigen Unterschied. Bis 2005 lebte ich überwiegend im Schaumburger Land, zuletzt genauer gesagt in Wiedenbrügge, also an der Südseite des Steinhuder Meeres und zog dann nach dem Kauf eines Hauses nach Linsburg. Der Weg zwischen Wiedenbrügge und Linsburg mag mit 23 km zwar gering sein, dennoch ist es rein mental eine etwas weitere Reise. In Linsburg ist das, was man gemeinhin die „nordische Mentalität" nennt, in den Leuten hier fest verwurzelt: eher wortkarg, das berühmte „Moin" omnipräsent, mit überschwänglichen Gefühlen und in der Kommunikation eher zurückhaltend. Für mein damals eher exaltiertes Naturell war das nach dem Leben im „Süden" erst einmal ein Kulturschock – und es hat einige Zeit, wenn nicht gar Jahre gebraucht, bis ich in Linsburg voll und ganz angekommen bin. Also eine Liebe auf den zweiten, vielleicht auch dritten Blick. Und die hält bekanntlich besonders lang. Wie sehr ich hier mittlerweile angekommen bin, zeigt sich nicht zuletzt dadurch, wie stark ich mich hier dem Leben und dessen Rhythmus angepasst habe bzw. wie dieser Ort meinen Lebensstil und Charakter tangiert hat. Und das durchaus positiv. Ich bin in Deckbergen am Fuße der Schaumburg geboren – und wie jeden Jugendlichen zog es auch mich zunächst in die Stadt. Doch schon im Alter von 30 Jahren trat ich den Rückzug aufs Dorf an: In der Stadt mag das Leben und die Kultur pulsieren – doch ich merkte, dass ich ein Refugium der Ruhe brauche, um zu leben und kreativ zu arbeiten. Für ein solches Leben ist Linsburg der ideale Ort. Das Erste, was man als Zugereister feststellt: Linsburg kannst Du aus allen Richtungen, direkt an der B6 gelegen und sogar mit eigenem, bestens funktionierenden Bahnhof, gut erreichen, selbst Richtung Hamburg geht es über die benachbarten Dörfer zur A7 recht flott. Hinzu kommt die Nähe zum Steinhuder Meer, das am besten per Rad zu erreichen ist und in das man nach fünfzehn Kilometern seine Füße stecken kann. Linsburg selbst ist ein durch Landwirtschaft geprägter Ort mit ca. 950 Einwohnerinnen und Einwohnern, von denen ein guter Teil wie ich aus anderen Städten und Dörfern zugezogen ist. Obwohl die Infrastruktur mit guten Verkehrsanbindungen, einem hervorragend geführten Dorfladen, einem mittlerweile brauchbaren Internet, einer Autowerkstatt und zahlreichen kleinen

Linsburg and the surrounding area

Sometimes just a few kilometers make a huge difference. Until 2005, I lived mainly in the Schaumburg Land, most recently in Wiedenbrügge, on the south side of the Lake Steinhuder Meer, and then moved to Linsburg after buying a house. The distance between Wiedenbrügge and Linsburg may be short at 23 km, but it is still a somewhat longer journey in mental terms. In Linsburg, what is commonly called the "Nordic mentality" is firmly rooted in the people here: rather taciturn, the famous "Moin" omnipresent, with exuberant feelings and rather reserved in communication. After living in the "south", it was a bit of a culture shock for my rather exalted nature at the time – and it took me some time, if not years, to fully settle in Linsburg. So it was love at second, maybe even third sight. And as we all know, that lasts a long time. The extent to which I've arrived here is shown not least by how much I've adapted to life here and its rhythm, and how this place has affected my lifestyle and character. And done so in a very positive way. I was born in Deckbergen at the foot of the Schaumburg – and like every young person, I was initially drawn to the city. But at the age of 30, I started to move back to the village: life and culture may pulsate in the city – but I realised that I needed a refuge of peace and quiet to live and work creatively. Linsburg is the ideal place for such a life. The first thing you notice as a newcomer: you can easily reach Linsburg from all directions, located as it is directly on the B6 and even with its own, well-functioning train station. Even in the direction of Hamburg it is quite quick via the neighbouring villages to the A7. In addition, it is close to the Lake Steinhuder Meer, into which you can dip your feet after fifteen kilometres, preferably having arrived by bike. Linsburg itself is an agricultural town with around 950 inhabitants, a good proportion of whom, like me, have moved here from other towns and villages. Although the infrastructure is exemplary with good transport connections, an excellently run village store, a now acceptable internet connection, a garage and numerous small specialist businesses, it quickly becomes clear that the bicycle is the ideal means of transportation here. Not only to get from A to B, but also to discover and enjoy the surroundings and nature. And there is plenty of that in and around Linsburg. First and fore-

↑ Der Grinderwald – ehemals Jagdrevier der Welfen und ab und an, wenn die meist in England weilenden Könige, Georg I. und II., im Kurfürstentum Hannover weilten, auch königlich genutzt.

↑ The Grinderwald – formerly the hunting grounds of the Guelphs and occasionally used for royal purposes when the kings George I and II, who were mostly in England, stayed in the Electorate of Hannover.

Fachbetrieben vorbildlich ist, wird schnell klar, dass das Fahrrad hier das ideale Fortbewegungsmittel ist. Nicht nur, um von A nach B zu kommen, sondern auch um Umgebung und Natur zu entdecken und zu genießen. Und davon gibt es in und um Linsburg eine Menge. Dazu zählt in erster Linie der Grinderwald – mit 1.000 Hektar Mischwald durchaus dazu einladend, sich ausgiebig zu verlaufen oder mit dem Rad zu verfahren, was für mich immer ein Glücksfall war, denn erst so habe ich alle Örtlichkeiten gut kennengelernt.

Vom Tourismus rund um das Steinhuder Meer ist Linsburg weitestgehend verschont geblieben. Dies mögen die ein oder anderen Geschäftsleute hier bedauern, erhöht für die hier Wohnhaften allerdings die Lebensqualität beträchtlich, zumal man es ohne große Mühen zum Einkaufen entweder nach Nienburg oder südlich zum Meer schafft.

Ebenso wie ich lange dafür gebraucht habe, hier wirklich anzukommen, so hat es fast ebenso lange gebraucht, mit der Umgebung und Natur zu verwachsen. Wirklich geholfen hat mir dieses Dorf nach einem einschneidenden körperlichen und mentalen Zusammenbruch im Jahre 2012 und mich dadurch auch erheblich, im positiven Sinne, geprägt. Ich bin mir sicher, dass ich mich an keinem anderen Ort seelisch und physisch so gut wiederhergestellt hätte wie hier. Geholfen haben mir dabei meine vielen Touren mit dem Fahrrad rund ums Meer.

Entgegen der These, dass man für das Leben auf dem Land

most, this includes the Grinderwald forest – with 1,000 hectares of mixed forest, it's a great place to get lost on foot or by bike, which was always a stroke of luck for me, as I got to know all the places really well.

Linsburg has remained largely untouched by tourism around the Lake Steinhuder Meer. One or two business people here may regret this, but for those who live here it increases the quality of life considerably, especially since it is easy to get to Nienburg for shopping or to the lake to the south.

Just as it took me a long time to really arrive here, it took me almost as long to get used to the surroundings and nature. This village really helped me after a drastic physical and mental breakdown in 2012, and it also had a significant, positive impact on me. I am sure that I would not have recovered as well mentally and physically in any other place as I did here. My many bike tours around the sea helped me in this respect.

Contrary to the theory that you have to be made for life in the countryside, I feel the exact opposite: the environment and the place where you live can shape and form you – if you allow it to. This also includes finding qualities of life in seemingly self-evident things, and appreciating them all the more the deeper you allow them to penetrate your life.

Linsburg is the ideal place to slow down and relax. No matter in which direction you leave it, after a few steps you come to densely wooded areas whose paths are also so well paved that it is the ideal place for hiking and – even more so – for cycling.

↑ Ein typisches Gehöft für diese Gegend mit zwei vielleicht nicht so typischen Straßenschildern.
↑ A typical farmstead for this area with two perhaps not so typical street signs.

← Mitten in Linsburg befindet sich ein verwachsenes Grundstück mit einer verwunschenen Ruine. Ein wunderbarer Spielplatz für Kinder – wenn sie denn dürften …

← In the middle of Linsburg is an overgrown plot of land with an enchanted ruin. A wonderful playground for children – if only they were allowed …

← Der Autor Ecki Stieg auf einer seiner ausgedehnten Radtouren.
← The author Ecki Stieg on one of his extensive cycle tours.

gemacht sein muss, empfinde ich das genaue Gegenteil: Die Umgebung und der Platz, an dem Du lebst, kann Dich prägen und formen – wenn Du dies zulässt. Dazu gehört es auch, dass man Lebensqualitäten in scheinbar selbstverständlichen Dingen findet, diese aber umso mehr schätzt, je tiefer man sie in sein Leben eindringen lässt.

Für die Entschleunigung, die es dafür benötigt, ist Linsburg das ideale Ambiente. Egal in welcher Richtung Du es verlässt, Du kommst nach wenigen Schritten in dicht bewaldete Gebiete, durch die befestigte Wege führen, die nicht nur Wandernde, sondern auch Radfahrerinnen und Radfahrer schätzen. Die Historie dieses Ortes lässt sich dabei nur noch erahnen: Linsburg wurde erstmals in einer Urkunde im Jahr 1263 erwähnt, es war ein herzogliches Jagdlager, das Ende des 17. Jahrhunderts von den Herzögen von Calenberg zum Jagdschloss erweitert wurde, das, nachdem Georg I. König von Großbritannien und Irland wurde, verfiel und abgerissen wurde. Heute erinnert nur noch wenig an diese Zeit, wie zum Beispiel einer der vier ehemaligen Schlossteiche (Foto). Besonders beliebt war Linsburg bei den Großstädterinnen und Großstädtern im 17. Jahrhundert nicht: So klagte selbst Sophie von der Pfalz über Langeweile und zu wenig Zerstreuung. Daran dürfte sich bis heute nichts geändert haben: Das Geheimnis von Linsburg offenbart sich nicht bei einem flüchtigen Besuch. Man muss hier leben und seinem Rhythmus folgen, um mit ihm zu verwachsen. Aber einen Versuch ist jeder Besuch wert.

The history of this place can only be guessed at: Linsburg was first mentioned in a document in 1263; it was a ducal hunting camp, which was expanded into a hunting lodge by the Dukes of Calenberg at the end of the 17th century; after George I became King of Great Britain and Ireland, it fell into disrepair and was demolished. Today, there are only a few reminders of this time, such as one of the four former castle ponds (photo). Linsburg was not particularly popular with city dwellers in the 17th century: even Sophie of the Palatinate complained of boredom and a lack of entertainment. This is unlikely to have changed to this day: the secret of Linsburg does not reveal itself during a fleeting visit. You would actually have to live here and follow its rhythm in order to grow into it. But every visit is worth a try.

S. 280–281   Auch das ist Linsburg – zumindest am Rande in nordöstlicher Richtung: Weite, Weite und nochmals Weite … Ein unreifes Getreidefeld unter sommerlichen Cumuluswolken.

P. 280–281   That too is Linsburg – at least on the edge in a north-easterly direction: vastness, vastness and more vastness … An unripe grain field under summer cumulus clouds.

↑ Seit mehr als 250 Jahren entzückt der Hainbuchen-Laubengang mit 70 m Länge die Besuchenden am Schloss Landestrost. Im Sommer saftig grün und Schatten spendend, im Winter ein knorriges Beispiel Gartenkunst.

↑ The 70-metre-long hornbeam pergola has been delighting visitors to Landestrost Palace for more than 250 years.

Neustadt am Rübenberge

Hans-Erich Hergt

Die geografischen Gegebenheiten für eine Besiedlung waren hier, auf dem Gebiet unserer Stadt, hervorragend geeignet. Alte Heerstraßen und mögliche Schifffahrtswege sind maßgebend gewesen für die Entstehung von Siedlungen. Hier gab es beides, die Leine, die bis Ende des 19. Jahrhunderts als Schifffahrtsweg diente und die Straße (B6) von Bremen, die über Hannover bis nach Prag führte.

Der Untergrund von Stadt und Schloss besteht aus einer Art Felsenbarre, ein Gemisch aus Schieferton, Sandstein und Geröll aus der letzten Eiszeit. Stadt und Schloss stehen also auf einem rauen Untergrund. Der 1493 urkundlich belegte Name „castrum (Burg) Roenberg", aus dem dann später durch Lautumwandlung der Zuname Neustadt „am Rübenberge" wurde, könnte auf die rauen Felsen hinweisen. Fest steht, dass etwa an der Stelle, wo heute das Amtsgericht steht, ein befestigtes Haus oder eine kleine Burg mit einer Siedlung der Grafen von Wölpe stand.

Einer Urkunde aus dem Jahr 1215 lässt sich entnehmen, dass Bernhard von Wölpe dem Kloster in Mariensee eine Mühle bei Neustadt schenkt. Damit beginnt der Eintritt Neustadts in die schriftlich überlieferte Geschichte. Die Stadt ist also plötzlich da. Die ersten Ortsansässigen stammen vermutlich aus drei Dörfern der näheren Umgebung, die nachweisbar um 1200 schlagartig aufgegeben wurden. Die Grafschaft Wölpe fällt um 1300 nach dem Aussterben der männlichen Linie an die Herzöge von Braunschweig-Lüneburg.

Eine Stadtrechtsverleihung gibt es nicht. Ein 1249 erwähntes Münzrecht wird nach Hannover verlegt. Im Jahre 1371 erhält Neustadt das Marktrecht und das Recht, einen Schifffahrtszoll

The geographical conditions in the area of our town were ideal for settlement. Old military roads and possible shipping routes were decisive for the development of settlements. Both existed here: the River Leine, which served as a shipping route until the end of the 19th century, and the road (B6) from Bremen, which led via Hannover to Prague.

The subsoil of the town and castle consists of a kind of rock bar, a mixture of slate clay, sandstone and rubble from the last ice age. The town and castle therefore stand on rough ground. The name "castrum (castle) Roenberg", documented in 1493, which later became Neustadt's surname "am Rübenberge" through a change in pronunciation, could refer to the rough rocks. It is certain that there was a fortified house or a small castle with a settlement of the Counts of Wölpe on the site where the district court stands today.

A document from 1215 states that Bernhard von Wölpe donated a mill near Neustadt to the monastery in Mariensee. This marks the beginning of Neustadt's entry into written history. Suddenly the town was there. The first inhabitants probably came from three villages in the neighbourhood, which are documented to have been abandoned abruptly around 1200. The county of Wölpe fell to the Dukes of Braunschweig-Lüneburg around 1300 after the male line dies out.

There is no granting of a town charter. A minting right mentioned in 1249 is transferred to Hannover. In 1371, Neustadt was granted market rights and the right to levy a shipping duty. The castle and town also controlled the Leine crossing, which also brought in money. In 1470, the future Duke Erich I was born in Neustadt Castle, who made Neustadt his resi-

↑ Die Bastion „Erichsberg" war ein wichtiges Bauwerk der Stadtbefestigung aus dem 16. Jahrhundert.
↑ The "Erichsberg" bastion was an important building of the town fortifications from the 16th century.

↑ Die 1859 errichtete Wassermühle wurde 1948 von zwei auf vier Geschosse aufgestockt und zählt zu den sehenswerten historischen Gebäuden von Neustadt.
↑ Built in 1859, the watermill was extended from two to four storeys in 1948 and is one of Neustadt's historic buildings worth seeing.

zu erheben. Burg und Stadt kontrollierten auch den Leineübergang, der ebenfalls Geld einbrachte. Im Jahre 1470 wurde im Schloss zu Neustadt der spätere Herzog Erich I. geboren, der 1495 Neustadt zu seiner Residenz machte. Auch sein Sohn Erich II. gab Neustadt den Vorzug vor seinen anderen Schlössern.

Erich I. reiste als Abenteurer und Söldnerführer durch die Welt. Als er 1549 auf dem Reichstag zu Hagenau starb, wollte der Wirt des dortigen Gasthauses seinen Leichnam nicht herausgeben, bevor nicht die Zeche bezahlt war. So wurde in Neustadt von der Bevölkerung das nötige Geld für die Auslösung der Leiche eingetrieben.

Sein Sohn, Erich II., prägte durch seine rege Bautätigkeit das Stadtbild bis in die Gegenwart. Um 1573 begann er mit dem Um- und Neubau von Schloss und Stadtbefestigung nach den neuesten militärischen Erkenntnissen der damaligen Zeit. Die Stadt wurde eine der modernsten Festungen. Die Neustädterinnen und Neustädter wurden für die Bauarbeiten zur Mitarbeit gezwungen. Wer in der Stadt leben wollte, musste sich einer Festungsordnung unterwerfen, die noch heute die Grundlage bildet für das größte Volksfest im Neustädter Land, dem Neustädter Schützenfest. Im Jahre 1609 erlebte die Bevölkerung Neustadts den ersten großen Brand.

1625 belagerten Tillys Söldner die Stadt und nahmen sie erst nach drei Wochen ein. Sie setzten sich für neun Jahre hier fest. Stadt und Umland wurden verwüstet.

Neustadt verliert 1636 den Status einer Residenz an Hannover.

dence in 1495. His son Erich II also favoured Neustadt over his other castles.

Erich I travelled the world as an adventurer and mercenary leader. When he died at the Imperial Diet (Reichstag) in Hagenau in 1549, the landlord of the local inn did not want to hand over his body until the bill had been paid. So the necessary money was collected from the citizens of Neustadt for the release of the body.

His son, Erich II, left his mark on the townscape to the present day with his lively building activities. Around 1573, he began remodelling and rebuilding the castle and town fortifications according to the latest military knowledge of the time. The town became one of the most modern fortresses. The people of Neustadt were forced to co-operate in the construction work. Anyone who wanted to live in the town had to submit to fortress regulations, which still form the basis for the largest public festival in the Neustädter Land, the Neustädter Schützenfest. In 1609, the people of Neustadt experienced their first major fire.

In 1625, Tilly's mercenaries besieged the town but three weeks were needed to conquer it. They took up residence here for nine years. The town and surrounding countryside were devastated.

Neustadt lost its status as a residence to Hannover in 1636. The town remained merely a small official residence.

In 1672, the bailiff of Neustadt received an order from Duke Johann Friedrich to lead a punitive expedition against the

↑ Der Wasserfall wurde als Wehr angelegt, um die Stromschnellen der Leine, die ein Hindernis für die Schifffahrt bildeten, über die Kleine Leine umfahren zu können.

↑ The waterfall was constructed as a weir so that the rapids of the Leine, which were an obstacle to shipping, could be bypassed via the Kleine Leine.

Die Stadt bleibt lediglich ein kleiner Amtssitz.

Der Neustädter Amtmann erhält 1672 die Order von Herzog Johann Friedrich, eine Strafexpedition gegen die Rodewalder Bevölkerung zu führen, die widerrechtlich Bier brauten. Das Braurecht lag ausschließlich bei der Bevölkerung Neustadts. Auf etwa jedem zweiten Haus in der Stadt lagen Braurechte. Der Verkauf von Bier war für die Menschen hier eine sehr wichtige Einnahmequelle. Etwa 30 Prozent der Haushalte in der Stadt lebten ausschließlich vom Bierbrauen. Landwirtschaft wurde nur im Nebenerwerb betrieben. Der Verkauf von Torf nach Hannover war eine weitere Erwerbsquelle noch bis Anfang der 1950er Jahre.

Im Jahre 1727 brennt die Stadt, bis auf zwei Wohnhäuser und die Kirche aus dem Jahr 1247, in Gänze ab. Die obdachlose Bevölkerung wurde auf die umliegenden Dörfer verteilt. Die Stadt erholte sich nur sehr langsam von diesem Inferno. Das Brauhaus und das Rathaus waren die ersten Gebäude, die wieder errichtet wurden. 1830 wurde zwischen Rathaus und Kirche ein Wachgebäude für die Nachtwächter und Polizei errichtet.

Noch einmal, im Siebenjährigen Krieg, erlangten die Wallanlagen eine kurze Bedeutung. Gegen ein heranrückendes französisches Heer sollte 1757 die Stadt in den Verteidigungszustand versetzt werden. Wieder wurde die Bürgerschaft zu Hand- und Spanndiensten verpflichtet. Was sie aber tagsüber an Material verbauten, wurde nachts zur eigenen Verwendung wieder abgebaut. Die Stadt wurde den Franzosen kampflos

people of Rodewald, who were brewing beer illegally. The brewing rights lay exclusively with the people of Neustadt. About every second house in the town had brewing rights. The sale of beer was a very important source of income for the people here. Around 30% of households in the town lived exclusively from brewing beer. Agriculture was only practised as a sideline. The sale of peat to Hannover was another source of income until the early 1950s.

In 1727, the town burnt down in its entirety, with the exception of two residential buildings and the church dating back to 1247. The homeless population was dispersed to the neighbouring villages. The town was very slow to recover from this inferno. The brewery and the town hall were the first buildings to be rebuilt. In 1830, a guardhouse for the night watchmen and police was erected between the town hall and the church.

Once again, during the Seven Years' War, the ramparts became important for a short time. In 1757, the town was to be put in a state of defence against an approaching French army. Once again, the townspeople were obliged to provide labour. However, the materials they used during the day were dismantled at night for their own use. The town was handed over to the French without a fight. There was billetting and looting.

As an administrative centre in the 19th century, Neustadt also benefitted from a large number of stagecoach connections. The "Alte Posthof" in Marktstraße is evidence of this period. It was not until 1913 that the stagecoach service was discontinued.

↑ Nordflügel von Schloss Landestrost. Erbaut um 1580 im Stil der Renaissance.

↑ The north wing of Landestrost Palace. Built around 1580 in the Renaissance style.

übergeben. Es gab Einquartierungen und Plünderungen.

Als Amtssitz im 19. Jahrhundert profitierte Neustadt auch als Knotenpunkt von einer Vielzahl von Postkutschenverbindungen. Ein Zeugnis aus dieser Zeit ist der „Alte Posthof" in der Marktstraße. Erst 1913 wurde der Postkutschenverkehr eingestellt.

Das Stift St. Nicolai, seit dem 15. Jahrhundert nachweisbar, diente der Versorgung der armen, alten und gebrechlichen Bevölkerung. Noch um 1850 konnten sich etwa 100 Personen der rund 1.500 Einwohnerinnen und Einwohner nicht selbst ernähren. Ein wichtiger Impuls für einen wirtschaftlichen Aufschwung war die Eröffnung der Eisenbahnstrecke von Hannover nach Bremen im Jahre 1847. Die Leineschifffahrt konnte zwar noch einige Jahrzehnte mit der Bahn konkurrieren, wurde aber gegen Ende des Jahrhunderts eingestellt. Ein wichtiges Bauwerk aus der Zeit der Leineschifffahrt ist die denkmalgeschützte Schleuse bei der Mühle. Torf aus dem Moor wurde nun industriell ausgebeutet und spielte weiterhin eine wichtige Rolle im Wirtschaftsleben der Stadt. Eine weitere große Bedeutung erlangte das Moor im Jahre 1914 durch die Einweihung einer Funkstation von Kaiser Wilhelm II. Die Radiogroßstation der Firma Telefunken war mit einer Höhe von 265 m eines der höchsten Bauwerke Deutschlands. Im Jahre 1931 wurde die Anlage abgerissen.

Das Steinhuder Meer spielte zunächst für die Neustädterinnen und Neustädter nur eine untergeordnete Rolle. Erst 1968, mit der Eröffnung einer befahrbaren Straße durch das

St Nicolai's Abbey, documented since the 15th century, was used to care for poor, old and infirm residents. As late as 1850, around 100 of the 1,500 inhabitants were unable to feed themselves. The opening of the railway line from Hannover to Bremen in 1847 was an important stimulus for an economic upswing. Shipping on the Leineschifffahrt was able to compete with the railway for a few more decades, but was discontinued towards the end of the century. An important building from the time of the Leineschifffahrt is the listed lock at the mill. Peat from the moor was now exploited industrially and continued to play an important role in the economic life of the town. The moor gained further importance in 1914 with the inauguration of a radio station by Kaiser Wilhelm II. The large Telefunken radio station was one of the tallest structures in Germany at a height of 265 metres. The station was demolished in 1931.

The Lake Steinhuder Meer initially played only a minor role for the people of Neustadt. This only changed in 1968 with the opening of a passable road through the moor. During the Second World War, the Lake Steinhuder Meer was used by the Allied bombers for guidance. This is where the bomber fleets split up in the direction of Hamburg, Magdeburg and Dresden.

Neustadt was very fortunate to have been largely spared major destruction during the Second World War, despite fierce fighting and heavy losses of British troops.

In 1940, the town had 3,849 inhabitants. The number rose to

↑ Links auf dem Foto in der Abendstimmung das „Storchenhaus", welches wahrscheinlich im 18. und 19. Jahrhundert als Schule für Mädchen genutzt wurde, und rechts die Liebfrauenkirche.

↑ On the left in the photo taken in the evening is the "Storchenhaus", which was probably used as a school for girls in the 18th and 19th centuries, and on the right the Liebfrauenkirche.

Moor, änderte sich das. Im Zweiten Weltkrieg diente das Steinhuder Meer den alliierten Bombern zur Orientierung. Hier teilten sich die Bomberströme in Richtung Hamburg und in Richtung Magdeburg und Dresden.

Neustadt hatte das große Glück, weitestgehend von größeren Zerstörungen, trotz heftiger Kämpfe und hoher Verluste englischer Truppen, im Zweiten Weltkrieg verschont worden zu sein.

Im Jahre 1940 hatte die Stadt 3.849 Einwohnerinnen und Einwohner. Durch Flüchtlinge und Ausgebombte stieg die Zahl 1947 auf 7.072. Um Platz für Wohnbebauung zu schaffen, wurden 1952 die Wallanlagen zwischen Erichsberg und der Leinstraße durch englische Pioniere abgetragen. Der Erichsberg mit seiner Kasematte ist ein sehenswertes Relikt einer einst starken Festungsstadt.

In den Folgejahren entstand eine Vielzahl von Neubaugebieten. Infolge des zunehmenden Kraftfahrzeugverkehrs durch die Innenstadt drohte die Stadt zu ersticken. Abhilfe schaffte erst der Bau einer Umgehungsstraße Anfang der 1960er Jahre. Widerstand gegen den Bau gab es allerdings von einigen Kaufleuten, die befürchteten, dass der Verkehr nun an der Stadt vorbeiläuft und niemand zum Einkaufen kommt. Diese Befürchtung war ein Trugschluss. Neustadt ist durch allgemeinen Tourismus und Veranstaltungen im Schloss ein gerne genommenes Ziel, sei es für Tagesausflüge oder auch für längere Aufenthalte.

7,072 inhabitants in 1947 due to refugees and those bombed out. In 1952, the ramparts between Erichsberg and Leinstraße were demolished by British pioneers to make room for residential development. The Erichsberg with its casemate is a relic of a once heavily fortified town that is well worth seeing. In the years that followed, a large number of new housing estates were built. Increasing motor vehicle traffic through the city centre threatened to choke the city. Only the construction of a bypass at the beginning of the 1960s provided a remedy. However, there was opposition to the construction from some merchants who feared that the traffic would now bypass the city centre and no one would come to shop. This fear was wrong. Neustadt is a popular destination, whether for day trips or longer stays, thanks to general tourism and events in the castle.

↑ Eine der ältesten Kirchen in den Grenzen des Naturparks, mit unterschiedlichen Baustilen, sowohl innen als auch außen.

↑ One of the oldest churches within the boundaries of the nature park with different architectural styles, both inside and out.

Liebfrauenkirche
Church of Our Lady

Peter Zenker

Die Liebfrauenkirche liegt an der Nebenstrecke des Pilgerweges Loccum-Volkenroda und wurde 1247 zum ersten Mal urkundlich erwähnt. Sie wurde zunächst als dreischiffige romanische Basilika erbaut und 1502 im gotischen Stil als Hallenkirche umgebaut. Im Zuge einer Restaurierung im Jahr 1997 wurden romanische Dekorationsmalereien mit Fabeltieren sowie weitere Ausmalungsreste aus dem 17. Jahrhundert entdeckt.

Der Mauerwerksbau wurde aus Hau- und Backsteinen dreischiffig mit Polygonalapsis und einem Satteldach über dem Mittel- und den Seitenschiffen gebaut. Strebepfeiler an Langhaus und Chor, am Schiff breite, am Chor schmale zweibahnige Spitzbogenfenster mit schlichtem Backsteinmaßwerk, gliedern die Fassaden. Im zweiten Joch von Westen sind reich ornamentierte spitzbogige Portale. Über dem Südportal finden sich drei figürliche Reliefsteine und eine Sonnenuhr.

Den gedrungenen Westturm, dessen Unterbau aus dem 13. Jahrhundert stammt, krönt ein verschieferter Turmhelm mit

The Liebfrauenkirche is located on the Loccum-Volkenroda pilgrimage route in and was first mentioned in a document in 1247. It was initially built as a three-aisled Romanesque basilica and rebuilt in 1502 in the Gothic style as a hall church. During restoration work in 1997, Romanesque decorative paintings with mythical creatures and other remnants of 17th century paintings were discovered.

The masonry building was constructed from brick and stone with three naves, a polygonal apse and a gabled roof over the nave and aisles. Buttresses on the nave and chancel, wide pointed arch windows on the nave and narrow double lancet windows with simple brick tracery on the chancel, organise the façades. In the second bay from the west are richly ornamented ogival portals. Above the south portal are three figurative relief stones and a sundial.

The squat west tower, whose substructure dates from the 13th century, is crowned by a slate spire with a four-sided base with small triangular gables with clock faces and sound open-

↑ An dieser Stelle ein Foto einmal nicht in Richtung Altar, denn selten gliedert sich eine Orgel so stimmig in ihre Umgebung ein wie in dieser Kirche. Man beachte die echten Kerzen in den Leuchtern.

↑ For once a photo not in the direction of the altar, because rarely does an organ blend in so harmoniously with its surroundings as in this church. Note the real candles in the candlesticks.

vierseitigem Ansatz nebst kleinen Dreiecksgiebeln mit Uhrziffernblättern und Schallöffnungen sowie einer achteckig ausgezogenen Spitze mit Kugel, Kreuz und Wetterhahn.

Der dreischiffige Kirchraum, überspannt mit Kreuzrippengewölben und seiner Apsis, beinhaltet auf der einen Seite ein vierjöchiges Seitenschiff mit dahinter folgender zweijöchiger Sakristei und auf der anderen Seite ein sechsjöchiges Seitenschiff. Das Mittelschiff wird mit spitzbogigen Arkaden von den Seitenschiffen getrennt und von achteckigen Pfeilern getragen, deren Kapitelle Tier- und Menschenköpfe schmücken. Der einachsige, barocke Altar von 1787 wird flankiert von zwei Säulen auf Postamenten. Die hohe Kanzel mit polygonalem Kanzelkorb befindet sich am nordwestlichen Chorpfeiler.

ings as well as an octagonal spire with a sphere, cross and weathercock.

The three-aisled church, spanned by ribbed vaults and its apse, contains a four-aisled side aisle on one side with a two-aisled sacristy behind it, and a six-aisled side aisle on the other side. The central nave is separated from the side aisles by pointed arched arcades and supported by octagonal pillars whose capitals are decorated with animal and human heads. The single-axis baroque altar from 1787 is flanked by two columns on pedestals. The high pulpit with polygonal pulpit basket is located on the north-west choir pillar.

↑ Eingebettet in das Grün der Gartenanlagen liegen die Klosterkirche aus der Gründungszeit und das barocke Konventgebäude. Der ehemalige Wirtschaftsweg des Klosters ist heute Ortsdurchfahrt.

↑ Embedded in the greenery of the gardens are the monastery church from the founding period and the baroque convent building. The former farm track of the monastery is now a thoroughfare through the village.

Kloster Mariensee

Peter Zenker

Das Kloster Mariensee wurde Anfang des 13. Jahrhunderts als Nonnenkloster gegründet, auf einem vom Grafen Bernhard II. von Wölpe gestifteten Gutshof erbaut und wohl schon seit 1215 nach den Gewohnheiten der Zisterzienserinnen geführt. Nach der Einführung der Reformation und dem folgenden Dreißigjährigen Krieg wurde das Kloster in ein Damenstift umgewandelt, in dem noch heute, über 800 Jahre später, ein evangelischer Frauenkonvent in geistlicher Gemeinschaft lebt.

Die weitläufige Anlage des Klosters Mariensee wird im Nordosten durch die mittelalterliche Klosterkirche mit dem barocken vierflügeligen Klostergebäude von 1729 dominiert. Nach Westen und Süden schließen sich umfangreiche Garten- und Weidelandflächen und verschiedene Nebengebäude an. Das Kloster ist Keimzelle des Ortes, der sich um das Kloster entwickelte und sein städtebaulicher Mittelpunkt.

Mariensee Monastery was founded at the beginning of the 13th century as a nunnery, built on an estate donated by Count Bernhard II von Wölpe and has arguably been run according to Cistercian practices since 1215. After the introduction of the Reformation and the subsequent Thirty Years' War, the monastery was converted into a convent for women, in which a Protestant women's convent still lives in spiritual community today, over 800 years later.

The extensive grounds of Mariensee Monastery are dominated in the north-east by the medieval monastery church with the baroque four-winged monastery building built in 1729. To the west and south are extensive garden and pasture land and various outbuildings. The monastery is the nucleus of the village, which developed around the monastery, and its urban centre.

↑ Banner im Klostermuseum schlagen die Brücke vom Mittelalter zur Reformationszeit. Tafeln in Buchform erläutern den Aufbau der kunstvollen Handschrift.
↑ Banners in the monastery museum from the Middle Ages to the Protestant Reformation. Panels in book form explain the structure of the ornate manuscript.

↑ Eine Sonderausstellung zum „Frauenort Äbtissin Odilie" stellt ihr Gebetbuch von 1522 vor, welches das Gebet der Frauen bis heute inspiriert.
↑ A special exhibition on the "Frauenort Äbtissin Odilie" presents her prayer book from 1522, which still inspires women's prayer today.

Es ist ein vielfältiger Ort, der nicht nur dem Gebet dient, sondern, dem Bildungsauftrag der Reformation folgend, auch der Vermittlung kultureller Inhalte und klösterlicher Kulturtechniken, wie zum Beispiel dem Klosterstich, der Kalligrafie und der Gartenpflege. Hier finden regelmäßig Seminare, Kunstausstellungen, Lesungen und Konzerte statt. Zudem ist es auch ein Ort der Einkehr und dient überdies als Unterkunft für Gäste.

Im Klostermuseum erfährt man viel über die Geschichte der norddeutschen Frauenklöster und darüber, wie Frauen in diesen ihren Glauben gelebt haben – in den Zeiten vor und nach Einführung der Reformation bis hin zum 19. Jahrhundert.

Als Baudenkmal ist das Kloster Mariensee in zweifacher Hinsicht von landes- und kirchengeschichtlicher Bedeutung:

Zum einen steht die Gründung für eine Welle von Klostergründungen durch den lokalen Adel im frühen 13. Jahrhundert und zum anderen für die Umwandlung bei der Einführung der Reformation im Fürstentum Calenberg-Göttingen durch Herzogin Elisabeth von Calenberg.

Als eines der fünf Calenberger Klöster gehört Mariensee zum Kernbestand des Allgemeinen Hannoverschen Klosterfonds, der seit 1818 von der Klosterkammer Hannover verwaltet wird.

Das Nebeneinander von mittelalterlicher Kirche aus der Gründungszeit und barockem Konventgebäude ist typisch für die Calenberger Klöster. Die Kirche wie auch das Konventgebäude haben sowohl als Einzelobjekte als auch als Teile der Klosteranlage eine hohe Aussagekraft für die Bau- und Kunst-

It is a multifaceted place that is not only used for prayer, but also for teaching cultural content and monastic cultural techniques, such as monastery engraving, calligraphy and gardening, in line with the educational mission of the Reformation. Seminars, art exhibitions, readings and concerts are regularly organised here. It is also a place for contemplation and accommodation in a guest area.

In the monastery museum you can learn a lot about the history of the North German women's monasteries and how women lived their faith in them – in the times before and after the introduction of the Reformation up to the 19th century.

As an architectural monument, Mariensee Monastery is of significance in terms of regional and church history in two respects:

Firstly, its foundation symbolises a wave of monastery foundations by the local nobility in the early 13th century and secondly, its transformation when the Reformation was introduced in the Principality of Calenberg-Göttingen by Duchess Elisabeth of Calenberg.

As one of the five Calenberg monasteries, Mariensee is part of the core holdings of the general Hannover Monastery Fund, which has been administered by the Hannover Monastery Chamber since 1818.

A medieval church from the founding period alongside a baroque convent building is typical of the Calenberg monasteries. Both the church and the convent building are highly significant for the history of architecture and art, both as individual objects and as parts of the convent complex, and are exemplary of the type of Protestant convent with a pre-Reformation church.

↑ Die Klosterkirche bietet – vor allem seit der letzten Renovierung von 1997 – ein geschlossenes Bild, in das sich verschiedene Elemente aus der Geschichte einfügen. Hier feiern Konvent und Kirchengemeinde Gottesdienst.

↑ The monastery church offers a cohesive image into which various elements from the history are integrated, especially since the last renovation in 1997. The convent and parish celebrate services here.

geschichte und sind beispielhaft für den Typus eines evangelischen Frauenklosters mit vorreformatorischer Kirche.

Das weitläufige Gelände ist fast unzerstört erhalten und in seiner Anlage mit Klostergarten, Weideland und Wasserläufen in seiner landschaftsprägenden Bedeutung an einem in die Leine fließenden Bachlauf gut nachvollziehbar.

Die Gartenanlagen des Klosters entsprechen in ihrem Aufbau der barocken Neuanlage aus dem 18. Jahrhundert. An die Abtei und jede der zwölf Wohneinheiten für die Konventualinnen schließt sich ein Ziergarten an. Außerdem ist jeder Einheit eine Parzelle im sogenannten Eichgarten zugeteilt. Hier wird Obst und Gemüse für den Eigenbedarf angebaut. Dort befinden sich auch Kräutergärten, die nach mittelalterlichen Vorbildern angelegt wurden und viele Besuchende anziehen.

Die Kirche des Klosters ist das einzige Gebäude, das aus der Gründungszeit erhalten geblieben ist. Äußerlich in recht schlichter, frühgotischer Backsteinbauweise erscheinend, bestimmt den Innenraum ihr monumentaler, dreijöchiger Backsteinsaal mit einem Chorpolygon aus der Mitte des 13. Jahrhunderts.

In den folgenden Jahrhunderten wurden noch diverse Bau- und Ausstattungselemente ergänzt. Die Kirche wurde im 18. Jahrhundert im Zusammenhang mit dem Neubau des Konventgebäudes vollständig umgestaltet: Die bisherige steinerne Nonnenempore wurde durch eine kleinere hölzerne ersetzt und die Innenausstattung barockisiert.

1867/68 wurde die Kirche durch einen Schüler des Architekten Konrad Wilhelm Hase neugotisch ausgestaltet. Die bisherige Damenempore wurde in das Innere des Konventgebäudes

The extensive grounds are still almost intact and the landscape of the monastery garden, pastureland and watercourses can be clearly traced along a stream flowing into the River Leine.

The gardens of the monastery correspond to the new Baroque gardens from the 18th century. An ornamental garden adjoins the abbey and each of the twelve residential units for the nuns. In addition, each unit is allocated a plot in the so-called "oak garden". Fruit and vegetables are grown here for personal use. There are also herb gardens, attracting many visitors.

The monastery's church is the only building that has survived from the founding period. Externally, it has a rather simple early Gothic brick construction and the interior is characterised by its monumental, three-bay brick hall with a choir polygon from the middle of the 13th century.

Various building and furnishing elements were added in the following centuries. The church was completely remodelled in the 18th century in connection with the construction of the new convent building: The previous nun's gallery made of stone was replaced by a smaller wooden one and the interior was baroqueised.

In 1867/68, the church was remodelled in neo-Gothic style by a pupil of the architect Konrad Wilhelm Hase. The previous ladies' gallery was moved to the interior of the convent building and an organ loft was built above the altar in place of the swallow's nest organ, on which a romantic Eduard Meyer organ can be played.

The exterior of the building is clearly structured. The brickwork of the façades is based on a profiled sandstone plinth. It

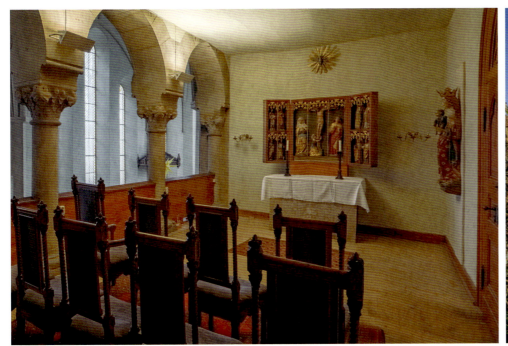 

↑ Auf der Damenempore befindet sich der mittelalterliche Altar und die Madonna, die aus dem 15. Jahrhundert stammt. Eine Legende sieht sie als Bewahrerin bei einer großen Flut.
↑ In the ladies' gallery is the medieval altar and the Madonna, which dates from the 15th century. One legend sees her as the protector against a great flood.

↑ Auf der Westseite trennt ein Seiteneingang zwei Hausgärten, die wie alle Gärten durch Einfassungen von Weißdornhecken klar strukturiert sind.
↑ On the west side, a side entrance separates two household gardens which, like all the gardens, are clearly structured by hawthorn hedge borders.

verlegt und anstelle der Schwalbennestorgel über dem Altar eine Orgelempore erbaut, auf der eine romantische Eduard-Meyer-Orgel erklingt.

Außen ist der Bau klar ablesbar gegliedert. Das Backsteinmauerwerk der Fassaden baut auf einem profilierten Sandsteinsockel auf. Es ist mit flachen Strebepfeilern gestaltet. Schlanke Spitzbogenfenster, die mit Glasursteinbändern eingefasst und in unterschiedlich und gestaffelt erscheinenden Gruppen angeordnet sind, bestimmen zusammen mit zwei Portalen das fast verspielt wirkende Äußere der nördlichen Längsfassade.

Der beachtliche Kirchenbau ist vor allem geprägt durch Baugedanken der zeitgenössischen Zisterzienserarchitektur, durch Einwirkungen des in Nordwestdeutschland während des 13. Jahrhunderts einflussreichen „Plantagenet"-Stils und durch charakteristische Elemente des norddeutschen Backsteinbaus.

Im Inneren der Kirche dominiert das mächtige, kuppelartig überhöhte Domikalgewölbe mit seinen zartgliederigen Rippen und bautechnisch ungewöhnlichen Details und Dekorationen in der Ausgestaltung. Der einschiffige Raum erfährt seinen Abschluss in einem mit hellen, schlicht dekorierten Fensteröffnungen versehenen Chorpolygon und dem neugotischen Holzaltar mit Abendmahlsrelief sowie einem Kreuzigungsbild.

Die hölzerne Kanzel mit Evangelistenfiguren auf steinerner Vierlingssäule auf der einen wie auch das Gestühl auf der anderen Seite, die Altarschranken, das Gestühl, die Brüstungen der Emporen sowie der Orgelprospekt entstammen der Zeit

is designed with flat buttresses. Slender pointed arch windows, framed with glazed stone bands and arranged in different and tiered groups, together with two portals, characterise the almost playful appearance of the northern long façade.

The impressive church building is characterised above all by the building ideas of contemporary Cistercian architecture, by the influence of the "Plantagenet" style, which was influential in north-west Germany during the 13th century, and by characteristic elements of north German brick construction.

The interior of the church is dominated by the mighty, dome-like domical vault with its delicately structured ribs and structurally unusual details and decorations. The single-nave room ends in a choir polygon with light-coloured, simply decorated window openings and the neo-Gothic wooden altar with a relief of the Last Supper and a crucifixion painting.

The wooden pulpit with figures of evangelists on a stone four-sided column on one side, as well as the stalls on the other, the altar rails, the stalls, the balustrades of the galleries and the organ's façade date from the restoration of 1867/68.

A larger-than-life wooden crucifix hanging on the north wall dates from the middle of the 13th century. A small vestibule cross and a finely carved Madonna and Child from the 15th century can be found in the ladies' gallery on the southern long side.

↑ Der Kreuzgang ist Ort der Stille und „Verkehrsweg". Und er bietet die Möglichkeit, wechselnde Ausstellungen moderner Kunst zu betrachten. Ein Treppenaufgang führt zum Bereich der Äbtissin und des Konvents.
↑ The cloister is a place of tranquillity and a "thoroughfare". It also offers the opportunity to view changing exhibitions of modern art. A staircase leads to the abbess and convent area.

↑ In der „Alten Küche" mit Regalen aus der Barockzeit lässt sich nachvollziehen, wie die Lebensmittel direkt aus dem Hausgarten weiterverarbeitet wurden.
↑ In the "old kitchen" with shelves from the Baroque period, you can see how food was processed directly from the home garden.

der Restaurierung von 1867/68.

Ein überlebensgroßes Holzkruzifix, an der Nordwand hängend, stammt aus der Mitte des 13. Jahrhunderts. Ein kleines Vortragekreuz sowie eine fein geschnitzte Madonna mit Kind aus dem 15. Jahrhundert finden sich auf der Damenempore an der südlichen Längsseite.

Unter der Orgelempore steht ein achtseitiger Taufstein aus dem 19. Jahrhundert auf einem Säulenbündel, über dem ein prächtiger Taufengel schwebt; ein Motiv, das vor allem im 17. und 18. Jahrhundert in lutherischen Kirchen verbreitet war.

Die Klosteranlage wurde im 18. Jahrhundert mit einem Konventgebäude ausgestattet, das die zisterziensischen Vorstellungen deutlicher widerspiegelt als der Vorgängerbau.

Jede Wohneinheit besitzt ein separates Treppenhaus; der zum Bereich der Äbtissin führende Aufgang ist der einzige, der nicht hinter einer Tür verborgen, sondern direkt vom Kreuzgang aus zugänglich ist.

Eine der geschichtlichen und kirchenrechtlichen Besonderheiten im niedersächsischen Raum besteht darin, dass es hier ungeachtet des Konfessionswechsels eine ungebrochene Klostertradition gibt, die sich bis zum heutigen Tage erhalten hat.

In diesem Zusammenhang stellt das Kloster von Mariensee eine Anlage von größter Harmonie dar – und ist unbedingt einen Besuch wert.

Below the organ loft is an eight-sided baptismal font from the 19th century on a cluster of columns, above which hovers a magnificent baptismal angel, a motif that was particularly common in Lutheran churches in the 17th and 18th centuries. In the 18th century, the monastery complex was equipped with a convent building that more clearly reflects Cistercian ideas than the previous building.

Each residential unit has a separate staircase; the staircase leading to the abbess's area is the only one that is not hidden behind a door, but is directly accessible from the cloister.

One of the historical and ecclesiastical peculiarities of the Lower Saxony region is that, despite the change of denomination, there is an unbroken monastic tradition here that has survived to this day.

In this context, the Mariensee monastery is a complex of the greatest harmony – and is definitely worth a visit.

↑ „Die Gärten sind uns Bild für die Gemeinschaft", sagt Äbtissin Bärbel Görcke: „Es gibt viel Raum einzuwurzeln und sich zu entfalten – in der Geschichte gegründet und offen für das, was kommt."

↑ "The gardens are an image for the community," says Abbess Bärbel Görcke: "There is plenty of space to take root and develop – grounded in history and open to what is to come."

↑ Am Anfang der Kräutergärten, gestaltet nach mittelalterlichen Vorbildern, lädt das „Paradiesgärtlein" zum Verweilen ein.

↑ When you enter the herb gardens, which were modelled after medieval examples, you will be invited to linger in "the little paradise garden".

↑↑ Das Toilettenhaus ist dem Gebäude vorgelagert und als eine weitere Besonderheit durch einen hier nicht sichtbaren, überdachten Gang mit diesem verbunden.

↑↑ The toilet block is located in front of the building and, as a further special feature, is connected to it by a covered corridor that is not visible here.

Danke!

Es ist das eine, eine Idee zu einem Buch zu haben, aber die Realisierung ist das andere. Und wie so oft im Leben geht es nur mit starken und engagierten Partnern!

Man spricht hier und dort über das Projekt, das Konzept und überraschenderweise findet sich dann plötzlich ein Kreis von Menschen, der diese Idee mitträgt und Unterstützung gibt.

Ohne euch, liebe Partner, Freundinnen und Freunde würde es dieses Buch nicht geben!

Als da sind ...

Natürlich zuerst die Partner, die sich auch finanziell engagiert haben – denn ohne sie ist ein Buch wie dieses in der heutigen Zeit nicht mehr denkbar und zu realisieren!

Die Kolleginnen und Kollegen der fotografierenden und schreibenden Zunft, teilweise Amateurinnen und Amateure, die aber gerade dann meist sehr persönlich und emotional einen Text verfasst haben oder ihre besten Fotos lieferten, wie einer der Tierfotografen, Bernhard Volmer (Naturfotograf des Jahres 2021), der beeindruckende Fotos beisteuerte, unter anderem das vom Seeadler.
Unter die ambitionierten Amateurinnen und Amateure fällt auch Alexander Fürst zu Schaumburg-Lippe, der nicht nur eine Erinnerung aus seiner Kindheit aufschrieb, sondern mir auch – voller Vertrauen – eine alte Holzkiste mit teilweise mehr als 100 Jahre alten Familienfotos und Postkarten zur Recherche übergab.

Sein Cousin, York Prinz zu Schaumburg-Lippe, beschaffte mir über seine Kontakte Fotos, die einmalig das besondere Schaffen von Graf Wilhelm – auch in Portugal – vor rund 300 Jahren dokumentieren.

Mein Freund Peter Zenker, der als Architekt und Teilzeitkunsthistoriker sein Wissen über die Kirchen und ein Kloster mit all ihren architektonischen Details beisteuerte, das so fundiert in Worte gefasst war, dass wir sie im Anschluss an sein Schreiben erst einmal mithilfe der Lektorinnen und Lektoren und dem Internet in verständliche Worte fassen mussten.

Thank you!

It's one thing to have an idea for a book, but realising it is another. And as so often in life, it only works with strong and committed partners!

You talk here and there about the project, outline the concept and then, surprisingly, you suddenly find a circle of people who support the idea and give their backing.

Without you, dear partners and friends, this book would not exist!

Among you are ...

First of all, of course, the partners who have also made a financial commitment - because without them, a book like this would be unthinkable and impossible to realise in this day and age!

The colleagues from the world of photography and writing, some of whom are amateurs, but who especially then have usually written a very personal and emotional text or provided their best photos, such as one of the wildlife photographers, Bernhard Volmer (Nature Photographer of the Year 2021), who contributed impressive photos, including that of the white-tailed eagle.
Among the ambitious amateurs is also Alexander, Prince of Schaumburg-Lippe, who not only wrote down a memory from his childhood, but also – full of trust – handed me an old wooden box with family photos and postcards, some of which were more than a hundred years old, for research.

His cousin, York, Prince of Schaumburg-Lippe, used his contacts to provide me with photos that uniquely document Count Wilhelm's special work – including his achievements in Portugal – some three hundred years ago.

My friend Peter Zenker, who, as an architect and part-time art historian, contributed his knowledge of the churches and a monastery with all their architectural details. His insights were so well articulated in his writing that we first had to put them into understandable words with the help of the editors and the Internet after he had finished his texts.

Die Lektorinnen und Lektoren sowie Übersetzerinnen und Übersetzer, die manchen Text überhaupt erst verständlich machten.

Der Grafiker Léon Auffenberg, der mich seit vielen Jahren mit seinen Entwürfen und Launen begleitet, seitdem er bei mir als Praktikant die ersten beruflichen Schritte machte und Jahre später bei dem herausragenden Prof. Markus Dreßen in Leipzig seinen Abschluss mit summa cum laude bestand – und sich heute trotzdem nicht zu schade ist, immer noch für mich zu arbeiten.

Der Motorbootfahrer Sebastian „Teddy" Tatje, der mit mir wenige Tage vor Weihnachten in Eiseskälte über das Wasser zum Wilhelmstein rauschte, damit ich noch Aufnahmen dort in der Festung machen konnte, weil mir der Fürst am Tag zuvor beim Glühwein von einer Idee für ein Foto erzählte ...

Die Druckerei Gutenberg Beuys, die immer alles gibt, um das zu Papier zu bringen, was in fast drei Jahren an Ideen, Fotos und Texten und Gestaltung zusammenkam.

Nicht zu denken wäre dieses Buch aber auch ohne die Geduld meiner Familie – ich erinnere mich gerne an die Worte meiner jüngsten (das Wort kleinen mag sie gar nicht!) Tochter, die zuweilen und immer wieder sagte:

„Papi, lass doch mal den blöden Rechner in Ruhe und spiel mit mir Mensch ärgere Dich nicht!"

Letztendlich danke ich jedem Menschen, der in irgendeiner Form, sei der Anteil auch noch so klein, zu diesem Buch seinen Teil beigetragen hat und den ich hier nicht erwähnt habe.

Heinrich K.-M Hecht

The editors and translators who made some texts comprehensible in the first place.

The graphic designer Léon Auffenberg, who has accompanied me for many years with his designs and whims, ever since he took his first professional steps with me as an intern and years later graduated Summa Cum Laude under the outstanding Prof. Markus Dreßen in Leipzig – and who still isn't too proud to work for me today.

The motorboat driver Sebastian "Teddy" Tatje, who rushed with me across the water to Wilhelmstein in the freezing cold a few days before Christmas, so I could take some shots there in the fortress because the Prince had told me about an idea for a photo over mulled wine the day before ...

The Gutenberg Beuys printing company, who always give their all to bring to paper what has come together in almost three years of ideas, photos, texts and design.

But this book would also be unthinkable without the patience of my family – I fondly remember the words of my youngest daughter (she dislikes being called "little"!), who would sometimes say over and over again:

"Daddy, why don't you leave the stupid computer alone and play Ludo with me!"

Finally, I would like to thank every person who has contributed to this book in any way, no matter how small, and whom I haven't mentioned here!

Heinrich K.-M Hecht

Die Autorinnen und Autoren / The authors

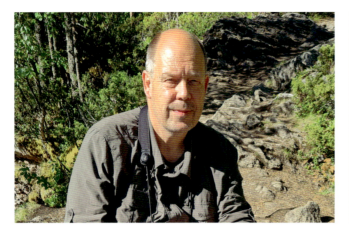

Dipl. -Biol. Dipl. -Ing. Thomas Brandt

geboren 1964 in Rinteln, studierte Biologie an der Universität Osnabrück und erfüllte so seinen schon als Kind gewachsenen Berufswunsch. Anschließend absolvierte er das Ingenieursstudium Ökologische Umweltsicherung an der GH Kassel/Witzenhausen. Seit 1994 ist er in der Ökologischen Schutzstation Steinhuder Meer (ÖSSM) tätig und als wissenschaftlicher Leiter unter anderem für die Bestandserfassung von Tieren und Pflanzen sowie für die Entwicklung und Umsetzung von Naturschutzmaßnahmen verantwortlich.

Thomas Brandt ist Autor von mehreren Sachbüchern, so auch von zwei Reiseführern mit den Titeln „Naturerlebnis Steinhuder Meer" und „Naturpfad Schaumburg" sowie vom Bildband „Das Steinhuder Meer – Bilder einer Landschaft". Darüber hinaus ist er Verfasser von mehr als 250 wissenschaftlichen und populärwissenschaftlichen Beiträgen zu verschiedenen Naturthemen und Redaktionsmitglied bei einer ornithologischen Fachzeitschrift.

Thomas Brandt ist dem Thema Naturschutz eng verbunden und seit vier Jahrzehnten auch ehrenamtlich im Naturschutz tätig. Seit 2017 ist er außerdem Vorsitzender der Niedersächsischen Ornithologischen Vereinigung (NOV).

born in Rinteln in 1964, studied biology at the University of Osnabrück, thus fulfilling his childhood dream. He then completed an engineering degree in Ecological Environmental Protection at the GH Kassel/Witzenhausen. He has been working at the Lake Steinhuder Meer Ecological Protection Centre (ÖSSM e.V.) since 1994 and, as scientific director, is responsible for recording animal and plant populations as well as developing and implementing nature conservation measures.

Thomas Brandt is the author of several non-fiction books, including two travel guides entitled "Naturerlebnis Steinhuder Meer" and "Naturpfad Schaumburg" as well as the illustrated book "Das Steinhuder Meer – Bilder einer Landschaft". He is also the author of more than 250 scientific and popular science articles on various nature topics and a member of the editorial board of an ornithological journal.

Thomas Brandt is closely associated with nature conservation and has been active in nature conservation on a voluntary basis for four decades. He has also been Chairman of the Lower Saxony Ornithological Association (NOV) since 2017.

Renate Braselmann

Geboren am 10. April 1951 in Langenfeld im Rheinland, aufgewachsen in Düsseldorf – und hat trotzdem die längste Zeit ihres Lebens in Münchehagen verbracht. Nach dem Abitur hat sie an der Pädagogischen Hochschule in Köln die Fächer Deutsch, Geschichte und Biologie für das Lehramt an Grund- und Hauptschule studiert. An der Gemeinschaftsgrundschule in Haan-Gruiten lernte sie ihren jetzigen Ehemann, Pastor Wolfram Braselmann, kennen und ging mit ihm nach Niedersachsen. Dort zogen sie zusammen ins Pfarrhaus nach Münchehagen, heirateten 1982 und bekamen vier Kinder.

Renate Braselmann war neben ihrem Beruf als Grundschullehrerin in Münchehagen aktiv in der Kirchengemeinde tätig und später auch in der Kommunalpolitik. Von 2011 bis 2021 war sie Ortsbürgermeisterin und initiierte mehrere ortsbezogene Projekte, leitete mehrere Jahre den Münchehäger Dörpverein, gründete eine Theatergruppe, einen monatlich stattfindenden Wochenmarkt, eine Bürgerinitiative, verschiedene Gesprächskreise und war deshalb bestens über das Leben in Münchehagen informiert.

Born on 10 April 1951 in Langenfeld in the Rhineland, she grew up in Düsseldorf – and yet has spent most of her life in Münchehagen. After graduating from high school, she studied German, history and biology at the University of Education in Cologne to become a primary and secondary school teacher. At the community primary school in Haan-Gruiten, she met her current husband, Pastor Wolfram Braselmann, and went with him to Lower Saxony. They moved into the vicarage in Münchehagen together, married in 1982 and had four children.

In addition to her job as a primary school teacher in Münchehagen, Renate Braselmann was actively involved in the church community and later also in local politics. She was local mayor from 2011 to 2021 and initiated several local projects, headed the Münchehäger Dörpverein for several years, founded a theatre group, a monthly farmers' market, a citizens' initiative, various discussion groups and was therefore well informed about life in Münchehagen.

Dr. Stefan Brüdermann

Geboren 1959 in Osterode, im schönen Harz, studierte er Geschichte und Germanistik an den Universitäten Göttingen und im wundervollen Wien. Nach seiner Promotion 1987 wurde er Archivar und arbeitete an den Staatsarchiven Wolfenbüttel, Hannover und Bückeburg und dem Deutschen Historischen Institut in Rom. Seit 2009 ist er Leiter der Abteilung Bückeburg des Niedersächsischen Landesarchivs und Vorsitzender der Historischen Arbeitsgemeinschaft für Schaumburg und lebt mit seiner Familie auch in Schaumburg.

Stefan Brüdermann publiziert über Universitätsgeschichte, Straßenverkehrsgeschichte und niedersächsische Landesgeschichte, derzeit vor allem über die Schaumburger Geschichte.

Born in 1959 in Osterode, in the beautiful Harz Mountains, he studied history and German at the universities in Göttingen and in beautiful Vienna. After his doctorate in 1987, he became an archivist and worked at the State Archives Wolfenbüttel, Hannover and Bückeburg and the German Historical Institute in Rome. Since 2009 he has been head of the Bückeburg department of the Lower Saxony State Archives and chairman of the Historical Working Group for Schaumburg and also lives in Schaumburg with his family.

Stefan Brüdermann publishes on university history, road traffic history and Lower Saxony state history, and currently above all about the history of Schaumburg.

Jürgen Engelmann

lebt seit fast 80 Jahren in Steinhude, segelt auf dem Steinhuder Meer, jetzt mit seinem P-Boot und zuvor in verschiedenen Klassen, zum Beispiel mit dem traditionellen Z-Boot, der 20er-Rennjolle. Im Segler-Verein Großenheidorn (SVG) ist er seit über 50 Jahren Mitglied und war dort über fünf Jahre Vorsitzender. Im SVG war er Mitorganisator für die Z-Boot-Regatten und die Holzbootregatten. Er war 30 Jahre lang in der Kommunalpolitik, als Ratsherr in Wunstorf und als Ortsbürgermeister in Steinhude, aktiv. Im Schaumburg-Lippischen Heimatverein engagiert er sich in der Seeprovinz für Heimatforschung und Heimatpflege. Beruflich konnte er in den letzten achtzehn Dienstjahren als Lehrer und Schulleiter der Haupt- und Realschule in seinem Heimatort tätig sein.

has lived in Steinhude for almost 80 years and now sails on Lake Steinhuder Meer with his P-boat and previously in various classes, for example with the traditional Z-boat, the 20er racing dinghy. He has been a member of the Großenheidorn Sailing Club (SVG) for over 50 years and was its chairman for more than five years. In the SVG, he was co-organiser of the Z-boat regattas and the wooden boat regattas. He was active in local politics for 30 years, as a councillor in Wunstorf and as local mayor in Steinhude. In the Schaumburg-Lippe local history association, he is involved in local history research and preservation in the maritime province. Over the past eighteen years, he has worked as a teacher and head teacher at the secondary school in his home town.

Die Autorinnen und Autoren / The authors

Dipl. -Geol. Benjamin Englich

ist bereits seit frühester Kindheit auf der Suche nach Fossilien und großer Dinosaurier-Enthusiast. Schon vor der Schulzeit stand fest: Er wird Paläontologe! Den Lebenstraum erfüllte er sich mit dem Studium an der Universität Bonn, durch welches er weltweit auf verschiedensten Grabungen und Gelände-Exkursionen unterwegs war. Seine zweite Passion, moderne Technologien, kombinierte er im Zuge seiner Abschlussarbeit mit der Neuaufnahme des berühmten Naturdenkmals „Saurierfährten" Münchehagen. Mittels Drohnen, hochauflösender Fotogrammetrie und Höhenfeldanalysen wurden zu den bereits bekannten 250 Dinosaurierspuren über 60 neue entdeckt und eine exakte 3-D-Erfassung der gesamten Fläche erzeugt. Diese Technik hat sich innerhalb der letzten zehn Jahre zum Standard in der Paläontologie entwickelt. Seit 2015 leitet Benjamin Englich die Grabungen auf dem Naturdenkmal. Seit 2022 ist er zudem wissenschaftlicher Leiter des Dinosaurier-Parks und somit auch für weitere Grabungen in ganz Niedersachsen, aber auch die Verwaltung der umfassenden Fossiliensammlung des Parks zuständig.

has been searching for fossils since early childhood and is an avid dinosaur enthusiast. Even before he entered school, he knew he wanted to be a paleontologist! He fulfilled his lifelong dream by studying at the University of Bonn, during the course of which he traveled the world on various excavations and field trips. He combined his second passion, modern technologies, with the re-survey of the famous natural monument "Saurierfährten" Münchehagen as part of his final thesis. Using drones, high-resolution photogrammetry and elevation field analyses, more than 60 new dinosaur tracks were discovered in addition to the 250 already known and an exact 3D survey of the entire area was created. This technique has become the standard in palaeontology over the last ten years. Since 2015, Benjamin Englich has been leading the excavations at the natural monument. Since 2022, he has also been the scientific director of the Dinosaur Park and is therefore responsible for several excavations throughout Lower Saxony, as well as managing the park's extensive fossil collection.

Klaus Fesche

ist Historiker und seit 2005 Stadtarchivar in Wunstorf. Seit vielen Jahren beschäftigt er sich historisch mit dem Steinhuder Meer, vor allem mit dessen Kulturgeschichte. Sein 1998 erschienenes Buch „Auf zum Steinhuder Meer. Geschichte des Tourismus an Niedersachsens größtem Binnensee" ist ein Standardwerk. Darüber hinaus hat er viele weitere Texte zum Thema verfasst. Andere Publikationen behandeln die lokale und regionale Geschichte, etwa die Geschichte der Expo-GmbH. 2010 erschien sein Buch „Geschichte Wunstorfs. Die Stadt, der Flecken und die Dörfer". 2021 gab er mit Hinrich Ewert das Buch „Wunstorfer Aufbrüche. Wendepunkte der Stadtgeschichte von 871 bis heute" heraus.

is a historian and has been the town archivist in Wunstorf since 2005. He has studied the history of Lake Steinhuder Meer for many years, especially its cultural history. His 1998 book "Auf zum Steinhuder Meer. History of tourism on Lower Saxony's largest inland lake" is a standard work. He has also written many other texts on the subject. Other publications deal with local and regional history, such as the history of Expo GmbH. In 2010, his book "Geschichte Wunstorfs. The town, the district and the villages" was published. In 2021, he and Hinrich Ewert brought out the book "Wunstorfer Aufbrüche. Turning points in the town's history from 871 to the present day".

Dr. Claudia Gondry

wurde 1953 in Hannover geboren. Als sie sieben Jahre alt war, zog sie mit ihren Eltern und drei Geschwistern in die alte Windmühle nach Schneeren, die ihre Familie im Laufe der nächsten Jahre sanierte. Dort ist sie aufgewachsen und erinnert sich vor allem an die endlosen Winterspaziergänge zum Steinhuder Meer. Während ihre Schwester ritt und ihre Brüder segelten, wanderte sie stundenlang durch die Gegend und entwickelte eine Vorliebe für die Landschaft, die sie später auch beruflich einbringen konnte.

1972 machte sie am Gymnasium Neustadt am Rübenberge ihr Abitur und studierte dann in Göttingen Kunstgeschichte und Klassische Archäologie. Im Rahmen ihrer Doktorarbeit ging sie 1979 mit einem Stipendium nach London – und blieb über 30 Jahre dort. Sie arbeitete beim Auktionshaus Christie's und als Dozentin an mehreren Universitäten. 2012 kam sie nach Schneeren zurück, um die alte Windmühle, die sie nach dem Tod ihrer Eltern mit ihren Geschwistern geerbt hatte, noch einmal zu renovieren.

was born in Hannover in 1953. When she was seven years old, she moved with her parents and three siblings into the old windmill in Schneeren, which her family renovated over the next few years. She grew up there and especially remembers the endless winter walks to the Lake Steinhuder Meer. While her sister rode horses and her brothers sailed, she spent hours walking through the area and developed a fondness for the landscape, which she was later able to put to good use in her career.

In 1972, she completed her A-levels at Neustadt am Rübenberge grammar school and then studied art history and classical archaeology in Göttingen. As part of her doctoral thesis, she went to London on a scholarship in 1979 – and stayed there for over 30 years. She worked at the auction house Christie's and as a lecturer at several universities. She returned to Schneeren in 2012 to renovate the old windmill that she had inherited with her siblings after the death of her parents.

Heinrich K.-M. Hecht

geboren am 25. August 1955 in Hannover, lebt Heinrich K.-M. Hecht heute mit seiner Familie im Schaumburger Land. Seine Begeisterung für die Fotografie entstand bei Familienausflügen an die Küste. Von 1966 bis 1986 war die Fotografie in Heinrich Hechts Leben ein Hobby. Nach zehn Jahren im Vertrieb und Marketing von Computerunternehmen beendete er 1986 seine bis dahin berufliche Laufbahn.

Seither ist die Fotografie Beruf und Berufung zugleich: Lieblingsthemen sind das Meer, Schifffahrt, Segeln, Architektur, Kunst und Automotive.

Er gehörte als Fotograf zum offiziellen Team der Dokumentation der Reichtagsverhüllung von Christo und dokumentierte unter anderem die Segelwettbewerbe der Olympischen Spiele und den America's Cup. Für die Weltausstellung EXPO 2000 war Heinrich K.-M. Hecht mit seinem Team verantwortlich für alle offiziellen Publikationen der EXPO-Gesellschaft.

Er veröffentlichte über zwanzig Bücher sowie mehr als 70 Kalender. Ausstellungen im In- und Ausland und Veröffentlichungen in internationalen Magazinen runden sein Schaffen ab.

born on 25 August 1955 in Hannover, Heinrich K.-M. Hecht now lives with his family in the Schaumburg region. His enthusiasm for photography developed during family trips to the coast. From 1966 to 1986, photography was a hobby in Heinrich Hecht's life. After ten years in sales and marketing for computer companies, he ended that particular professional career in 1986.

Since then, photography has been both his profession and his vocation: his favourite subjects are the sea, shipping, sailing, architecture, art and automotive motifs.

As a photographer, he was part of the official team documenting Christo's wrapping of the Reichstag and documented the sailing competitions at the Olympic Games and the America's Cup, among others. For the EXPO 2000 world exhibition, Heinrich K.-M. Hecht and his team were responsible for all official publications of the EXPO organisation.

He has published over twenty books and more than seventy calendars. His work is complemented by exhibitions at home and abroad and magazines.

Die Autorinnen und Autoren / The authors

Hans-Erich Hergt

Vorsitzender des Museumsverein Neustädter Land e.V., in Neustadt 1950 geboren und aufgewachsen. Hans-Erich Hergt hat mit anderen Kindern aus seiner Straße in den 1960er Jahren am Steinhuder Meer Flöße gebaut und Pirat gespielt. Am Weißen Berg wurde gezeltet und man hat dort mit Freude einen großen Teil der Sommerferien verbracht.
Über 35 Jahre im Rat der Stadt und eine langjährige ehrenamtliche Tätigkeit als Vorsitzender des Museumsverein, in dem Herr Hergt seine Ambitionen für die Geschichte der Stadt Neustadt einbringen konnte, war und ist für ihn selbstverständlich.

Chairman of the Museumsverein Neustadt Land e.V., born and raised in Neustadt in 1950. Hans-Erich Hergt and other children from his street built rafts and played pirates on the Lake Steinhuder Meer in the 1960s. They camped on the Weißer Berg and enjoyed spending a large part of their summer holidays there.
Over 35 years on the town council and many years of voluntary work as chairman of the museum association, in which Mr Hergt was able to contribute his ambition for the history of the town of Neustadt, was and is a matter of course for him.

Stefan Ibold

Jahrgang 1961, segelt quasi seit Geburt an am Steinhuder Meer. Bis Ende der 1980er Jahre war er am Nordufer beheimatet, bevor er danach an das Südufer wechselte, wo er auch heute noch aktiv ist und inzwischen dort auch lebt.
Er ist seit vielen Jahren eng mit der Wettfahrtvereinigung Steinhuder Meer, deren Sportwart er ist, verbunden, so dass er die Entwicklung des Wassersports auf dem Steinhuder Meer gut verfolgen kann.
Neben seiner beruflichen Laufbahn als Dachdeckermeister und öbuv-Sachverständiger für das Dachdeckerhandwerk hat er sich auch als Autor von Fachbüchern und Fachartikeln im Bereich Segeln – seine große Leidenschaft – betätigt. Für den Segler-Verband Niedersachsen und den Deutschen Segler-Verband bildet er Schiedsrichterinnen und Schiedsrichter sowie Wettfahrtleiterinnen und Wettfahrtleiter aus und ist bei beiden Tätigkeiten national und international unterwegs. Dabei entstand seine weitere Liebe zur Fotografie, die er überwiegend bei Regatten ausübt.

Stefan Ibold, born in 1961, has been sailing on the Lake Steinhuder Meer practically since birth. Until the end of the 1980s, he was based on the north shore before moving to the south shore, where he is still active today and where he now lives.
He has been closely involved with the Lake Steinhuder Meer racing association, of which he is the sports director, for many years, so that he can follow the development of water sports on the Lake Steinhuder Meer closely.
In addition to his professional career as a master roofer and öbuv expert for the roofing trade, he has also worked as an author of specialist books and articles on sailing – his great passion. He trains referees and race organisers for the Lower Saxony Sailing Association and the German Sailing Association and travels nationally and internationally in both activities. This also gave rise to his love of photography, which he mainly pursues by taking photos at regattas.

Doreen Juffa

wurde 1976 in Rostock an der Ostsee geboren – Wasser gehört zu ihrer DNA und ist quasi der blaue Faden in ihrem Leben.
Sie begleitet den Naturpark Steinhuder Meer seit 2014 beruflich für die Region Hannover und ist seit 2020 Geschäftsführerin des Naturparks. Neben ihren Aufgaben schätzt sie besonders den Blick auf das Steinhuder Meer aus ihrem Büro des Naturpark-Hauses in Mardorf.
Sie ist ferner Sprecherin der Arbeitsgemeinschaft der Niedersächsischen Naturparke und seit 2022 im Vorstand des Verbandes Deutscher Naturparke (VDN).
Ideen entwickeln, Netzwerke aufbauen und Projekte umsetzen, Partner gewinnen und Interessen ausgleichen – das sind ihre beruflichen Stärken und sie decken sich quasi mit den Leitlinien des Naturparks Steinhuder Meer.

Born in 1976 in Rostock on the Baltic Sea, water is ingrained in her DNA and is essentially the blue thread running through her life.
She has been supporting the Lake Steinhude Nature Park professionally at the Hannover Region since 2014 and has been Managing Director of the Nature Park since 2020. In addition to her duties, she particularly appreciates the view of Lake Steinhuder Meer from her office in the Nature Park House in Mardorf.
She is also the spokesperson for the working group of Lower Saxony's nature parks and has been on the board of the Association of German Nature Parks (VDN) since 2022.
Developing ideas, building networks and implementing projects, gaining partners and balancing interests – these are her professional strengths and they virtually coincide with the guidelines of the Lake Steinhude Nature Park.

George Kochbeck

Jahrgang 1955, wuchs bis zum Abitur in Gütersloh auf.
Mit vierzehn gründete er seine erste Band – und kam vom Musikmachen nie wieder los.
Ab 1978 zog es ihn nach Hamburg und er startete dort im passenden musikalischen Umfeld seine Profikarriere.
In den 1980ern spielte er mit vielen berühmten Künstlerinnen und Künstlern der Neuen Deutschen Welle zusammen.
1986 landete er einen Hit mit seiner Band Georgie Red.
Seit den 1990er Jahren und bis heute ist Kochbeck erfolgreicher TV-Filmkomponist und hat alleine für die TV-Krimiserie SOKO Leipzig über 100 Folgen erfolgreich vertont. Nebenher engagiert er sich in der Organisation von Konzerten mit weiteren erfolgreichen Musikerinnen und Musikern und spielt von Zeit zu Zeit die Kirchenorgel in der wunderschönen Kirche von Bergkirchen.
George Kochbeck lebt mit seiner Familie in Wiedenbrügge in der Nähe des Steinhuder Meeres und ist inzwischen überzeugter Schaumburger.

Born in 1955, he grew up in Gütersloh until graduating from high school.
He founded his first band at the age of fourteen – and has never stopped making music.
In 1978 he moved to Hamburg and started his professional career there in the right musical environment.
In the 80s he played with many famous artists from the Neue Deutsche Welle.
In 1986 he landed a hit with his band Georgie Red.
Since the 1990s and to this day, Kochbeck has been a successful TV film composer and has successfully scored over a hundred episodes for the TV crime series SOKO Leipzig alone. At the same time, he is involved in organising concerts with other successful musicians and from time to time plays the church organ in the beautiful church in Bergkirchen.
George Kochbeck lives with his family in Wiedenbrügge near the Lake Steinhuder Meer and is now a committed Schaumburger by conviction.

Die Autorinnen und Autoren / The authors

Frank Ludowig

ist gebürtiger Wunstorfer und Jahrgang 1967. Seine berufliche Laufbahn wurde ihm quasi in die Wiege gelegt. Wie schon sein Vater, sein Großvater und auch sein Urgroßvater ist er selbstständiger Fleischermeister und dem Handwerk sehr verbunden. Neben seinem eigenen Handwerksbetrieb, in dem es heute hauptsächlich um Nachhaltigkeit und Tierwohl geht, ist er in der Branche unter anderem als Sachverständiger und in Aufsichtsräten tätig sowie ehrenamtlich sozial engagiert. Zum Segeln kam er erst recht spät, als zwei seiner vier Kinder mit dem Wassersport am Steinhuder Meer anfingen. Mit großer Begeisterung wurden dann jedoch sämtliche Urlaube gemeinsam mit der Familie auf Charteryachten verbracht. Eigene Boote liegen seitdem in der Baltischen Segler-Vereinigung in Großenheidorn und werden von der Familie intensiv genutzt.

was born in Wunstorf in 1967. His professional career was practically laid out for him from the cradle. Like his father, his grandfather and his great-grandfather, he is a self-employed master butcher and is very attached to the craft. In addition to his own craft business, which today mainly focuses on sustainability and animal welfare, he also works in the industry as an expert and on supervisory boards, as well as being involved in social work on a voluntary basis. He only came to sailing quite late, namely when two of his four children started doing water sports on the Lake Steinhuder Meer. With great enthusiasm, however, all vacations were thereafter spent together with the family on charter yachts. Since then, their own boats have been kept in the Baltic Sailing Association in Großenheidorn and are used intensively by the family.

Landesbischof Ralf Meister, Abt zu Loccum

wurde am 5. Januar 1962 in Hamburg geboren und ist seit dem 26. März 2011 Landesbischof der Evangelisch-lutherischen Landeskirche Hannovers. Er war zuvor drei Jahre Generalsuperintendent in Berlin und sieben Jahre Propst in Lübeck. Bis 1996 war Meister in der Arbeitsstelle „Kirche und Stadt" am Seminar für Praktische Theologie an der Universität Hamburg tätig. In dieser Zeit entstanden zahlreiche Veröffentlichungen zu religions- und stadtsoziologischen Fragestellungen. 2018 wurde Meister zum Leitenden Bischof der Vereinigten Evangelisch-lutherischen Kirche Deutschlands gewählt. 2020 wurde er als 65. Abt des Klosters Loccum eingeführt.

was born on 5 January, 1962 in Hamburg and has been regional bishop of the Evangelical Lutheran Regional Church of Hannover since 26 March 2011. He was previously general superintendent in Berlin for three years and provost in Lübeck for seven years. Until 1996, Meister worked in the "Church and City" department at the Seminar for Practical Theology at the University of Hamburg. During this time, he produced numerous publications on religious and urban sociological issues. In 2018, Meister was elected Presiding Bishop of the United Evangelical Lutheran Church of Germany. In 2020 he was installed as the 65th abbot of the Loccum monastery.

Marion und Derek Meister

Marion Meister, Jahrgang 1974, hat an der Filmhochschule „Konrad Wolf" in Potsdam-Babelsberg Animation studiert. Seit 2006 veröffentlicht sie Romane bei verschiedenen Publikumsverlagen im Bereich Fantastik.

Für ihren Near-Future-Thriller „White Maze", der unter dem Pseudonym *June Perry* erschienen ist, erhielt sie 2019 den Glauser Preis für den besten Jugendkrimi und die *Goldene Leslie*, den Jugendliteraturpreis des Landes Rheinland-Pfalz.

Als gebürtige Bayerin hat sie inzwischen in Niedersachsen, am Steinhuder Meer, Wurzeln geschlagen.

Ihre Erlebnisse aus Natur und Landleben finden immer wieder Eingang in ihre Romane.

Derek Meister, Jahrgang 1973, ist in Hannover geboren und zog Anfang der 2000er Jahre in die Nähe des Steinhuder Meeres nach Münchehagen. Er arbeitet seit 1999 als freier Autor und studierte Film- und Fernsehdramaturgie an der Filmhochschule Potsdam-Babelsberg. Schon während des Studiums entwickelte er für SAT1 die beliebte Serie „Mit Herz und Handschellen" mit. Es folgten zahlreiche hoch budgetierte TV-Movies unter anderem für RTL und PRO7.

Der Abenteuerfilm „Die Jagd nach dem Schatz der Nibelungen" (2008) wurde in vier Sparten zum Deutschen Fernsehpreis nominiert. Seit zwanzig Jahren schreibt er außerdem Bücher und mittlerweile sind im Kapitänshaus etliche Krimis, Thriller sowie historische Romane entstanden. Zu seinen bekanntesten Werken zählt die mittelalterliche Krimireihe um den Ermittler „Rungholt" sowie die Krimiserie um „Polizeitaucherin Svea Roth".

Marion Meister, born in 1974, studied animation at the "Konrad Wolf" film school in Potsdam-Babelsberg. Since 2006 she has been publishing novels with various publishers in the field of fantasy.

For her near-future thriller "White Maze", which was published under the pseudonym *June Perry*, she received the Glauser Prize in 2019 for the best young adult crime novel and the *Golden Leslie*, the youth literature prize of the state of Rhineland-Palatinate.

As a native of Bavaria, she has now put down roots in Lower Saxony, on the banks of Lake Steinhuder Meer.

Her experiences of nature and country life repeatedly find their way into her novels.

Derek Meister was born in Hannover in 1973 and moved to Münchehagen near Lake Steinhuder Meer in the early 2000s. He has been working as a freelance author since 1999 and studied film and television dramaturgy at the Potsdam-Babelsberg Film School. While he was still studying, he helped develop the popular series "With Heart and Handcuffs" for SAT1. Numerous high-budget TV movies followed, including for RTL and PRO7.

The adventure film "The Hunt for the Nibelung Treasure" (2008) was nominated for the German Television Award in four categories. He has also been writing books for twenty years and has now created a number of crime novels, thrillers and historical novels in the Captain's House. His best-known works include the medieval crime series about the investigator "Rungholt" and the crime series about "Police diver Svea Roth".

Die Autorinnen und Autoren / The authors

Stuart C. Orme

wurde am 02. Februar 1976 in Bremen geboren, drei Jahre nach der Einwanderung der Eltern aus England nach Deutschland.
Die Familie, im Golfgeschäft aktiv, hat einige Umzüge hinter sich. Seit 1989 waren sie in Hannover ansässig und zogen 1997 nach Mardorf um.
Heute leitet Stuart Orme, gemeinsam mit seinem Bruder David, ein Unternehmen, das Golfanlagen baut, pflegt und vermarktet. Sie beschäftigen über 30 Mitarbeitende und setzen sich mit der Familie und dem Unternehmen aktiv für den Naturschutz ein. Ihre Golfanlagen sind nicht nur CO_2-neutral, sondern tragen auch zur CO_2-Reduktion bei: Vogel-, Echsen- und Insektenschutz sowie das Aufforsten von Bäumen und Heckenpflanzen stehen bei ihnen im Mittelpunkt.
Nach über 25 Jahren in Mardorf ist die Familie Orme fest in der Gemeinschaft verankert und engagiert sich in lokalen Vereinen. Stuart Orme spielt in seiner knappen Freizeit selber Golf und erkundet gerne die schöne Gegend rund um das Steinhuder Meer mit seinem Motorrad.

was born on 2 February 1976 in Bremen, three years after his parents emigrated from England to Germany.
The family, active in the golf business, has moved several times. They had been based in Hannover since 1989 and moved to Mardorf in 1997.
Today, Stuart Orme and his brother David run a company that builds, maintains and markets golf courses. They employ over 30 people and are actively involved in nature conservation with the family and the company. Their golf courses are not only CO_2-neutral, but also contribute to CO_2 reduction: bird, lizard and insect protection, as well as the reforestation of trees and hedgerow plants are at the centre of their activities.
After more than 25 years in Mardorf, the Orme family is firmly anchored in the community and is involved in local associations. Stuart Orme plays golf in his spare time and enjoys exploring the beautiful area around Lake Steinhuder Meer on his motorbike.

Alexander Fürst zu Schaumburg-Lippe

geboren am 25. Dezember 1958 in Düsseldorf, ist ein deutscher Unternehmer sowie Land- und Forstwirt.
Gemeinsam mit seiner Ehefrau Mahkameh, Fürstin zu Schaumburg-Lippe, bewohnt er das Schloss Bückeburg im Schaumburger Land. Neben vielzähligen Schirmherrschaften von diversen Hilfsprojekten, welche der Fürst inne hat, wie zum Beispiel Interhelp, gilt seine Leidenschaft der Musik. Im Speziellen der Jazz- und Klaviermusik, die er gemeinsam mit seiner Ehefrau – die eine ausgebildete Pianistin ist – tagtäglich lebt und mit seinem Freundeskreis teilt.

born on 25 December 1958 in Düsseldorf, is a German entrepreneur as well as a farmer and forester.
Together with his wife Mahkameh, Princess of Schaumburg-Lippe, he lives in Bückeburg Castle in the Schaumburg region. In addition to his numerous patronages of various aid projects, such as Interhelp, his passion lies in music. Specifically, he is passionate about jazz and piano music, which he shares and lives daily with his wife, who is a trained pianist, and with friends.

York Prinz zu Schaumburg-Lippe

ist der Cousin von SHD Alexander Prinz zu Schaumburg-Lippe.
Seine Großeltern Fürst Wolrad und Bathildis lebten und liebten das Schloss Hagenburg. Ebenso die Enkelkinder York und seine Schwester Tatjana.
York Prinz zu Schaumburg-Lippe ist immer noch mit dem Wasser verbunden und liebt diese idyllische Ruhe des am Stichkanal liegenden Anwesens mit all den reichhaltigen Facetten der Natur.
Heute kümmert er sich in erster Linie um sein Unternehmen mit hochwertigen Armbanduhren und Schmuck sowie, wenn es seine Zeit zulässt, mit der Organisation von Oldtimer-Rallyes. Seit 2013 folgt er den Spuren Graf Wilhelms, der in Portugal der Erbauer des großen Bruders des Wilhelmsteins ist: das Fort de Lippe in Elvas, auch genannt Forte de Nossa Senhora da Graça.

is the cousin of SHD Alexander, Prince of Schaumburg-Lippe. His grandparents Prince Wolrad and Bathildis lived and loved Hagenburg Castle. As did his grandchildren York and his sister Tatjana.
York, Prince of Schaumburg-Lippe, is still connected to the water and loves the idyllic tranquillity of the estate on the Stichkanal with all the rich facets of nature.
Today, he primarily looks after his company with high-quality wristwatches and jewellery, as well as organising classic car rallies when his time allows. Since 2013, he has been following in the footsteps of Count Wilhelm, who built the big brother of the Wilhelmstein in Portugal: the Fort de Lippe in Elvas, also known as the Forte de Nossa Senhora da Graça.

Ecki Stieg

lebt seit seiner Geburt im Schaumburger Land und seit mehreren Jahrzehnten in der Nähe des Steinhuder Meeres.
Er begann seine journalistische Laufbahn im Jahr 1981, war von 1987 bis 1997 eine der prägenden Stimmen von radio ffn (Sendung „Grenzwellen") und ist seit 2014 Moderator bei Radio Hannover.
Neben dieser Tätigkeit ist er freier Autor und Medienarbeiter.
Ecki Stiegs Passion ist das Radfahren und das Leben mit und in der Natur.

has lived in the Schaumburg region since he was born and has lived near the Lake Steinhuder Meer for several decades.
He began his journalistic career in 1981, was one of the defining voices of radio ffn from 1987 to 1997 (the music programme "Grenzwellen") and has been a presenter at Radio Hannover since 2014.
In addition to this activity, he is a freelance author and media worker.
Ecki Stieg's passion is cycling and living with and in nature.

Die Autorinnen und Autoren / The authors

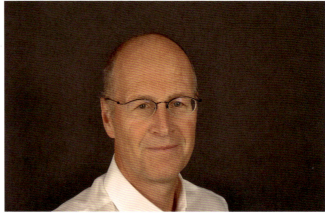

Regine Stünkel

Die Moderatorin, Journalistin und Reporterin Regine Stünkel verbrachte ihre Kindheit und Jugend in Steinhude. Dort entdeckte sie ihre Leidenschaft für das Moderieren. Die Journalistin präsentiert im Norddeutschen Rundfunk eine Sendung über das Glück. Diese hat sie konzipiert, um in herausfordernden Zeiten positive Impulse zu setzen. In ihre Sendung fließen auch Glücksmomente aus ihrer Heimat Steinhude ein. Zuvor moderierte Regine Stünkel mehr als zehn Jahre im Radio das NDR-Gesundheitsmagazin Visite und die Call-in-Sendung Ratgeber. Für ihre Moderation bekam Regine Stünkel den Journalistenpreis der Deutschen Gesellschaft für Ernährung. Der NDR hat zudem ihre Fernsehdokumentation „Freiheit für Schwerverbrecher?", die sie gemeinsam mit Gerald Pinkenburg realisierte, für den Grimme Preis eingereicht. Beim NDR verantwortet sie als Redakteurin tagesaktuelle Magazin- und Nachrichtenformate und trainiert in der *ARD.ZDF. medienakademie* regelmäßig Journalistinnen und Journalisten. Als ausgebildete Veranstaltungsmoderatorin führt sie seit vielen Jahren durch Kongresse, Podiumsdiskussionen und Festakte vor großem Publikum wie auf der Berlinale oder in der Nationalen Akademie der Wissenschaften Leopoldina.

The presenter, journalist and reporter Regine Stünkel spent her childhood and youth in Steinhude. It was there that she discovered her passion for presenting. The journalist presents a programme about happiness on Norddeutscher Rundfunk. She created this programme to provide positive impetus in challenging times. Her programme also includes moments of happiness from her home town of Steinhude. Previously, Regine Stünkel presented the NDR health magazine Visite and the call-in programme Ratgeber on the radio for more than ten years. Regine Stünkel was awarded the German Nutrition Society's journalism prize for her presenting work. NDR also submitted her television documentary "Freiheit für Schwerverbrecher?", which she realised together with Gerald Pinkenburg, for the Grimme Prize. As an editor at NDR, she is responsible for daily magazine and news formats and regularly trains journalists at the *ARD.ZDF. medienakademie*. As a trained event presenter, she has been hosting congresses, panel discussions and ceremonies in front of large audiences for many years, such as at the Berlinale or at the German National Academy of Sciences Leopoldina.

Prof. Dr. Henning Windhagen

geboren 1965 in Essen, ist orthopädischer Chirurg und leitet die Orthopädische Klinik der Medizinischen Hochschule Hannover am Annastift. Seit der Jugend ist er begeisterter Wassersportler mit Ursprüngen am Dümmer See und heute am liebsten am Steinhuder Meer. Ambitioniert unterwegs war er in der FD-Klasse und findet heute den besten Ausgleich zum intensiven Beruf auf Regatten der 15er-Jollenkreuzer. Mit der ebenso wasseraffinen Familie zieht es ihn permanent auch an die guten Küstenspots für das Windsurfen, eine weitere Leidenschaft.
Seit 2020 ist er im Vorstand des Yachtclubs Steinhuder Meer und engagiert und erfreut sich dort an einer erfrischenden Seglergemeinschaft mit zahlreichen gemeinsamen Aktivitäten, einem ereignisreichen Clubleben und intensivem Segelsport.

was born in 1965 in Essen and is head of the Orthopaedic Department at Hannover Medical School / Annastift. Since his youth he has been an enthusiastic sailor with early experience at the Dümmer Lake, and is now happy exploring the Lake Steinhuder Meer. In competitive sailing, he moved from FD-sailing to the 15er Jollenkreuzer class, identifying regatta participation as best possible therapy against modern workload stress. With his family, all keen about watersports, he also likes to go windsurfing along the Baltic and North Sea coasts.
Since 2020 he is board member of the Lake Steinhuder Meer Yachtclub and enjoys the club´s hospitality, friendship and commitment to sailing.

Dip.-Ing. Peter Zenker

Geboren 1955 als Sohn eines klassischen Musikers in Alexandria und im Alter von sechs Jahren in Deutschland gelandet, wo er seitdem im Hannöverschen sein Zuhause gefunden hat. Nach dem Abitur am Kaiser-Wilhelm-Gymnasium hat er einige Semester Kunstwissenschaften an der Georg-August-Universität in Göttingen studiert, um sich dann aber dem Architekturstudium zu widmen. Er ist freischaffender Architekt und lebt mit seiner Familie in Lüdersen, einem kleinen Dorf im Calenberger Land. Beruflich wird er, neben vielen anderen Projekten, immer wieder mit denkmalrechtlichen Aufgaben betraut, was ihm wegen seiner ausgeprägten Affinität zu bauhistorischen Themen große Freude bereitet. Er engagiert sich besonders für das Bauen im ländlichen Raum. So hat er gemeinsam mit Mitwirkenden den Verein Dorfentwicklung und Baukultur in Lüdersen gegründet, dessen Ziel es ist, die Bedeutung der Gesamtqualität von Architektur bei Bauprojekten mit städtebaulichen Auswirkungen auf das Dorf und seine Umgebung zu vermitteln und Interessierte zu beraten.

Born in 1955 as the son of a classical musician in Alexandria, he landed in Germany at the age of six, where he has since found his home in Hannover. After graduating from the Kaiser Wilhelm Gymnasium, he studied art at the Georg August University in Göttingen for a few semesters before devoting himself to studying architecture. He is a freelance architect and now lives with his family in Lüdersen, a small village in the Calenberg region. In addition to many other projects, he is regularly entrusted with tasks relating to listed buildings, which he enjoys because of his pronounced affinity for historical building topics. He is particularly committed to building in rural areas. Together with fellow campaigners, he founded the Lüdersen Village Development and Building Culture Association, whose aim is to communicate the importance of the overall quality of architecture in construction projects with an urban development impact on the village and its surroundings and to advise interested parties.

Partner / Partners

Danke an alle Partner, die uns tatkräftig oder finanziell unterstützt haben. Ohne euch wäre dieses Projekt nicht möglich gewesen.

Thank you to all our partners who have supported us actively or financially. This project would not have been possible without you.

augenklinik.org

bauwo.de

getec.de

eigensinnig.com

hannover.de

klocke-lingemann.de

liebe-hannover.de

stadtwerke-wunstorf.de

meerradio.de

schweerbau.de

volksbank-hameln-stadthagen.de

fw-wesling.de

Quellenverzeichnis / Bibliography

Großenheidorn

Schettlinger, Hans: *„Großenheidorn gestern und heute"*. Arbeitskreis 750 Jahre Großenheidorn

Sachsenhagen

Röver, Manfred (1998): *Sachsenhagen Schlossturm: Bestandsaufnahme und Nutzungskonzept*

Alle Kirchentexte / All church texts:

Dehio, Georg (1992): *Handbuch der Deutschen Kunstdenkmäler, Bremen Niedersachsen*. München. Neuaufl. bearb. von Gerd Weiß unter Mitarb. von Karl Eichwalder. (Reihe: Handbuch der Deutschen Kunstdenkmäler)

Nöldecke, Arnold; Kiecker, Oskar; Karpa, Oskar; Clasen, Carl-Wilhelm; Kiesow, Gottfried (1958): *Die Kunstdenkmale des Kreises Neustadt am Rübenberge*. München, Berlin. (Reihe: Die Kunstdenkmale des Landes Niedersachsen)

Landeskirchliches Archiv Hannover (LkAH): Kirchengemeindelexikon.
kirchengemeindelexikon.de

Niedersächsisches Landesamt für Denkmalpflege: Denkmalatlas Niedersachsens.
denkmalatlas.niedersachsen.de/viewer

Wikipedia – Die freie Enzyklopädie: Bearbeitungsstand: 10. Dezember 2023.
de.wikipedia.org

Bildnachweise / Picture credits

Alle Fotos Heinrich K.-M. Hecht, außer:
All photos Heinrich K.-M. Hecht, except:

Airbus: S. 114
Archiv Regine u. Werner Stünkel: S. 127
Achim Süß: S. 300 rechts
Alexander Fürst zu Schaumburg-Lippe, privat: S. 306 rechts
Andreas Bröer: S. 78 oben links
Andreas Müh: S. 93
Beeke Fitschen: S. 53
Ben Scheurer: S. 66, 69 unten
Benjamin Englich, privat: S. 300 links
Bernd Wolter/Region Hannover: S. 8 oben, 10
Bernhard Volmer: S. 13, 28, 30–31, 32/33, 34/35, 36–39
Bettina Seidensticker: S. 60/61
Carola Faber: S. 295 links u. unten
Claudia Gondry, privat: S. 301 links
Claus Kirsch, Christian Stahl/Region Hannover:
S. 8, 18/19, 59, 118, 124, 128, 243
Dietmar Seegers: S. 150/151
Dinopark: S. 208
Emke Hillrichs: S. 65
Eva Lührs/ÖSSM: S. 298 links
Fabian Hoppe: S. 78 unten rechts
Frank Ludowig, privat: S. 304 links
Hans-Erich Hergt, privat: S. 302 links
Heiko Höhn: S. 97
Heinrich K.-M. Hecht/Guido Hiller: S. 132, 137
Hendrik Tesche: S. 301 rechts
Henning Windhagen, privat: S. 308 rechts
Jacinto Cesar: S. 144
Joachim Sölter: S. 185 unten
Jörg Albach: S. 102 oben links
Jörg Schneider/Region Hannover: S. 264
Jürgen Engelmann, privat: S. 299 rechts
Kaliwerk Sigmundshall: S. 148 unten
Kloster Loccum, Archiv: S. 229 unten
Kulturerhaltungsverein Bad Rehburg e.V.: S. 219 oben rechts
Kurt Prenzler: S. 68
luftwaffe.de: S. 110–112
Michael Kalla: S. 221
mono-photography.de: S. 72, 74–75
Mönkehäger Dorpverein: S. 190, 193, 195
Peter Zenker, privat: S. 309
Philipp Schröder/Region Hannover: S. 6
Region Hannover: S. 303 links
Renate Braselmann, privat: S. 298 rechts
Sammlung Dr. Edler, Stadthagen: S. 162
Schloss Bückeburg: S. 134
Stadt Rehburg-Loccum: S. 218 unten, 219 (sw)
Stadtarchiv Wunstorf: S. 83 oben, 98, 123 links, 138, 173 rechts
Stefan Andreas, BSV: S. 62, 64
Stefan Brüdermann, privat: S. 299 links
Stefan Ibold: S. 52, 69 oben, 80, 302 rechts (privat)
Stuart C. Orme, privat: S. 242 oben rechts
Susanne Kußmann: S. 184 rechts (2)
Thomas Hoppe: S. 9, 70, 143, 173
Tim Rudloff: S. 157 rechts
Ulrike Fiedler-Meyer: S. 162 oben
Wilfried Rave/Region Hannover: S. 12, 20/21, 36, 290
York Prinz zu Schaumburg-Lippe, Archiv: S. 172 (sw), S. 307 links (privat)

Impressum / Imprint

Herausgeber: Leuenhagen & Paris
Redaktion und Art-Direktion: Heinrich K.-M. Hecht
Grafikdesign: Leon Auffenberg
Lektorat: Imke Schaffors, Hannover und
Michaela Horst, Stadthagen
Englisches Lektorat: Dr. Andreas Urscheler, Zürich (CH)
und Smith Translations, Hildesheim
Druck: Gutenberg Beuys Feindruckerei, Langenhagen
Printed in Germany
© Heinrich K.-M. Hecht, 2024
Alle Rechte vorbehalten

ISBN: 978-3-945497-28-9